PRAISE FOR
THE GRAY BIRD OF BAGHDAD

"Steve Monteiro deftly leads the reader through the halls of power in Washington, the sands of the desert in Iraq, and the steamy beaches of South Florida in a true tale of patriotism and international intrigue. The risks to life and country are real. The telling of the story is honest and personal. The story of the rescue of one of Saddam Hussein's bio-weaponeers and his contribution to US national security, and of a team led by a true-life secret agent, will have you on the edge of your seat."

—KIMOTHY SMITH, DVM, PhD, former Senior Advisor for International Biodefense, US Department of Homeland Security

"Stephen Monteiro's *The Gray Gird of Baghdad* is a satisfying read on many levels. It is a page-turning story of a mission to rescue an Iraqi scientist, an in-depth look at war's innocent victims and the destructive tugs of bureaucracy, and, most important of all, a heart-warming story of an unusual friendship."

—LINDA CASHDAN, former journalist, Voice of America, and author of *Special Interests*

"Stephen Monteiro's masterful memoir is more than a page-turning manhunt for a missing Iraqi scientist. It is also a sobering—and sad—exposé of bureaucratic turf wars and political infighting that seemed determined to prevent him and his team from succeeding—and thus confirming uncomfortable truths about Saddam Hussein's biological warfare program. By focusing on one mission involving just one scientist, Monteiro has contributed greatly to our understanding of America's costly war in Iraq."

—MEL LAYTNER, former foreign correspondent for NBC News and United Press International and author of *What They Didn't Burn*

THE GRAY BIRD OF BAGHDAD

An Ex-Secret Service Agent's
Desperate Mission to
Save an Iraqi Scientist

STEPHEN PHILLIP MONTEIRO

Published by SparkPress, a BookSparks imprint,
A division of SparkPoint Studio, LLC
Phoenix, Arizona, USA, 85007
www.gosparkpress.com

Published 2022
Printed in the United States of America
Print ISBN: 978-1-68463-151-3
E-ISBN: 978-1-68463-152-0
Library of Congress Control Number: 2022904510

Interior design by Tabitha Lahr

For my wife, Carmela,
and my sons, Ryan and Jared, who put up with my antics,
absences, and crazy moods . . . I love you and thank you.

And for my wonderful parents, George and Emily, to whom
I owe everything.

"War demands sacrifice of the people.
It gives only suffering in return."
—Frederic Clemson Howe

AUTHOR'S NOTE

THE EVENTS DESCRIBED IN THIS book are real. The book's primary events spanned an eight-year period, from 2001 to 2008, and took place in Iraq, Syria, New York City, Virginia, Florida, and Washington, DC. The names of some of those in the story have been altered for their safety and out of respect for their privacy. I've omitted some details that make them identifiable.

I've endeavored to keep the dates, times, and basic events in this book as accurate as possible; however, given the dynamics of the violent conditions in Iraq during that time period, and the difficulty of recalling specific details during such an extensive time span, gaps and inaccuracies may exist. The dialogue throughout does not come from audio recordings or transcripts, and is not meant to be taken as verbatim, but rather as recreations of this story's facts and experiences as Thamer and I remember them.

Chapter 1

BAGHDAD, IRAQ—MARCH 2003

THEY HUDDLED UNDER THE STAIRWELL, Thamer, his wife, and their three children, sick with fear as they listened to the low rumble of bombs in the distance. Death was not far beyond their door, and they all knew that at any moment they might hear its knock. So they prayed. For a moment Thamer Imran cursed himself—he could have sent his family north to Erbil where it was safer. But no, he really couldn't have. Splitting up the family wasn't an option. If death was coming, they would die together.

Earlier that day, in the wee hours of March 20, 2003, Thamer Abdul Rahman Imran woke to the undeniable blasting sounds of his country, his city, his home under attack. It was the first day of the Iraq War.

Thamer lived in a small, but respectable, two-bedroom home in Al-Basateen Hay, a quiet Baghdad neighborhood in the Al-Shaab district, where most residents were government employees or military officers. Thamer was proud to live among people of education and achievement. More than that, he was grateful that his neighbors were more than mere acquaintances who exchanged casual hellos, but instead were warm friends who enjoyed spending a Saturday evening sharing a meal, helping each other with their vegetable and fruit gardens, and offering another set of eyes under the hood.

There in the dark morning hours when America and its allies invaded Baghdad, Thamer felt a pang for the hard work it had taken him to reach this place. He dreaded that at any moment this life he built and everyone in it might be blown off the map. It would be hours before they all returned to their beds, and almost dawn by the time he and Eman fell asleep, holding each other in the smoky, nighttime glow of the invasion.

Although Thamer was a jovial man, he was by no means a simple man. Thamer was a microbiologist for Iraq's National Monitoring Directorate, which had been established to work directly with the United Nations Special Commission—a commission created after the first Gulf War to ensure Iraq didn't develop weapons of mass destruction. Thamer's job sounded ominous, but to him, it was like any other position in Iraq's Military Industrialization Corporation; the job offered a degree of stability to a non-political man in a country where most good jobs went to those fiercely loyal to the regime. Thamer had the training and the skills for his post, but he also possessed another very important skill, a secret skill. One that was different from that of his colleagues. It was not a skill he chose but it was one that would come to upset his life in ways unimaginable.

Although Thamer was a thinking man, he wasn't political. If he had thoughts about Saddam Hussein or negative thoughts about Iraq in general, he kept them to himself—as any astute employee of the Iraq government would. Or any smart Iraqi. Saddam's barbarity was well documented and started as soon as he became president in 1979 with his purge of the Iraqi parliament. His enemies real or perceived were imprisoned, tortured, murdered, or they just plain disappeared. Thamer was careful. He knew the wrong word to the wrong person could be fatal in the brutal dictatorship that engulfed Iraq.

On work days, Thamer always woke earlier than he needed to, and he loved to linger in bed and watch the rising sun define the curves of his wife lying next to him. But on that first morning of the second Iraq War, the city had already been glowing for hours with rampant fires, so the rising sun gave him no pleasure. Outside the window, a hazy and smoky sort of sunrise spilled across the garden, and over the date tree he had nurtured from a young sapling into an old timer sagging with fruit. The bombing had stopped, but the ear-ringing silence that remained was disturbing, and he felt a sick foreboding that his gentle sunrise mornings would now be nothing more than memories. He crept from the comfort of his bed, careful not to awaken Eman, and steeled himself to be ready to do whatever was needed to protect his family should bad news or even a bomb come flying in their direction.

He walked into the kitchen and stared at the familiar kettle and bowl of fruit. His breakfast routine was humble, just tea and plums, but today the churning of his stomach told him to leave the kitchen. He tiptoed back to the bed and whispered, "I love you," into Eman's long, thick, dark waves of hair, which always smelled like flowers but today carried the additional scent of smoke.

Then he stepped out his front door into a neighborhood that looked as if today were just another day in the peaceful neighborhoods of Iraq, as if the bombing sounds had been only a bad dream. But the usual bustling activity of his neighbors preparing to go to work was missing. In its place was an eerie, unsettling silence.

Despite Thamer thinking of his family as his greatest asset, for twenty years they had taken a backseat to his career. Now they were all he could think about. In the early days after the invasion, he moved them to the house of Eman's father in Al-Bunouk Hay. Thamer believed it was safer there than in their own home in Al-Basateen, which he thought could become a target because so many of its residents worked for either the government or military.

With the addition of Thamer's family, his father-in-law's home became extremely crowded, but huddling together made the family feel more secure. To add to their troubles, kidnappings in and around Baghdad had begun to increase; some of the kidnappings were motivated by politics and some by revenge, but most kidnappers were in it for the money and took advantage of the confusion and social upheaval brought on by the start of the war.

As weeks passed, the combination of frequent bombings, roadside improvised explosive devices (IEDs), rocket attacks, and mortar fire made Baghdad one of the most dangerous places in the world. With death or disfigurement always one wrong turn or errant bomb away, Thamer no longer viewed the future in terms of years but of days and weeks. With conditions in the city deteriorating quickly and an insurgency gaining traction, he knew that his only hope was getting out.

Hussein ordered tanks and anti-aircraft batteries to take positions in the more populated areas of the city: inside schools, outside hospitals, near homes. He claimed this was to protect his people from being bombed. But Thamer knew that this was to ensure that—should the West's coalition forces bomb Iraqi forces—Hussein could declare to the world (with righteous indignation) that the Westerners were savages who attacked innocent civilians. It was a dangerous strategy. Anyone could see that Saddam was drawing the war closer to those innocent civilians. But no Iraqi would dare utter this aloud.

In the months after the invasion, Thamer and his family tried to carry on with their normal lives, despite the life-threatening turmoil that swirled around them. Thamer's main concern was making sure his money didn't run out. Goods were much more expensive as supplies dwindled, and looters took over the city. Thamer carpooled to work every day with his colleague, Jassim, who lived nearby. Together they drove through the bombed-out city to their offices in a building in Al-Jadriya. The offices sat along the Tigris River in the heart of the city, close to the University of Baghdad. Black smoke rising from never-ending fires was a constant sight as military forces penetrated farther into the city.

Pilings of concrete riddled the streets, and buildings on the verge of collapse made the journey perilous.

All normal business and work for a microbiologist had ended for Thamer when he and his colleagues became security guards for his Directorate. And they never missed a day despite the danger of traveling through the war-torn city, because, quite simply, they were still being paid. Their families needed the money, so Thamer and his fellow scientists, despite the war raging around them, reported for work. Thamer was grateful they did. It gave him a sense of security in numbers and the comfort of sharing the confusing and increasingly stressful experience with peers. And if things went from bad to worse, he felt this was a group he could trust.

Thamer's workplace became his family's only point of contact with the outside world. The US employed a "shock and awe" strategy, which involved dominating the enemy by use of overwhelming power and a spectacular display of force, and it was working. Communication was almost non-existent as bombs rained down and destroyed Iraq's communication grids. Every day Thamer and his colleagues swapped whatever information they had about friends and relatives that had been injured or killed and information on where to get benzene and kerosene, supplies they desperately needed for heating and cooking. They tried to piece together what was going on throughout their city, their country, and the world.

Although Thamer's work as Chief of Biologists was suspended, he still had workplace responsibilities. The Directorate issued him a rifle to protect their facility against the looters who plagued the city as law and order ceased to exist. He accepted the rifle, but only because he was certain it would be more dangerous to turn it down. He didn't want to appear unwilling to defend his own country, and he certainly didn't want to feel vulnerable should looters overtake their building. It was happening all over the city as desperation moved in and any sense of calm and order moved out. But Thamer knew he could never shoot anyone, least of all any of his fellow countrymen. His two older brothers had been killed in the Iraq-Iran War. First, Mohammed in 1983, and then Abdul Ameer in 1988. The loss of his brothers was devastating to Thamer and his family. He dearly loved the brothers who used to watch over him as a boy, making sure he stayed in school and out of trouble. He missed their long talks over tea and fruit as they tutored young Thamer in the ways of the world. Thamer knew the price of war, and it frightened him.

America's "shock and awe" strategy overwhelmed Iraqi forces in short order. Even Saddam Hussein's elite Republican Guard broke and ran. On April 9, 2003, just under three weeks after the first bombs started falling on Baghdad, coalition forces from forty-nine countries led by the US, took over the Republican Palace and several ministries. The military takeover was large, fast and overwhelming. With thousands of support and contractor personnel, it was truly an invasion. Iraqis toppled the twenty-foot-tall, bronze statue of Saddam Hussein that had stood in Firdos Square. Sharif al-Jabouri, a champion Iraqi powerlifter with the medals to prove it became famous for taking a sledge hammer to the statue, signifying an end to a savage regime. Many Iraqis cried as they beat the statue with their shoes, a gesture considered to be a supreme insult in Iraq.

Over the next several weeks as lawlessness started to creep across the city, Iraqi civilians looted and burned palaces, museums, libraries, and even hospitals. By April 14, the United States declared victory, and Hussein's dictatorship came to an end. Hussein himself vanished, despite claiming in early March 2003 that the faithful would be victorious against the aggression. He went into hiding soon after the invasion, speaking to his people only through occasional audiotape.

Then, on July 22, 2003, Saddam's son, Uday, and his youngest son, Qusay, whom many believed was being groomed as his successor, were killed when they fought it out with military forces in the Northern city of Mosul. Five months later, on December 13, US soldiers found Saddam Hussein hiding in a six-to-eight-foot spider hole nine miles outside his hometown of Tikrit. A soldier at the scene described him as "a man resigned to his fate."

For Thamer, the news in May of 2003, that major combat operations had ended and that the Americans had declared victory, was the answer to his prayers. He, along with his family, colleagues, and neighbors, believed the US declaration of victory meant the fighting would now end. He was so sure of this that he took his family home to Al-Basateen. He and his neighbors gathered outside their homes to shout and laugh with astonishment at this sudden upending of the world they knew. They were bewildered by the fact that the tyrant who had been the unchecked mastermind of twenty-four years of destruction and murder throughout their country had now been run off in under three weeks. This extraordinary change in his country gave Thamer renewed hope.

"Now that Saddam has been defeated, the fighting will stop, and this will all be over," he told Eman as they lay side-by-side in their old familiar bed.

But two, large, looming issues nagged at Thamer's renewed optimism. One, he was an employee of a government that was in complete disarray. Would he still have a job? Would he be able to support his family? He and Eman often talked quietly about their fears after the children had gone to bed. His job had been to facilitate inspections of Iraq's weapons programs—was there a future for this kind of work? And if not, what might he be asked to do next? Already it had been several weeks since his job had involved any consistency, any clarity. And since Hussein's downfall, Thamer's pay had become erratic; on some paydays, he'd received a check for an unexplainable amount, and on others, he'd received no check at all. Thamer was running out of money. The other dark thought that nagged him, Thamer kept to himself. The horrors of the terrorist attacks on the United States on September 11, 2001 were burned into the memories of Americans

and countless others around the world. And for many, the finger
of blame pointed straight at Iraq. The attacks on 9/11 took the
lives of almost three thousand people and forever darkened and
destroyed the lives of countless others. Thamer always assumed
that vengeance was being plotted in the shadows.

Two months after the fall of Saddam Hussein, nothing
resembling peace had yet to arrive in Iraq. Although resistance
efforts by the Iraqi army had waned, and many Iraqi soldiers
defected to aid the West's coalition forces, a new threat emerged.
Armed insurgents and warring street gangs were amassing, and a
large coalition of foreign fighters from other Muslim countries,
including Syria, Iran, Lebanon, and Afghanistan were streaming
into Iraq to join the Jihad to expel the infidels from Iraq. The
violent group Al-Qaeda in Iraq (AQI) attracted thousands of foreign fighters to their cause, and the quick rise of this insurgency
took coalition forces by surprise. Iraqis, and those who joined
them, fought not only the Westerners, but also each other, as the
gangs and insurgent groups fought for control.

The country's Sunni-Shiite bloodletting drove many Iraqis
to commit a shameful act: change their names. Intensification of
sectarian violence forced many to adopt other identities to avoid
harassment and death, forcing desperate Iraqis to pay bribes to
secure documents that could pass inspection.

The Shiite-Sunni divergence dates back to June 8, 632 AD
with the death of Mohammed, and a subsequent argument over
who should become Islam's new religious and political leader.
Although their differences were religious in nature—with many
Sunnis believing that Shiites are not true Muslims—it now has
less to do with religion, and more with obtaining power. Iran, a
predominantly Shiite country, pitted itself against Saudi Arabia, a
predominantly Sunni country for dominance in the region. This
split led to Iraqis having less of a sense of nationalism. In its place
they developed a strong relationship and loyalty to their sect and
tribe. This became even more evident during the war with each

side trying to outmaneuver the other for control of the country. Getting stopped by someone outside your sect could cost you your life.

Like many Iraqi civilians, Thamer and his family had little choice but to wait, watch, and cope with increasing uncertainty. They watched as food supplies dwindled, first in the markets, then on their kitchen shelves. Electricity was available for only a few hours each day, which meant inconsistent refrigeration, no air conditioning, no fans, and no ice. They napped during the afternoons as the oppressive heat of impending summer choked their house in its sweaty fist.

One reason Baghdad had capitulated so quickly was that the coalition forces' bombing campaign had targeted civilian infrastructure; not only had communications and power grids been blasted to bits, but water purification and sewage treatment plants had been destroyed. The lack of clean water and sanitation contributed to an outbreak of diarrhea and hepatitis throughout the city. People became desperate and began stripping trees to use as fuel against freezing. The Tigris River, long since poisoned by pollution, became both a well and latrine for many Baghdadis living without power, sewerage, or clean water. The air smelled like rotting garbage. What medical services existed were soon overwhelmed with over a hundred Iraqis an hour flooding into Baghdad hospitals.

Thamer had no idea when the carnage would end, and his sense of powerlessness worried him. He could offer no words of security to his wife who turned to him for answers. The thought of not being able to take care of his family was a cause of great shame to Thamer, and he knew that the conditions were only going to get worse.

During those first nights of the assault on Baghdad, the people of Iraq quickly learned a terrifying new word: smart bomb. These bombs were supposed to seek and destroy their targets with great precision. But Thamer understood that despite their sophistication, no bomb was smart enough to figure out who was a soldier or who was a civilian, who was old or young, who deserved to die and who didn't. What he hadn't known was that something could frighten him more than the threat of fast death by bombing; Thamer began to fear what would happen to his family if the money ran out or when their food and clean water were gone? What would happen when the millions of people left in Baghdad became desperate?

Chapter 2

BAGHDAD, IRAQ—JUNE 2003

THE JOURNEY TO AND FROM WORK WAS dangerous, but if Thamer and Jassim wanted to support their families, they had to keep showing up. They had carpooled together for years, and in the days before the war, they would talk nonstop during the ride to work. Now, they said almost nothing as they traveled, as if talking would weaken the vigilance they needed to reach their destination alive.

One day in April, about a month after the invasion, Thamer and Jassim arrived at their office to find the building abandoned. They followed their instincts to turn around and head home by way of a route that took them close to Al-Tahir Square. It was an unfortunate choice. They ran into American tanks crossing the bridge, and the tanks opened fire in order to disperse a crowd. The rounds came dangerously close to their car, and Thamer and Jassim narrowly escaped. As they sped through the narrow streets to get away from the attack, Thamer felt his chest pounding like a hammer hitting an anvil, and his hands shook uncontrollably as they fled the chaos. He thanked Allah that they'd been spared but worried his luck wouldn't hold out much longer.

Neither Thamer nor Jassim had been supporters of Saddam Hussein, but they worked for his government, and Thamer knew that anyone with ties to the ousted regime was at risk of capture, torture, and even murder. Many Iraqis had suffered under Hussein's brutality, and Thamer and his colleagues knew that they might be targets of massively impassioned retaliation.

The country had split into factions divided along religious lines, primarily Shia Muslims versus Sunni Muslims. The Sunnis were in the minority, but they'd held power under Saddam, who was also Sunni. Now they found themselves powerless and were eager to wrest that power back from the Shia, who began to take control after Saddam's demise. The Shia, meanwhile, were looking for revenge against Saddam and the Sunnis, who had repressed them for the past two dozen years. Thamer was a Shia but had worked for the Sunnis, so he figured everyone was against him. It didn't matter whether or not he had supported Saddam's government; if he ran into the wrong people—from either side—they would consider him guilty by association and that meant a death sentence.

On June 3, 2003, Thamer and Jassim did like they had every day since the war started. They left the Al Shaab district headed to work for another day of boredom. As they drove, they stared at their city through dust-shrouded windows. Once strung with jewel-like palaces and mosques, colorful roofs, and graceful arches, the bustle of commerce and community, now Baghdad was a husk of burned and crumbling ruins. Huge craters lay splayed open where buildings had been ripped from the earth. Charred metal skeletons of cars and trucks littered the roads. Massive explosion after massive explosion boomed throughout the city, and the dust from the bombs lingered in the air, drying eyes and choking lungs. Thamer felt sickened by the unrelenting ugliness that stared back at him.

Coalition forces sometimes crossed their path, plowing through the city with tanks and armored personnel carriers. That morning, Thamer sighed with relief when they once again arrived safely at work. But his relief was soon upended by a terrible event that would turn his life upside down.

As they had since the invasion, Thamer and his colleagues gathered each morning outside the Directorate building. They took guard shifts throughout the day, as assigned by their supervisors—a handful of them at a time, standing between looters and their building. Luckily, no looters attacked their unremarkable building, so he and his colleagues spent most of their time standing around and talking about what was going on in their respective neighborhoods, trying to stave off boredom.

Around 9:00 a.m., just after Thamer started his guard duty shift, a military convoy pulled to a stop in front of the Directorate. Thamer watched in bemusement as a uniformed man exited one of the vehicles and walked toward the Directorate entrance. The soldier was tall. An American, he guessed. He wasn't surprised that coalition forces had arrived, only that it had taken them this long. He'd been expecting a visit from Western military forces as they penetrated deeper and deeper into the city, taking control of government buildings and institutions. Still, he was unprepared for what came next.

The soldier walked straight up to him. "Thamer Abdul Rahman Imran?"

Thamer nodded, startled that the man knew his name. The soldier motioned for Thamer to follow him off the street and inside the gate. At once, Thamer caught a glimpse of the paper in the soldier's hand. It was a photo of himself along with his name in bold. More curious than worried, he tried to read the rest of the print, but the page kept shifting in the man's hand. Thamer thought it looked like posters he had seen in the old American Westerns he'd loved to watch as a child: "Wanted: Dead or Alive!"

The soldier relieved Thamer of his weapon. As much as the gun had unnerved Thamer, this unnerved him more. Then the soldier stopped and turned to study him more carefully, looking from his face to the photo and back again.

"Do you work here at the Directorate?"

"Yes, I do."

"What is your job?"

"I am a biologist," Thamer answered without hesitation. He had nothing to hide.

The soldier turned and nodded to a fellow soldier, as if Thamer had confirmed something much more serious than his name and profession. The tall soldier pulled a cell phone from his pocket and made a call.

"The gray bird is in the net," he said.

Thamer spoke some English, but didn't understand this strange phrase. He wondered, am I the gray bird? Why gray? Because of my hair? Why bird? Why do I have a code name? What net am I in? And *why me*?

As if in answer to his unspoken questions, the tall soldier, still on his mobile phone nodded to the handful of armed soldiers that had followed them into the yard. They surrounded Thamer, staring at him as if he were a prize catch to be admired. Thamer stood silently, waiting for instructions. The guards grew impatient with this vigil and began milling about until a Westerner wearing khaki pants and a brown t-shirt appeared.

"My name's Jack," he told Thamer, smiling as he extended his hand. "I'm from the DOD."

Thamer shook his hand. He assumed Jack was a soldier, just one in a different kind of uniform, but he had no idea what "dee-oh-dee" was.

"Do you know where Colonel Sinan Muhie is?" Jack asked, looking at a paper with a list of names. "Is he here today?"

"Yes, he is," Thamer answered as casually as he could, though a chill ran through him. This was the moment he realized the coalition forces surrounding him were not making a random stop at a government building. Whatever this was, it was a coordinated effort.

"Okay," Jack told him. "We're going inside. We want to ask you more questions."

Inside, they walked to the office of one of Thamer's longtime colleagues, Dr. Ala Mahdi Al Saeid, who was already waiting at his desk with Colonel Muhie. Colonel Muhie had been temporarily put in charge of the Directorate. Several Western soldiers armed with rifles crowded into the room. Jack led Thamer into their midst.

"We want to talk to you about your backgrounds and some of the work you have been doing," Jack announced to the assembled group. "It shouldn't take more than a couple of hours. We have some routine questions, but we need to move you to another location."

The soldiers flanked Thamer and marched him back outside. Nobody told him where they were taking him, and surrounded by weapons, he felt too intimidated to ask. To tamp down his growing alarm, Thamer reminded himself that Western military forces were in control of Baghdad, at least for now. As a government worker, Thamer knew that these forces were in essence his bosses. He assumed that the occupiers needed to account for each government agency, to know who worked there and what they did, and that today they had simply gotten around to his Directorate. They probably started with him because he was the first person they saw. Thamer soon saw two colleagues emerge from the complex under similar escort and he silently sighed in dismay.

He and his colleagues were loaded into the back seats of three armored vehicles, each scientist flanked by two armed soldiers. Heavy-duty vehicles had become ubiquitous throughout Baghdad, symbols of the coalition's control over the city. This small convoy, comprised of a half dozen such vehicles, crossed the Tigris River over the four-lane Al Jadriyah Bridge. They didn't drive far. On the other side of the bridge, they pulled up to the American-occupied Republican Palace.

Thamer had never been to the palace, and despite his mounting fear, he couldn't help but be awed by the massive edifice with its two giant bronze heads of Saddam Hussein standing watch from the pillared main gates, the massive sandstone blocks that defined the main building, and its decorative blue dome and flowing fountain. It was a gaudy, overbuilt facade meant to hide the three-story, air-raid bunker below it.

The convoy came to a stop, everyone got out, and several soldiers flanked Thamer and his fellow scientists to march them inside. They walked through vast halls scattered with military personnel and up broad, echoing stairs. Then his guards separated him from his colleagues and led him into a large high-ceilinged room, empty of all decoration or furnishings except for a small table with three chairs in a far corner.

Thamer's escorts exited to guard the door as two new men entered. More Americans, but not wearing uniforms. Still, they had a military air. They wore fatigues, more of those brown t-shirts and khaki pants. He guessed that both were in their mid-thirties. One was short and fair, and the other tall and dark. The tall one wore glasses. Both were all business. Without pre-amble, they began asking rapid-fire questions:

"What is your full name? Where do you work? What are your duties?"

Thamer answered the first few. Then they rattled several more questions, to which he politely replied, "Excuse me, I've already answered these questions."

"Not for us. Please just cooperate."

"I don't understand. Why am I here?"

"That's what we're trying to determine. Just answer the questions."

The two men in khakis continued their questions, repeating them again and again, and Thamer repeated his replies almost verbatim. Still the questions kept coming. He had no idea how long this went on—maybe two hours—before his throat grew sore and dry.

"May I please have some water?" he asked, his voice scratchy and weak to his own ears.

The shorter of the two men strode out, returned with a bottle of water, and set it in front of Thamer without comment.

"Thank you," Thamer said. He gulped most of it in one long drink, pausing only to catch his breath.

The questions continued. The men asked Thamer about microbiology, his knowledge, his research, and how it applied to his work. His heart rate slowed and his breathing calmed, so relieved was he to finally talk about a familiar topic he knew and understood so well. At first, their questions made him believe he was sharing knowledge with fellow scientists and was therefore helping the people who had freed his country from tyranny. But it didn't take long for their inexpert questions to reveal their scientific ignorance. These men weren't trying to learn about his department. They didn't care to share scientific knowledge or to pursue a spirit of collaboration. The truth behind the interview hit Thamer like a mallet to the chest: they believed Saddam Hussein had weapons of mass destruction hidden somewhere and that Thamer knew about it. This wasn't an interview. It was an interrogation.

"Do you know the location of any stockpiles of biological agents?" they asked.

"I am sorry, I do not," he replied. "To my knowledge, they destroyed them in 1991." As far as he knew, this was true, but clearly it wasn't what they wanted to hear.

"We already know they exist," said the tall one with the glasses. "We just want to know the locations. If you tell us, we can help you return to your family."

As far as Thamer knew there were no bioweapons in Iraq, and his inability to point his interrogators toward such weapons was putting him in danger. But he told himself that the truth was his best defense.

"I don't think you understand," he told the stern-faced men. "My job was to assist the United Nations in verifying *that there were no* bioweapons."

"We don't think *you* understand," said the short one, tight-lipped, tense. "We already know there are. We *know* you lied to the UN. So just tell us the truth."

The more they pushed him, the more he despaired. What were they going to do to him if he couldn't point them to any bioweapons?

Underneath the questions of his interrogators, Thamer could hear the muffled voices of his colleagues seeping through the walls. He wondered if they felt as depleted as he did. He wondered if the terror was beginning to rise in their chests.

Hours passed. Thamer did his best to cooperate, answering every question thoroughly, honestly, even politely. Oddly, fear and exhaustion made him even more polite. But the problem remained: he couldn't tell them what he didn't know. "Okay, that's enough," the short interrogator said, and Thamer felt momentary relief. This ordeal was wrapping up. Soon he could go home to his family. Then the interrogator barked, "Stand up and empty your pockets!"

A hot jolt of adrenaline shot through Thamer. Why did he have to empty his pockets if he was about to be released? He reached into his back pocket and pulled out his wallet. Then he emptied his other pockets of his flip-phone, stray coins, keys, and a pocket knife.

His interrogators called in a uniformed soldier from the hall. Thamer watched in silence as the young man methodically noted in a log each of his possessions. The man then placed them all in a clear plastic bag and carried it out of the room. It occurred to Thamer that he now had no identification, no proof of who he was. He could be anybody. Or nobody.

Two armed guards escorted him downstairs toward the entrance, and without warning, a guard grabbed Thamer's wrists and handcuffed him with plastic zip ties. Another guard strapped a black blindfold over his eyes, and his world went dark.

"What's happening? I have done nothing! Where are you taking me?" Thamer shouted. It felt as if a dozen hands were hustling him outside, and the brisk pace caused him to stumble and fall down several steps, then bash his knee against cement.

Then hands reached under his armpits to haul him back onto his feet, then hurried him along again.

"We're taking you to another location," a new male voice replied.

"Why?" Thamer pressed.

"To refresh your memory."

Thamer's heart beat against his chest with such unbearable terror that he thought he might drop dead right there. A new location? Wasn't that what they always said to someone before the captive disappeared? His mind raced to grasp a positive thought. Maybe someone had witnessed his arrest, someone who could convince these authorities that he knew nothing about weapons of mass destruction, someone who could tell his family where he was. Would Eman ever know what happened to him? What would happen to Eman? To their children?

"Climb in the back," a male voice ordered.

The back of *what* was unclear since Thamer was now in the dark. But he did as he was told, stepping up onto a bumper and then taking a seat in what felt like the bed of a truck.

Then he heard a familiar voice. "What's happening?" The Arabic words were spoken in a whisper, but he recognized the voice of one of his colleagues and friends, Sinan.

"Where are they taking us?" asked another voice he couldn't place, though it was familiar.

"They told me to empty all my pockets," Sinan said.

"Me too," said Thamer. He wanted to ask if anyone had seen Jassim, who had driven with him to work just hours ago.

But a voice ordered, "Be quiet! You're not permitted to talk." Then the vehicle began to move.

Chapter 3

NEW YORK CITY, NY—SEPTEMBER 2001

THE FIRST THING THAT REGISTERED when I walked onto Ground Zero was the air, or rather the wall of haze and filth that now took the place of air. It was air full of jet fuel, pulverized glass, concrete ash, mercury, and burned plastics—every modern toxin imaginable. And flimsy government-issued masks were all that stood between our team and that murky cloud of poison.

I staggered blindly through the wasteland of floating dust and twisted debris, my hands working overtime to keep my goggles clear. My labored breathing made me sound like Darth Vader. And all around me were people unrecognizable in hazmat suits, head gear, and masks of all kinds: from industrial gas masks to makeshift face coverings made of ripped cloth. If my own mother had been standing next to me, I wouldn't have known it. Everybody looked like space creatures.

Small fires smoldered amid the debris, and the clouds of smoke and layers of floating dust gave the entire site an eerie atmosphere of apocalyptic surrealism. But breathing was only one of the physical challenges caused by the destruction. Walking through the grimy haze without turning an ankle called for great focus.

Massive chunks of ragged rubble lay where lean, elegant buildings had once stood. Iron, concrete, and steel now lay in gargantuan piles several stories high, dwarfing the remnants of crushed police cars and fire trucks. The carnage all around was overwhelming, sickening—unfathomable and I was standing right in the middle of it. Fifteen acres of complete devastation. The entire scene looked, sounded, and smelled like the end of the world.

It was the largest crime scene in American history, completely unstable and seething with hot explosive gas pressure that continued to build. One small shift, and it could all go up again. The sheer size and weight of the buildings that had collapsed created a dangerous situation. Whenever a piece of steel or concrete was moved, it introduced oxygen into the hyper pressurized environment, which often resulted in spontaneous fires. It was like blowing air on a hot ember that was just waiting to ignite. Every so often a deafening wail would sound, a rising and falling shriek, that meant we had to scatter or risk getting blown up. Yet running off the pile was also dangerous, with the chance of plummeting through a gap and getting sliced open, burned, or buried.

There were twelve men on my team, all of us Secret Service agents, and we were there on a very clear mission: to find anyone who may still be alive and recover those that perished. How do you sift through story-high piles of debris? One bucket of broken concrete and mangled steel at a time.

Sweat poured down our faces as we dug with only our hands. The rubber masks chaffed the sweaty skin around our mouths and foreheads. It was nearly impossible to work for long with them on and breathe at the same time. The filters clogged within minutes anyway, so many of us took them off. That exposed us to the toxic air, but none of us wanted to slow down for a second. It seemed foolish, even then, trying to clear tons of rubble by hand, but we did it anyway, in the hope that by some miracle we'd find someone still alive underneath it all. I was in awe of the NYC firefighters, as I watched them digging with their hands, crawling through holes, and totally exhausted but never giving up. As the days passed and hope of finding anyone alive faded, horrible thoughts entered my mind. I was praying that no one was still alive under the tons of wreckage. I knew we couldn't get to them in time and the thought that they were suffering while hoping to be rescued was unbearable.

Over the next several weeks we worked twelve-hour shifts, sifting through endless wreckage. And we didn't find even one survivor. So we looked for bodies and for anything the dead had left behind. We rarely came across human remains. When we did, not much was left that bore any resemblance to a person; instead, we found small pieces of flesh and bone. When we found parts of a person, rescuers would gather around to hold hands and pray over the deceased. Not only did we never know who the body parts belonged to, we couldn't even tell if they'd been part of a man, woman, or child. But we took comfort in a moment of silence and prayer, as if we were giving the dead some semblance of a dignified death.

Once the prayer ended and the remains were bagged and tagged, it was back to work. We searched not only for victims, but also for personal property—jewelry, pocketbooks, wallets, photographs, cell phones. We hoped these things might help identify the dead, give comfort to their families, and serve as evidence that might shed light on this inexplicable crime or its perpetrators.

Each day brought something new in the way of evidence and bad news. The death toll continued to rise, and hospitals were overwhelmed with the injured. Many people were unaccounted for, and normal communication was overloaded as people desperately tried to contact their friends and relatives. But one thing that never changed was the presence of the hovering dust cloud. No matter how we looked when we arrived, we always wore a chalky white coat of armor when we left. We couldn't escape it. Our clothes were so contaminated that we threw them away rather than try to salvage them. Fortunately for us, the government and private companies moved in quickly with supplies likes clothes, helmets, socks, pants, and boots.

At the end of each day, we returned to our temporary living quarters. That could mean a hotel near lower Manhattan or a ship in the harbor; the government moved us around a lot as rooms were scarce. By night, away from the smoke and rubble, we continued to live and breathe the heartbreak of the terrorist attacks. We watched endless news broadcasts and sat in heartbroken silence listening to fathers, mothers, brothers, sisters, sons, daughters, and friends plead for information. I would end every day completely exhausted, physically depleted and emotionally gutted. But it wasn't long before my sadness gave way to rage. This wasn't an accident. It was a carefully executed plan that had been designed and plotted for years. In those early days, solid information eluded us, but we felt certain the attackers had Middle Eastern, perhaps Afghani, connections. And as the information trickled in, I grew more and more consumed with hate and thoughts of vengeance.

But as much as the events of 9/11 led to despair and fear across the city, the country, and the world, it also cultivated a sense of community. Each morning as we trekked back to Ground Zero, hundreds of New Yorkers waved, honked, saluted, cheered, and thanked us. I felt embraced by a wave of patriotism I had never before experienced. The response from the country, and the world, was a balm to our aching bodies and hearts. There was a growing feeling of being in it together.

Every day, donations poured in for us first responders. People sent boots, clothing, masks, shovels, gloves, batteries, helmets, water, and food. Lots of food. Some people risked driving right up to Ground Zero to deliver pans of homemade casseroles and cookies. The relief tents scattered around the city's lower end filled up with enough comfort food to feed an army. We often walked into stores in Manhattan to buy personal items, and the store managers would wave away our money, "No charge!" Every person I encountered found some way to extend me goodwill. The best of America emerged on September 11, 2001 and the days that followed. It made me feel that this is what it must have been like during World War II, when people across the United States felt united by a cause. In the fall of 2001, the entire country came together to try to lift each other up from hell. And hell it was, a hell that took hold of me and refused to let go. Long after I stumbled out of the hellscape of Ground Zero, it continued to burn a raging hole in my psyche.

Some of what clung to me wasn't just a feeling or memory. The Environmental Protection Agency had assured us the air wasn't that bad, but of course, it was. I'm one of the lucky ones, at least so far. I paid a price for my time at Ground Zero like many others who worked there, but not the ultimate price, as did many of my colleagues and other first-responders who died from breathing poison air that sent over 2,500 contaminants into previously healthy lungs. To this day, the 9/11 body count grows.

On September 14, three days after the Twin Towers fell, I listened as President George W. Bush spoke to the rescue workers at Ground Zero. He hadn't planned a speech, but seeing the magnitude of the devastation, he grabbed a bullhorn to declare that America was on bended knee, in prayer for the lost, for the rescue workers, for the families who mourned.

As he continued, someone shouted, "We can't hear you!"

President Bush shouted back, "I *can* hear you! *I can* hear you! The rest of the world hears you! And the people—" he paused to let the crowd's rousing cheer subside, "—and the people who knocked these buildings down will hear all of us soon!"

I was proud of my president that day. Proud of his confident defiance even as he stood atop the wreckage of unimaginable defeat. At that moment, he was the unified voice of my country.

In the weeks after my time at Ground Zero ended, my initial surge of patriotism sank under the weight of gut-wrenching reality. The emotion was overwhelming every time I watched the media replay images of the towers falling. But I grew tired of that feeling, and fast. I was no victim; I was a Secret Service agent. So I decided that every time I watched the towers fall, I'd replay the president's words in my head: " . . . the people who knocked these buildings down will hear all of us soon." I wanted payback, and I wasn't alone. I felt the collective anger boiling over in us all. You hit America, we hit you back ten times harder.

In the early days after the attacks, we didn't know exactly who was behind them, so my hatred was indiscriminate. I was suspicious of every Middle Easterner of every stripe: Afghanis, Iranians, Iraqis, Yemenis, members of Hamas, Hezbollah, the Taliban. As far as I was concerned, they were all the enemy.

Sometime after the 9/11 attacks, the FBI discovered the plot was hatched by Al-Qaeda, the extreme Islamist terrorist organization led by Osama Bin Laden. Then, on October 7, 2001, the United States struck a blow against Afghanistan to make it impossible for the Taliban to offer safe haven to Al-Qaeda forces; we invaded Afghanistan with the goal of hunting down Osama Bin Laden and those that supported him. It was a start, but not enough to convince me our country was safe, and certainly not enough to assuage my anger. I was raring for the justice the president promised, and although I supported our troops, I was no longer one of them. I was a Secret Service agent with a job to do, so I kept my rage to myself.

After several weeks, my time at Ground Zero ended. My team dispersed, and we returned to our duty stations around the country. We were changed men: immeasurably changed. Standing on the graves of almost three thousand people will do that. I served in the Navy during the Vietnam War, but Ground Zero marked my first time on the ground in a war zone. I felt pride seeing American flags fluttering everywhere, but the image no longer conjured uncomplicated nostalgia. The sense of security and strength I'd once felt took a serious blow—a blow I felt would change things forever. Now, more than anything I felt lost innocence and bitterness. Gone were the days of feeling safe because oceans separated us from our enemies. A new enemy had woken us to how vulnerable we were, so my days of sleeping easily were over. For weeks after 9/11, I would lie awake at night, impatient, waiting, and thinking—it's retribution time.

A YEAR AND A HALF LATER THAT DAY finally arrived. It was March 20, 2003. I was at my home in Annapolis relaxing on the couch with my wife Carmela. She leaned against me, and the scent of her shampoo drifting up to me was calming; in fact, just about everything about Carmela is calming. She's the rock of my life. She's stuck with me through all the rough and tumble and the moments when I've felt at my lowest. That night, she'd succeeded in talking me into watching a romance movie with her. I generally try to avoid that kind of "entertainment" any way I can, but some-times I give in, and the sweet time with my wife is worth enduring the shlocky content of the Hallmark-type movies she loves. We were comfortable and enjoying a relatively quiet night together when the news flashed on the screen: Wolf Blitzer announced the start of the Iraq War. We sat watching as Baghdad's black sky burst into orange light in the darkness before dawn as a reporter broke the news on the American forces' first onslaught on Iraq. The sleeping city behind him exploded into flames, white smoke, and echoing thunder as bomb after bomb struck strategic targets.

With each flash of America's so-called shock and awe tactics, my chest surged with an intense blend of celebration and sadness. No doubt the Iraqis on the receiving end were in "shock," but I doubt they or anyone else in the world felt much in the way of "awe." We knew Iraqis were dying under those bursts of light and that many Americans and Iraqis would die in days to come. To me it all made sad but necessary sense. This was the payback the president had promised, and I was all in. I was ready to do my part in the president's War on Terror, whatever form that might take.

Chapter 4

WASHINGTON, DC—DECEMBER 2005

IT WAS DECEMBER 2005. I WAS wrapping up my second act in law enforcement and getting ready to begin a career as a civilian, this time as a consultant with the well-respected firm of Booz Allen Hamilton. As I packed up the office, ending a career I'd worked in for more than twenty years, I thought about endings. Ever since the weeks I'd spent searching the fatal wreckage of Ground Zero for answers, I'd spent a lot of time thinking about how nothing lasts. Getting older was heavy on my mind, and in three days I'd attend my retirement party to celebrate the end of my career with the Secret Service. What better reminder that time moves on?

I looked around my office to make sure I was leaving nothing important behind. Only two boxes to hold twenty years of my life? A few personal photos, a couple of name plates, a coffee mug, and my memories—that was it. I loved the job, but it was time to move on. Still, I couldn't help thinking my desk looked abandoned, particles of dust outlining the places where open files used to sit, like chalk outlines of bodies you see in movies. It reminded me of the victims whose cases kept me up at night.

My time at Ground Zero unfortunately wasn't my first expo-sure to the evil in the world. Before I was a Secret Service agent, I was a cop. I dealt with murders, rapes, child abuse, robberies, assaults, and every sort of mayhem imaginable. In my years as a police officer, I never once received a call because something good had just happened. It was a career defined by the negative. Some of the cases you forget, some you barely remember, and some stick to you like super glue. I didn't know any of the initial 2,996 victims murdered on 9/11—though I worked side-by-side with others who died later in the aftermath of the toxic cleanup— but I'll never forget walking over the wreckage that became the final resting place for so many. I felt connected to them all, just as I did with all the victims of the horrible crimes that were part of my life as a cop. I wanted to help them get justice.

I'd had mixed feelings the day I left my police career behind too. It's always nerve-racking looking ahead into the abyss, and now on the day of my retirement party, I experienced that familiar old friend: trepidation. Even though I had my next job lined up and set to start the following Monday, I wasn't sure what my first assignment would be, and the lack of knowing what came next left me feeling shaky on my feet. My new employer had assured me I'd need all the skills listed on my resume. But to use for what?

Tonight, I'd try to forget all that and prepare myself for the roasting and ribbing that go with retirement parties. When I walked into the Grand Hyatt Hotel in downtown Washington, DC, dozens of my colleagues, Carmela and our sons, Ryan and Jared, greeted me with deafening cheers. It was a night to kick back and reflect, and I was ready to enjoy it.

Because there are so many Secret Service Agents in Wash-ington, and therefore retirement parties almost every week, there's a long-standing joke at the agency: *your retirement party will be three guys taking you out for a beer—and you won't know two of them!* I took the huge turnout as a great compliment. My colleagues gave me the usual plaques and praise. They shared stories about the millions of miles we traveled together, the endless midnight shifts, standing post in the cold, the boredom of a lonely stakeout, feeling overworked and underpaid, and most of all, never having a life that belonged to you. Truth be told, during some stretches I spent more time with these guys than I did with my own family. But I would not have wanted to do anything else. Being a Secret Service agent as one colleague eloquently put it, is like "standing next to history." Carmela, Ryan, and Jared stood closely by me during the litany of speeches, smiling the entire time, and that was the most humbling gift of all: feeling their love and support stronger than ever despite all the missed family dinners, holidays, events, and the long assignments that kept me away from home and sometimes made me feel like a stranger when I came back. Ryan spoke and said how lucky they felt to have me as a dad. I felt proud, and relieved—that they had seen me not as an absentee dad, but as a man devoted to service.

I threw back a few beers, shared plenty of hugs and handshakes, and made lots of promises to keep in touch. And with that, the proudest chapter of my work life was over. Taking a last look around me at familiar faces, feeling the old esprit de corps, it was hard to let go. I felt the weight of knowing that I might never again be part of something so important and so much bigger than myself.

After the party, I went to dinner in Georgetown with my family. We talked about my career and how quickly time had passed since we'd transferred to Washington, DC, in 1993.

"Dad, you can finally relax now and not be a stuffy suit-and-tie man," Jared joked.

My sons often teased me about my rigid personality and boring business attire. Once when Jared was a teenager, I had several Secret Service friends over for a party. Jared came downstairs and said, "You guys all look alike even when you're not working. You even wear the same shoes." My colleagues and I looked each other up-and-down, and it was true; every one of us wore pressed khaki slacks, button-down shirts, and loafers with no socks. We busted up laughing.

Now, sitting in the restaurant with my two sons dressed in their own suits and button-down shirts, made me proud. Ryan had followed in my footsteps by beginning a career with the Secret Service, and Jared was a junior at Towson University. Jared would also take up a career of public service. In 2011, he graduated from law school and became a prosecutor. We used to joke, "law enforcement, all in the family." I wished my parents were alive to share this moment with us. They would have been so proud of their grandsons.

We had all sacrificed a lot, my sons, my wife, and I. But here we all were, together, still a devoted family. We agreed it would be good to have me around more, now that I'd be working for a private government contractor and was likely to keep more normal hours.

I knew little about my first assignment. When I asked for details my interviewer was blunt. "I can't give you specifics, only that you'll be the point man for a highly sensitive operation."

He seemed confident that I was the perfect man for this mission, but waiting to learn the details was my idea of the fifth ring of hell. My family was used to not always knowing the precise nature of my assignments. I was not. The following week couldn't come soon enough.

That Monday morning, I sat in my new cubicle staring at a blank computer screen. The IT guys hadn't gotten around to giving me a password, so I sat there stupidly gazing into an electronic void, still wondering what the hell I was supposed to be doing. It was January of 2006. The company that hired me was well-known and respected, which gave me some comfort, but otherwise, I was in the dark. I took the job on a leap of faith.

I was assigned to the government's Science and Technology Directorate in the Department of Homeland Security. More precisely, the Office of Research and Development. So I knew that much, and it sounded interesting, maybe even challenging. The office was headed by Dr. Maureen McCarthy, a physicist who had previously served as Chief Scientist for the National Nuclear Security Administration, coordinating non-proliferation programs. She was also the first Defense Policy Fellow of the American Association for the Advancement of Science. Word had it she was a force in her own right, with no patience for excuses or for anyone who offered them.

After more than a week at my new job, I still had a blank computer screen and still knew nothing about the so called "sensitive operation." Nobody in my section had much to say to me except "good morning" and "good night." Apparently, camaraderie and conversation weren't on the agenda. I wondered how long the silent treatment would last. And I thought Secret Service agents were stiff! I was sure it would get better given some time, at least I hoped it would. About a week later, I got a visit from an administrative aide.

"The Deputy Director wants to see you," he said. "Can you come by his office in fifteen minutes?"

"Can you tell me what this is about so I can get ready for it? Do I need to bring anything with me?"

"No, just bring yourself."

"Ok, I'll be there," I said. I thought to myself, they should change the name of this division from "Research and Development" to "Run Silent, Run Deep."

I walked into his office, more eager than nervous, ready to just do something already. With a friendly wave of his hand, he invited me to sit. We had something in common, we were both Navy veterans. He was a submariner. I was cryptologist. I hid my impatience as we spent a few minutes exchanging pleasantries about our time in the Navy. Then, without warning, he fell silent, stood, and crossed the room to a gray government safe in the corner. He bent down and deftly spun the dial through what seemed like a very long combination until the handle clicked. He pulled open the heavy door, reached inside, took out a slender white binder and handed it to me.

"Here you go. See what you can do with this. Read it, and you'll understand."

I nodded, hoping he'd offer a bit more explanation. The binder didn't weigh much.

"Oh, by the way, you'll be reporting to Dr. Maureen McCarthy who's heading up this project." I took it to be the same Dr. McCarthy I'd heard rumors about, tough and unrelenting. That was the extent of my briefing.

I took the binder to my desk but sat there for a moment before I opened it. This was so weird. Never before had I been handed a briefing document without a word of explanation. I hoped it would hold something interesting. Above all, I prayed it would be something I could accomplish. I began reading, and with each page I turned, I got more of a nervous feeling in my stomach. Each page drew me in deeper, increasing my interest and apprehension. The operation outlined in the document was clearly a serious endeavor, something that would normally be handled by a team. Well, I wanted to work on something interesting and important. Check. But was I the right guy for the job?

A chilling thought gripped me: surely, they don't expect me to do this by myself? No, of course not. I didn't have the authority for something like this. I slowly closed the binder. Why was there no mention in this file of a team, squad, support staff, partner, or any other person or entity? In the binder was a photo of the gray-haired, middle-aged Iraqi who was apparently the man described in these pages. That, plus one direct instruction for me:

"Find a missing, Iraqi, bioweapons scientist somewhere in Iraq and convince him to cooperate with us."

They wanted me to turn an Iraqi enemy into an American asset.

I muttered aloud, "What, seriously?"

With a sigh, I opened the file again to read it more closely, hoping to understand who he was, this Arab who I thought looked about ten years older than I, though he was two years younger. The man in the photo had a serious look on his face, which I disliked on sight. After 9/11, after breathing in the dust of the fallen at Ground Zero, I was not disposed to like anyone from *that* part of the world. More than four years had passed, but I was still raw. And I was still prone to moments of despair and anger. And my distasteful job now, it seemed, was to convince this one that we should be friends.

The pages in my hands offered precious little info on this guy's life, his connections, or why he was so important. It would take me months to find out all the answers to how Thamer Abdul Rahman Imran ended up on my desk. I closed the binder for a second time, leaned back in my chair, folded my hands behind my head, and let out a breath of air. The words *unexpected* and *overwhelming* rattled around inside my head. Well, the mystery of my assignment is over, now where to begin, I thought. I had a photo and a name but not much else.

Chapter 5

WASHINGTON, DC—JANUARY 2006

I COULDN'T GET THE FACE OF IRAQI bioweapons scientist Thamer Imran out of my head. I had barely started my new assignment, and I was already beginning to regret my leap of faith in accepting it. This was different from any case I'd handled before. I was not simply tasked to find this man—by all accounts an enemy of America—but to convince him to become an asset. This was a brutal request to make of a guy like me, particularly at a time when we were at war with Iraq and my wanting revenge for 9/11 was still strong. Beyond that, neither my training nor my experience had really prepared me for this mission. I usually gathered evidence to lock up bad guys, not go on search and recovery missions. Now I was being asked to obtain this Iraqi's cooperation and turn an enemy into a best buddy.

My assignment was code-named Project Zebra. I wondered what hidden meaning this name carried, if it referred to some special characteristic of the man I'd be looking for, of the secrets we wanted him to divulge, or of the military defense we wanted him to bolster. I was told later that Dr. McCarthy had a picture of a zebra in her office, "Hey why don't we call it Project Zebra?"

someone asked. Sure, why not? Sometimes cloak and dagger tactics are all cloak, no dagger.

The day after I received my assignment, Dr. McCarthy called me into her office for a meeting. She told me I was the replacement for a former army intelligence officer who wasn't moving fast enough to find the missing Iraqi scientist.

"I want this guy found, we need to talk with him, and the guy you're replacing hasn't done squat," she said.

"I understand."

"It's your job now."

"Ok," I said. "I'll take it from here."

My subsequent meetings with Dr. McCarthy were the same as my first—short. I decided to meet the man I was replacing to get more details on what he'd done so far, his take on what the holdup was, and whether there were any avenues he might suggest I try next to find this missing Arab, who apparently was important to someone. I was careful not to convey an attitude of blame or superiority.

I needn't have worried. He was more than happy to hand the assignment off to me. That was partly because, for as many doubts as Dr. McCarthy had conveyed about his competence, he had at least as many doubts about hers. Where she felt he was moving too slowly, he felt she lacked an understanding of the intensive nature of the work involved. If anything, he felt her constant pressure was slowing him down by preventing him from following the steps he thought necessary. In response to my comment that, as a physicist, Dr. McCarthy was obviously intelligent and must have a handle on all this, he remarked, "Intelligence work requires a different kind of intelligence." I smiled.

He respected my background but didn't think it would be helpful. In fact, he expressed doubts about my ability to get approval to carry out the mission.

"Steve," he said, "this is a job typically handled by other government agencies. We technically don't have the jurisdiction to do this." I had no retort. He was right. It was odd that this mission found its way to the R&D section in the Science and Technology Directorate of DHS.

My predecessor was concerned about crossing legal lines and getting in trouble. He wanted no part of this effort. His concerns weren't without merit. Returning to my office, I slumped into the chair, and rubbed my eyes, sensing the start of a stress headache. I wondered what I'd just walked into. I thought, ok we have legal *and* jurisdictional issues, and my predecessor running away as fast as he can. The image of a big, fat, shit sandwich started to take shape in my mind. Taking a job on a leap of faith with no idea of what the hell you're supposed to do is not something I would recommend. But here I am, I thought. Just keeping moving dude, keep moving forward.

The fact that my target was an Iraqi, and we were fighting a war in Iraq wasn't lost on me. It would be an understatement to say that the war added just a bit more stress to the situation. The year 2006 would turn out to be one of the most violent years of the war. It had been less than five years since the 9/11 attacks, and less than three since we'd invaded Iraq. My brothers and sisters in arms were dying in Iraq and Afghanistan, and I categorically despised both of those countries. The entire Middle East was a mess as far as I was concerned.

My role in Project Zebra was mostly about the logistics and mechanics of finding a man who didn't want to be found, and I knew that learning why he was so important was a good first step to finding him. So, I started by learning what I could about the Iraqi government's scientists.

As a result of the US invasion of Iraq, many Iraqi scientists with the kind of skills that could do us harm were now displaced, on the run, and scared. The institutions they once supported were no longer functional because we'd bombed them out of existence. The first year after the invasion was marred by chaos, confusion, death, and a fear of the unknown—on all sides of the conflict.

"Sides," in fact, were hard to identify. This new reality had no clear outlines, no clear boundaries, and no clear end in sight. This was the environment the scientists found themselves in. They had few options, no hope and no future, at least not in their home country. They had families, but no way to support them. They were adrift in a country torn apart from the outside by war, and from the inside by an insurgency. From an American perspective, all of this made them more dangerous to our interests than ever. Desperate scientists with deadly skills running around in a country at war? What could go wrong, I thought? I continued digging deeper.

A chemist's mutilated body was dumped on a street in Basra; a physicist shot twice in the back in Baghdad; a dean of engineering kidnapped by a hit squad and his body left on his wife's doorstep. Without a doubt, these were parts of a systematic effort to eliminate or exile a group crucial to the country's reconstruction. One of the first academics murdered was Muhammad al-Rawi, president of Baghdad University. On July 27, 2003, he was assassinated in his clinic by an unknown hit team. In the chaos of Iraq, exact body counts were impossible to tally, but observers recorded several hundred assassinations of academics. There was a campaign to kidnap or kill all of the scientists in Iraq.

To me, these scientists represented the culmination of my worst fears. As chemical specialists, missile delivery experts, conventional weapon experts, and bioweapons scientists, they were the people who ran the Weapons of Mass Destruction (WMD) programs that threatened the security of our nation and the world. Where would they go? Who would they work for? And what havoc could they wreak was a scary unknown.

Because of their association with the former regime and the skills they possessed, scientists like Thamer Imran were targets for kidnapping. And it was no secret that the insurgents wanted these scientists to contribute their skills to the Jihad. In an open communiqué, Al-Qaeda called for these scientists and technicians to join the fight against the infidels.

The superiority of our US forces was without question, and the insurgents understood that they couldn't stand forever against such military dominance, overwhelming in both size and technology, so they needed to adopt a new strategy, a strategy designed not to defeat our forces militarily, but to change American policy in the region. Al-Qaeda's use of conventional weapons (IEDs) although deadly to our troops, wasn't enough to chase us out, but the use of unconventional weapons could be a different matter. The sight of US forces donning full chem/bio protection suits to ward off blisters, vomiting, respiratory failure, skin sores, mental deterioration, horrible pain, and even death that could result from such an attack might sway the opinion of the American people that's it was time to pack it in and leave.

Scientists who possessed military skills were being kidnapped and forced to join the Jihad. And scientists who didn't possess military skills were being killed as part of the strategy to prevent the new Iraqi government from being successful. If you want a new government to fail, one way to achieve that is to wipe out their brain power. After learning what was happening to Iraq's scientists, I had no doubt that the danger Thamer faced was real. I needed to find him and find him fast.

This risk of "losing" Thamer and other scientists like him to the insurgents eventually got the attention of highly placed military and intelligence experts in DC who were convinced that it was important that *we* find the scientists who possessed WMD skills, learn what they were up to, and eliminate the chance that they could pass on their tradecraft to the bad guys or countries hostile to the US. I agreed with all that. But the military and intelligence brass also seemed convinced it was important to get these scientists on our side. To me, it was a strategy fraught with danger. I saw no point in cooperating with anyone from the enemy's side, because there was no way we could trust those guys. It was impossible to say how many weapons scientists remained loyal to Saddam or sympathized with the insurgency. But I knew it was likely that hundreds of them felt caught in the middle; they were unemployed and diminished, terrified that they'd be targeted if they worked with the US-led coalition, yet unsure whether the United States could be trusted. We were having plenty of problems in Afghanistan with so called "friendlies" turning against us. The Taliban were able to successfully infiltrate Afghan security forces with their own fighters and carried out a number of "insider attacks" resulting in the deaths of Americans and Afghan military and police. How could we trust any of them to work for us? How could we know that they weren't poised to turn against us?

I never told my boss about my misgivings, and I justified my silence this way: my assignment was to find this guy and bring him in, nothing more.

JUST A FEW WEEKS AFTER I RECEIVED my remarkably limited briefing, Dr. McCarthy stopped me in the hallway outside my office.

"Stephen, we're going to the White House to brief on Project Zebra, and you're going to give the brief."

I was floored. "To who?"

"The Homeland Security Council." Shit, this wasn't good.

"I'm tired of getting beaten up," she added.

Great. I guess it was time for someone else to leave blood on the floor, I thought.

"When?" I asked.

"Two hours."

"You've got it!" I said. But what I really thought was, oh shit. I wasn't even close to being prepared for this.

There was no time for me to gather any new information beyond the little I'd read and what I'd learned during my conversations with my predecessor. But I knew this is what they hired me for, to stand and deliver. So I rushed to draft, proof, and print briefing packets. Dr. McCarthy had done much of the prep work ahead of time, and I was going with her because she just needed a new delivery boy.

A couple of hours later, I stood at the head of a long mahogany table, handed out the briefing packets, and faced several of President Bush's Homeland Security advisers who'd been appointed to a council he himself had formed in the wake of the 9/11 attacks.

I had a fair amount of experience conducting briefings, and it never bothered me to speak in front of people, so I stuck to Dr. McCarthy's five-minute script. Then for the next forty-five minutes I hung in there, extolling and defending the value of our plan to find Iraqi scientist, Thamer Imran, while the council did their best to find holes in it, and finding holes wasn't difficult. I hadn't yet had time to create my own plan, so we were more or less selling the old one.

"I think you're wasting your time," one council member said. "Imran has already been interrogated. I'm sure we have all the information we're ever going to get from him."

I replied, "That may be true, but as a criminal investigator and polygraph examiner specifically trained to extract information from people, I'm never sure that I get it all."

The room fell silent. I could see on their faces that they took my comment as an insult, but I didn't flinch because I knew I was right; anyone who is sure they're so good at interrogating that they'd never miss anything is wrong. I knew I'd taken a risk firing that shot across the bow of this ship of power, and right away I saw that the shot had landed someplace important. After a stunned moment, their expressions shifted to curiosity as I continued to make the case for how important it was to find Thamer and the knowledge he possessed. The council member who had called me out said nothing for the rest of the briefing. Dr. McCarthy wore a faint smile that told me she respected fighters. Good to know.

It wasn't the last battle we'd have with the HSC. At the time, I didn't understand the resistance we were facing. Why would they not want us to find him and learn as much as we can from him? The answer to that question would be revealed later, much later.

AT FOLLOW-UP MEETINGS, THE SECRETARY of Homeland Security, Michael Chertoff, Bush's second in as many years, was the only one who seemed responsive to our plans. The Secretary expressed concern about the lack of solid intelligence regarding the activities and whereabouts of scientists and technicians with WMD skills, and he insisted the council develop a full-blown strategy to track these scientists if not to help us, at least to prevent them from working against us. He was afraid that people like Thamer Imran might sell their skills to countries unfriendly to the United States, or that they might actually find their way into the US. The vast unpatrolled sections of our border with Mexico worried him. Iraqis had been picked up trying to enter the US using established drug smuggling routes in the northern Mexican desert. The thought of drug smugglers and terrorists working together worried DHS, and frankly, scared the shit out of me.

Other federal agencies tried weighing in on our operation, complaining that Homeland Security was overstepping its jurisdiction. They argued that foreign affairs were the purview of the State Department and that the Department of Homeland Security should stick to the homeland. The Secretary was having none of that. He made it clear that the President had charged him with the total security of our homeland, and he would stretch as wide a net as necessary to do that without wasting time to argue over whose turf he stepped on. Chertoff was essentially asking, why wait for a problem to wash up on a New Jersey beach before we acknowledge we have a problem? When it came to biological weapons, that could be far too late.

My Secret Service training taught me to address any threat as far away as possible from whatever I've been assigned to protect, and if that meant traveling halfway around the world to prevent danger from reaching anyone under our protection, that's what I'd do. The Secret Service doesn't wait for a threat to come knocking.

Despite my questions about why the HSC was blocking us, I had questions about Thamer. What information did Thamer have that was so important, and why would he ever give it to us? But I wasn't given a lot of reasons; it was made clear that my job was to find him. This is how classified operations are run. You're told what you need to know and nothing more.

As I continued my investigation, I made contacts at the US State Department, and those led me to contacts at the Embassy in Baghdad. I became familiar with a State Department program called the Iraqi Interim Center for Science and Industry, IICSI for short. The program was created to keep track of all the WMD scientists and other "intelligentsia" of Iraq and find out what they were up to, and that involved paying these guys to show up and check in with us. The US did not want their skills and knowledge to fall into the wrong hands, and at the same wanted them to help build a new Iraq government assisted by the US. While their payments kept them from starving and kept us aware of what they were doing, the system was hardly a guarantee that they weren't doing double duty and working against us.

I began to understand how big a footprint we had in Iraq. Another shot at nation building, when will we ever learn, I thought to myself as I dug deeper into the program. The insurgents, on the other hand, wanted to use scientists with WMD skills and conventional weapons skills and then kill the rest of the scientists who couldn't help them militarily. They didn't want to build a new Iraq that would be a puppet of the US, and eliminating the best and brightest was one way to do it. The IICSI attempted to assuage the scientists' fears and uncertainties by paying them a monthly stipend to keep them at bay. Better than nothing, I thought, but hardly a long-term strategy.

The more I read Thamer's file, the more uncertain I became about why he'd been imprisoned for over two years. I learned that while in prison, Thamer was visited by US government officials. I also learned that he had information that was important and that an agreement had been made to relocate him to the US in return for his cooperation.

Why did they decide to release him, and what happened to the promise to help him? I reviewed every report, evaluation, and assessment I could get my hands on.

After weeks of digging, I found some of the original staff members who visited him in prison. I learned their take on his value and let them explain why they didn't follow up on his release. What I had gleaned from these interviews was that they'd moved on to other things and had all but cast Thamer out of their memories. To them, it seemed, he was just another dead-end task in an endless stream of dead-end tasks. Ok, I thought to myself, Thamer was visited in prison and determined to be of value, and then suddenly it all went away. And here we come along, this small group headed by Dr. McCarthy, looking to bring it all back. There was no doubt that our presence was rattling some cages, and I was beginning to get the impression that someone wanted this whole thing to go away.

It didn't help that I was working alone to unlock this mystery. From the moment I opened Thamer's file, it was clear to me that this was not a one-man job. So why was I working it alone?

One day Dr. McCarthy stopped me in the hallway.

"Steve, I know you need help."

No shit, I thought, as she handed me a piece of paper.

"Give this guy a call and see what you think." She walked on, only to turn around abruptly at the end of the hall and shout, "He's spent time in Iraq!"

I became hopeful as I opened the piece of paper and read, *Immigration and Customs Enforcement, Special Agent Kevin Kelly.* Partnering with someone from Immigration and Customs made sense; we were going to have immigration issues if we ever brought Thamer in, and this agent's experience in Iraq would be a plus. I called the number.

Chapter 6

WASHINGTON DC—JULY 2006

KEVIN KELLY WAS AN UPBEAT, dynamic talker in his late-thirties, and he struck me as a guy who could adapt to almost any situation. My decades of experience in policing and conducting thousands of interviews of people with every kind of background imaginable, gave me an ability to size up people quickly, and right away I felt comfortable with Kevin. He'd been a Marine and had fifteen years as a Special Agent with ICE. Our similar experiences gave us common ground, and I felt an instant rapport. Although his immigration experience was important, what appealed to me most was that he came off as someone who wasn't hung up on rules and regulations, a plus for two men venturing into uncharted territory where the usual rules might need to be, well, bent. I later learned that he was also skilled in the art of dynamic persuasion, a refined term for getting people to do what he needed them to do by whatever means. I didn't know it then, but this gift would indeed come in handy.

Dr. McCarthy had already explained to him the gist of our mission, and Kevin was eager to dive in. Over the next week or so, Kevin and I exchanged phone calls, careful not to say too much over the phone because parts of the mission were classified. In one particular call, he suggested we add another person to our team, namely Jim Elseth, a friend of his, and at the time a Lieutenant Colonel in the Marines who was assigned to a special task force at the Department of the Treasury that dealt with financial investigations in Iraq. Kevin assured me that all we needed was a little push from Dr. McCarthy to persuade Jim's superiors to let him join the team. She did just that, and soon the three of us arranged to meet at Homeland Security headquarters.

When I saw the two of them waiting for me in the lobby, I was reminded of the Twin Towers. Both Kevin and Jim were at least six-foot-three, and solidly built, and together they cast a huge shadow. Kevin had red hair, and his no-nonsense haircut, impeccable dark suit, and sunglasses made him look like a Secret Service agent straight out of central casting. Meanwhile, Jim's haircut and upright, shoulders-back bearing announced from a mile away the unstoppable confidence of a Marine, although his civvies forced me to stifle a grin.

Jim suffered from a problem I'd noticed plaguing many Marines, including my brother: an inability to dress themselves like adults when out of uniform. He wore a sport coat that didn't match his pants, a bright colored shirt that fought with both, and a striped tie too short for the decade. We retreated to a basement office that I had reserved. I'd prepared as in-depth a briefing as I could offer, given that I knew little. I was hoping that by the end of my briefing I would have a team that would help me find this "missing person."

As we sat down, I reminded myself that appearances aren't the measure of a man, and I smiled, shaking my head slightly at Jim's plaids, stripes, and six-inch tie. Jim had an easy, outgoing personality—the opposite of what I was expecting of a Marine. I took to him right away. We talked about his experiences since the war started, his background and assignments in the Marines, and his work at Treasury conducting financial investigations in

Iraq. When it came to discussing business, his mature sense of conviction impressed me. We talked a bit about 9/11, the event that ultimately brought the three of us together.

For Jim, 9/11 was even more personal than it was for me. His brother, Robert, had been a naval officer assigned to the Pentagon. That morning, after learning of the attacks in New York, Robert had picked up the phone to call his sister who worked in Manhattan urging her to stay home because they didn't know if there were more planes being used in the attack. Minutes later, Lt. Commander Robert Elseth, US Navy, was dead. He was killed when American Airlines's Flight 77 plowed into the Pentagon. Devastated by this news, Jim left his managerial job, went back on active duty, and ended up fighting in Iraq in the battle of Fallujah. I didn't know Robert but immediately felt a kinship with him. We were Navy brothers. Listening to what happened to him brought back a flood of angst over the heavy price America paid. Despite all that upheaval and trauma around Robert's death, Jim wasn't followed by a dark cloud; instead, he had a bright, energetic, up-beat personality that quickly drew me in. He took his work seriously, but it was clear he saw a sense of fun as an important component to hard work.

Jim's first questions got straight to the point, "So we're looking for a missing scientist, and he's a microbiologist?"

I nodded.

"And this scientist has something we need?"

"We think so."

"And our job is to find him and learn what he knows?"

"Yup, and it's important that the bad guys don't learn what he knows before we do."

"I get it," Jim said. "And any idea where he is now?"

Kevin, who knew as much as I knew, rolled his eyes.

"We have no idea," I confessed. "We've gotten reports that he could be somewhere in Syria." I shrugged. "He could also be dead."

"Are you kidding me?"

"No," Kevin and I answered in unison.

"So, we're looking for one man somewhere in the Middle East who might be dead?" Jim asked.

"You got it," I told him, "And we'll be pretty much solo on this one. We have little support, no budget to speak of, and, so far, no help from anyone else. As a matter of fact, it appears from where I'm sitting, that the people who've assigned me this task don't want this to go off, and I don't know why."

Kevin grinned at his friend. "Getting more interesting, huh?"

"Okay," Jim held up his hand and ticked off each fact on his fingers. "So, no money, no top cover, no plan, no help from any other agencies?"

"That about sums it up. And that's the easy stuff."

"What do you mean?"

"Even if we manage to find him, I'm not sure he's going to want to talk to us."

"No shit?"

"No shit."

Kevin and Jim looked at each other and then back at me.

"You guys still interested?"

There was a pause.

"Hell, yeah!" Jim said, as he clapped his hands and rubbed them together as if someone had just brought him a juicy steak. Kevin grinned and shook his head, and we all laughed. We were three very different men, but the chemistry was already working. I knew that wherever this project led next, these men would have my back.

Although I had a team, we each spent hours alone, pondering the puzzle of Thamer Imran. A big concern for us was that even if we were lucky enough to find him, he may not want to talk to us. I wondered, since when does the US government lock a guy up for two years without ever charging him with a crime? He wasn't a combatant. He never took up arms against us, yet we made him a prisoner. That might be reason enough for him not wanting to cooperate. With no way to provide for his family and no future to speak of and his country in turmoil, his bitterness and resentment toward us wouldn't be surprising. Although I didn't know exactly where he was, I was hoping he'd have the strength to keep going. Thamer started to become a person to us rather than a target. And this missing person was looming larger and larger in my life.

ONE OF THE MOST TELLING PIECES of information I learned about Thamer was that he combined two demographics: he was a Shia Muslim, and he was also a member of Saddam Hussein's Ba'ath Party. The Ba'ath party was the power in Iraq and was owned by one man, Saddam Hussein, whose power was built on familial and tribal loyalties. Hussein was a Sunni Muslim, so Hussein's Ba'ath party was dominated by Sunnis. Shia Muslims had little to no power in his regime, and were regarded with suspicion. Thamer had joined the Ba'ath party despite all this because he had to. Being a member of the party was the only way to get the kind of position he had studied for and dreamed of. But he was no party loyalist, just a scientist who wanted to provide his family a better life.

What would happen to Carmela and my sons if I were whisked off to jail for no valid reason? *For two and a half years?* This project was beginning to feel not only like a professional assignment, but a personal mission that raised a lot of questions, and it was growing harder to tell who were the good guys and who were the bad guys.

I was most disturbed by hearing reports about some of our interrogation techniques. The Abu Ghraib prison scandal made world-wide headlines when CBS broke the story of human rights violations and war crimes being committed by the US against imprisoned Iraqis. The crimes included physical and sexual abuse, torture, rape, sodomy, and the killing of Manadel al-Jamadi, an Iraqi national who was tortured to death while being interrogated. I always view news reports with a healthy dose of skepticism, as there is generally more to the story, but when the photos appeared of some of our troops gleefully abusing and degrading Iraqi prisoners in the most sickening ways, it could not be denied or ignored. While I wanted those responsible for 9/11 to be punished, the revelation that we were torturing prisoners was hard to swallow. It was tough to put my finger on everything that bothered me about this case; so much was unwritten and unsaid. But my instincts were already hinting that I was about to question the idea of justice in a way I never had before. When the Abu Ghraib prison scandal photos were released, the danger to our troops increased tenfold as thousands of foreign fighters poured into Iraq, incensed and looking for revenge. The treatment of prisoners at Abu Ghraib also led to sickening acts of retaliation against our troops and support personnel. The abuses at Abu Ghraib came with a heavy price tag.

The rationale for invading Iraq was falling apart. No weapons of mass destruction were found. Saddam Hussein had nothing to do with 9/11. He hated Al-Qaeda and the Taliban and kept them out of his country. So why were we there? Why were our soldiers dying? Why were Iraqis being killed? I thought back to my time in the military near the end of the Vietnam War. So much death and destruction in that faraway war, and to what end? What did we accomplish? It was troubling to think that we could be heading down that road once again. It gave me a sickening feeling.

As far as I could discern, Thamer's only mistake was bad timing. He was arrested at the beginning of the war when the US was frantically seeking evidence of the weapons of mass destruction that our intelligence community had assured the president were in existence. Bush used this information as his justification for invading Iraq. At first, I also believed that Iraq possessed WMDs, believed our intelligence community had done their due diligence and had no reason to lie. It seemed Thamer's questioners believed it too, or needed to, so much so that perhaps they gave no credence to other possibilities.

I didn't need to meet Thamer to know he'd been roughed up. Nobody was trying to hide it from me. The Abu Ghraib Prison scandal had made it clear that some people on our side weren't above abusing prisoners, and I'd heard plenty of whispers from colleagues about how "enhanced interrogation techniques" were being used against prisoners who withheld potentially vital information. Long before I'd heard of Thamer Imran, I'd thought about what I would do if I had to interrogate a prisoner I believed had information about the location of a dirty bomb set to go off. I played the scenario in my head: I have to convince some guy to tell me where a bomb is, and if I don't, thousands of people could die. The thought of children being torn apart from some massive explosion sickened me. How far would I go? I didn't like thinking about it. Torture went against everything I believed in from a moral standpoint, and I wouldn't want it done to our guys if they got captured. But after 9/11, I figured everything was on the table.

Chapter 7

CAMP CROPPER, IRAQ—JUNE 2003

THE MILITARY CONVOY MOVED QUICKLY through the dangerous streets of Baghdad. With Thamer's arms shackled behind his back, his shoulders were on fire and each bump in the road was agony. He heard the distant rattle and crack of small arms fire, but that had become a constant all over the city, so it offered no clue to where they were headed.

The truck jerked to a stop, and a guard ordered, "Move!"

Thamer rose to unsteady feet. Then he hesitated, unable to see through the blindfold tightly wound around his head. Hands yanked him down from the truck bed onto pavement, where he stumbled but kept his balance, as they hurried him into a building. His ears rang with the comparative quiet after the loud droning of the truck engine. The ride hadn't been long but not short either, maybe half an hour. He wondered if he was still within city limits.

"May I call my family so they will not worry?" he said in English to the person beside him, who kept a firm grip on his arm. No reply.

The plastic cuffs pressed hard into his wrists and cut off circulation. His hands felt icy and stabbing pains gave way to numbness. He feared permanent nerve damage, but he said nothing. Thamer feared any complaint might only antagonize his captors.

Calm down, he silently ordered himself. You've done nothing wrong. They've made a mistake. As soon as they figure that out, everything will be okay.

Inside the building, two men hustled him into a cold room. He knew it was small, because of the way the sounds of his shuffling feet bounced sharply off the walls. They asked a few cursory questions about his health, wrapped a pressure cuff around his arm to take his blood pressure, and checked his pulse. The "physical" was over in a few minutes. One of his guards ordered, "Don't move," and then left.

Thamer remained standing upright and alone for several hours. He wanted to find a way to rest but feared that even feeling around for a place to sit might lead to punishment for disobeying the order not to move. After a while, his legs shook violently. Arrows of pain shot through his back. Then before he could stop it, his body slumped to the ground. He felt rough concrete under his hands.

"Stand up!" a male voice shouted.

He hoisted himself back onto his feet, which cost him considerable pain and effort. Soon, the relentless darkness and tightness of the blindfold made him dizzy. He swayed and dropped to the floor again.

"Stand!" the voice ordered again. The coldness of the cell sank deeper into his bones until Thamer shivered uncontrollably. The distinct sound of tumblers turning in a metal lock was followed by the voices of several men in tense discussion.

It was true what he'd heard about the senses, how lack of one intensifies the others. Being blinded for hours had heightened his hearing and his ability to feel people shifting the air around him. This time, his interrogators didn't introduce themselves. They only asked questions. The same questions.

"Where did you hide the WMDs?"

"I didn't hide anything." He struggled not to sound panicked, enraged, or pained, though he felt all those things.

"You're a WMD scientist, right?"

"Yes, sort of. I mean, we don't call it that . . . "

"Just tell us where the biological weapons are. Soon as you tell us, you can leave."

"I wish I had information to give you. I do. My job has been to cooperate with the United Nations to ensure there are no weapons of mass destruction. I know you freed us from Saddam Hussein. I know you're our friends. If there were WMDs, I would be glad to tell you."

"Then tell us. We have the intelligence. We know you have them."

The more he insisted he didn't know anything, the more it seemed to anger them. Their voices became louder and more menacing. He was aching with hunger and dry with thirst. The cinched blindfold hurt his temples. He knew they had not only blindfolded him to prevent him from seeing *them*, but to keep them from seeing *him*. He thought, if they looked into my eyes, they'd see me as human, and it would be more difficult to bully and harass me.

As fast as it began, the questioning stopped, and Thamer's body went limp with relief. Then a fist crashed into the side of his head and knocked him to the concrete floor. A burst of light exploded in his darkness. Shocked and in pain, Thamer couldn't believe what was happening. He had cooperated. Had answered every question he was capable of answering. He'd told them about his education, training, and responsibilities and the names of his supervisors.

Why were they doing this to him?

AROUND THE TIME THAMER'S interrogators were throwing a second punch and then a third, his wife, Eman, was standing at their kitchen table, staring at their children gathered around her for dinner: nineteen-year-old Farah, sixteen-year-old Mustafa, and eleven-year-old Usama. She ladled soup into three bowls, unable to hide her shaking hands. Then she sat down in front of her own bowl, which she'd left empty. Her three children looked from their anxious mother to her empty bowl, to each other, young faces creased with doubt. Nobody moved.

"Go ahead, eat while it's hot. I'm going to wait for your father." Eman looked across the table at the empty chair where her husband usually sat.

Usama spoke first. "Where's Dad? He's usually home by now."

"Probably working late," Eman said, trying for a cheerful tone. She glanced from face to face and saw she wasn't fooling anyone, not even Usama, her little one. They were all growing up so fast. Of course, they were. They lived in a war zone.

She rose from the table, unable to bear the tension any more. Her mounting fear for her husband, her need to lie to the kids—it was all too much. She rose from the table and walked into the front room.

"I'll be right back," she called over her shoulder in the same false lighthearted tone.

What she had told them could very well be true; Thamer often worked late. But when he did, he always called. Eman paced, paused to peer out the window, paced some more. No, not always, she reminded herself. How many times had she paced like this before, only to have everything turn out fine? One time, Thamer had stayed for a late meeting and when he'd come home, he'd said, "Remember, I told you about it this morning?" Another time she forgot that he'd promised to take Usama to soccer practice. "Remember, I told you about it this morning?" But that was all before the war.

This was a different Baghdad. Since the war started, Thamer made a point to be specific about his whereabouts. When he had left this morning, he'd said nothing about working late. She looked at the clock: 7:30. More than an hour late. A hundred things could have happened, and her mind raced with words like violence, gunfire, death. How had these concepts become normal thoughts any time her husband was late for dinner? She heard footsteps behind her and spun on her heels, startled to see Farah right behind her. She put a hand to her heart, as if to hold it in.

Eman tried smiling, but her daughter's pained expression reflected Eman's true feelings—blood-tingling terror, and her terror was made worse because she knew she wasn't overreacting. Thamer held a government job that had something to do with weapons, and the government he worked for had just been defeated in a war. Eman had always known this moment might come.

She glanced toward the kitchen, eyes begging Farah to say nothing to upset the boys. Neither woman said a word. But a voice in Eman's head probed, are you sure you were paying attention this morning, Eman? You're sure he didn't say something important? Worst of all, she couldn't remember his last words before he'd left for work. She hoped they'd been, "I love you," but no, it hadn't been that kind of morning. She was pretty sure all either of them had said was "Goodbye."

THAMER LAY ALONE ON THE ICY floor, bound and blindfolded with no sense of whether it was day or night, no idea how long he'd been in custody. All sense of time and place were lost. All he knew was that his time alone on that floor—lonely and painful as it might be—was a temporary reprieve. His interrogators hadn't been satisfied with his answers, even though they'd all been true. He knew they'd be back with their questions and their fists.

Thamer thought, if these guys are sure there are weapons of mass destruction in Iraq, they know something I don't know. Were they right? Had his government been hiding information from him?

Cold and terrified as he was, he grew more terrified at the thought of what these people might be doing to his family. Had soldiers stormed their home? Kidnapped his wife and children? Were they being interrogated? Beaten? Starved? Worse? The questions joined the questions of his interrogators to create a dust storm in his head, a *shamal*, the kind of sand storm that howls and darkens the skies for days.

What was happening to him didn't seem real. Who were these people subjecting him to humiliation and brutality? These were the guys who had come to free Iraq? Although these weren't his countrymen, until just hours or days ago, until the moment of his arrest, he had believed they shared the same ideals, the same hopes for freedom, justice, and a better world. Every punch felt like a betrayal: an extremely confusing betrayal.

Thamer didn't know what these guys planned to do with him, but he knew he wasn't going to be released anytime soon; otherwise, why would they have taken all his possessions, blindfolded him, and moved him to this place? No, he was going to be here for a while, he thought.

What he didn't know was that more than two and half years would pass before he would once again be free.

Thamer was more of a scientist than a religious man, but for the first time in a long time he prayed. He prayed that Allah would see him through this and return him to his family. Alive.

The now-familiar clang of the lock opening sent a jolt of adrenaline through his body. Terror. More than one person entered his cell. He heard two men talking, though there could have been a third. Did someone sit there silent, someone whose only job was to watch? His breathing came shallow and quick. The questions began again:

"Where are the bio stockpiles located? We know you know!"

"I swear I've told you all I know."

"Tell us now, and save yourself a lot of pain."

"I cannot tell you what I do not know," he pleaded.

"No, we want him awake," Thamer heard one of them say. To what was he referring? A needle? Drugs? He heard the shuffle, then felt the body heat and smelled the deodorized sweat of his attackers moving toward him again. They punched and kicked him from all directions. He couldn't move his bound arms or fold himself up fast enough to cover every target, stomach, chest, arms.

At first, the vile name-calling that accompanied the beatings had shocked and offended Thamer. Now he was beyond caring, the foreign words almost mundane, like bad dialogue in a cheap action movie: "Lying fucker. Sand monkey. Raghead bastard."

Through the beating, though bound, he tried to protect his face and stomach but to no avail. Every inch of him was wounded, battered. And though he hadn't seen his own face in days, he knew if Eman saw him now, she'd barely be able to recognize him. After another brutal kick, he felt something shift strangely in his abdomen and worried that his insides were bleeding. He slumped to the floor and closed his eyes, praying to Allah to let him pass out. No such mercy was forthcoming. The voices of his captors amplified and faded as he drifted in and out of consciousness.

"May I please have some water?" he gasped again.

"You want water?" one of the voices yelled. "We'll give you water!"

"Yeah, give him water!"

Someone took hold of his neck and shoulder. Still bound, he tilted his head back and opened his mouth like a baby bird eager for nourishment. Rough fingers opened his mouth wider. Someone shoved the neck of a water bottle between his lips and poured the contents down his throat. It choked him until he felt like he was drowning. Thamer coughed and gagged as he struggled for air, water spilling half-in, half-out of his mouth.

"Please . . . I can't breathe!" He jerked free from the cruel grip of many hands.

Three voices hooted and guffawed as someone forced another bottle into his mouth, water gushing into his nose and lungs. Everything became a blur, and then one of his prayers was answered: he passed out.

Later, he awoke alone, cold, and wet in his cell. How much later was it? A day? An hour? A week? He had no idea. Another man visited him. At that point he couldn't distinguish who was a soldier and who was a Department of Defense bureaucrat. They were all the same to him now. Whenever someone entered the cell, torment and humiliation followed.

But this time someone removed his blindfold and restraints. He squinted, eyes almost shut, blinded by the bluish-white fluorescent light. The room was only a few paces wide in each direction. Four walls and a ceiling that appeared to have been white at one time but now was dingy and dirty. He could have been anywhere.

"Would you like a cigarette?"

"Yes, please," he responded, grateful for the first kind gesture since his capture. Finally, someone has decided to believe me, he thought.

Then, without warning or cause, the man grabbed the back of his head and smashed Thamer's face into the cell wall. A brilliant flash of light exploded across his vision and blood poured from his nose, soaking the front of his shirt. Blinded by a sharp pain above his left eye, he placed his hands over his face, desperate to protect his broken nose from another blow. He willed himself to lose consciousness again. It didn't work.

"Are you married?" the interrogator demanded.

"Yes."

"Do you have any children?"

"Yes."

"How many?"

"I have three, a daughter and two sons."

"Well, then, you won't need these anymore," the man laughed as he kicked Thamer in the testicles with heavy boots. Then again. And again.

Thamer collapsed to the ground, pulling up his knees to his groin, which gave little protection, as the man kicked and kicked. The pain was unbearable.

I'll never be a man again, Thamer thought in agony as he curled into a ball and threw up on the floor. Moaning and lying in his own vomit, he heard the heavy door bang shut.

AS INCAPABLE AS THAMER WAS OF tracking the passage of time, Eman counted every hour. Night turned into day. Days turned into a week. Not only did Thamer fail to call, nobody called. After he failed to answer her calls, she called the only two of his colleagues for whom she had numbers. They didn't answer. She called his brothers and sisters. None of them had heard from him. She now knew that something horrible had happened to her husband, but what? Was he dead? Kidnapped? As chaos took over the city, many people were being kidnapped for ransom. This thought set her heart racing. She had no money to pay.

She tried to reassure the children. "If something bad happened to him, someone would tell us. I'm sure your father will call soon."

She composed angry speeches in her head, which she would deliver to him upon his return. "Shame on you for making me worry!"

Eman convinced her brother, Saad, to make the trip with her to Thamer's office. Saad warned her they'd be taking their lives in their hands by venturing onto the streets, but Eman explained that the uncertainty was tormenting her family, that her children wrung their hands and paced in silent, wide-eyed fear. As their mother, she could no longer stand by and hope. She swore to her brother she wouldn't ask him to drive anywhere else to look for Thamer, just to his office.

"Please, Saad!" she pleaded. "Someone at his office will know where he is."

Saad relented.

Eman had avoided venturing far from home since war had begun, and she now noticed a similar tense caution in her brother as he traversed the scarred, city streets. It was clear that his talk of the dangerous streets came from experience. He refused to stop the car to ask anyone for help, including other Iraqis, so he and Eman made slow progress. A once, fifteen-minute drive now took them more than an hour.

They arrived at the Directorate, but nobody there knew what had happened to Thamer or any of the others. The faces of his colleagues who hadn't been arrested told her they weren't hiding knowledge of his whereabouts, that they were just as mystified and worried as she was. They were polite as they tried to wrap up the conversation and show Eman and Saad to the door. She knew what that meant: they were too scared to voice their suspicions.

Many more days passed before she received a phone call from one of Thamer's colleagues at the Directorate. He whispered that he heard Thamer had gone to a meeting with a group of American scientists. That's all he said before he hung up.

She clung to this new information with renewed hope. The US government needed his help. It was something important and secret. They were keeping him hidden for his own safety!

Then, more friends called. "Eman, I think he's been arrested," one caller said. Another said Thamer and some of his colleagues were being detained in the south, in the province of Basra.

Eman broke her promise to her brother. She walked to Saad's house to beg him to help her search again. "Please! Just one more trip. Now I know where he is. Please take me to Basra!"

"Eman, it's too dangerous, and you don't know for sure that he's even there."

"I can't sit and wait like this, not knowing if he's dead or alive. He's my husband!"

"And if something happens to you? Who will take care of the children?"

Eman paced. Her brother was right, but how could she do nothing to help her husband?

"I have an idea," Saad said. "Let's go to the Red Cross. They can help us. Nobody ever attacks the Red Cross."

The next day, they went to a Red Cross office in Baghdad. Nobody there had any idea what had happened to Thamer. They told her that the Americans were keeping most prisoners in Baghdad. It was somewhat encouraging information and convinced Eman to abandon the trip to Basra. She would have to wait, but for how long nobody would even venture a guess. And, she had a more immediate problem. How was she to keep her children alive and safe in the chaos of a war?

Chapter 8

CAMP CROPPER PRISON, IRAQ—JUNE 2003

IN A HAZE OF DARKNESS AND EXTREME cold, Thamer heard a guard enter his cell. "Thamer, I have good news for you," he said. "Your son, Usama, has come to visit you."

Thamer breathed a sigh of relief. His family had found him! But Thamer's initial joy quickly turned to confusion. Why was Usama the one here? He was a young boy. This made no sense. Where was Eman? Was she dead? She would never let their young son near a place like this. She would never endanger any of their children.

"An escort is bringing him to you."

Thamer looked down at his shackled ankles, and his face burned with shame. "Could you please take off my shackles?" he asked. "I don't want my son to see my like this."

To Thamer's surprise, the young man said, "Sure," and bent down to unlock the restraints. Moments later, two soldiers escorted Usama to Thamer's cell. Before him stood his handsome, athletic, outgoing teenage son, smiling as if nothing was wrong with the world.

"Usama! So good to see you!" Thamer held out his arms, but before he could embrace his son, something warm and wet splashed his chest.

He glanced down to see his T-shirt drenched in blood. He felt no pain. Where was all this blood coming from? He looked up to see Usama gripping his throat, face pale, and mouth wide open, gasping for breath. His throat had been slashed. Blood spurted from the wound. Thamer screamed like a wild animal as the guards dragged Usama's limp body away. Crazy with grief he leaped forward and flung himself over his son while screaming his name, "Usama! Usama! Usama!" Then he called out to Allah, his cries the only sound in the universe.

Thamer's eyes snapped open. He lay on the floor of his cell in a fetal position, covered in sweat, still shaking uncontrollably. Everything was silent except the buzz of the bright fluorescent light overhead. His mind whirled. Was it real? Had they brought him here after he passed out? He looked down. His shirt was crusted with blood, yes, but old blood, *his* blood, and his shirt was no bloodier than it had been since his last beating a few hours earlier.

Still, he wasn't sure of anything. Had his child been murdered? It took until sunrise for Thamer to accept that it had been a nightmare. He closed his eyes and thanked Allah. Usama was alive. This was the first thing he'd felt grateful for since his arrest, and he realized the irony: the only thing he had to feel grateful for was the realization that a horror created by his own mind hadn't actually happened. He knew that if he were held here much longer, he would lose his mind.

Sometime later—who could know how long—a new guard entered Thamer's cell.

"Here take this," said the new man, handing him an apple and a large bottle of water. Thamer opened the bottle and gulped the water, stopping only to take a huge bite from the apple. No water or apple had ever tasted better. He paused in the middle of his second bite, looked up at the guard, wary. What was the catch? What was this guard up to?

"Would you like a shower?"

"Yes, thank you." Thamer tensed, waiting for a blow to the chest or gun to the head.

He was astonished when the guard led him out of the cell and down the hall to an actual shower. The man stood by while, with shaking hands, Thamer removed his dirty, blood-splattered dress shirt, pants, and underwear. The guard took the clothes from him with a grimace of disgust, saying he would have them washed. Thamer wasn't sure he wanted them back. He stepped into the shower and because he was in so much pain, delicately washed his body, trying to rid himself of the filth of all that had been done to him. It seemed no amount of soap would make him clean again. He felt coated in shame. As warm water rolled over him, he tried making sense of this new guard, waiting outside the stall. Was his kindness yet another prelude to cruelty? He tried to pray, but his mind couldn't hold onto what to pray for. It was all too big.

He stepped out of the shower, and the guard handed him what looked like hospital scrubs. His other clothes had vanished. To his shock, the man shook his hand, wished him well, and left.

Another guard blindfolded him, cuffed his hands so tight they went numb, and loaded him clumsily into the back of a truck. Intense sun beat down, and Thamer took a deep breath, letting himself enjoy the comforting contrast to the constant chill of his cell. Then, his ease was scorched by a terrifying thought, he'd given his captors no useful information—were they now driving him to his execution? Until recent days, he never would have considered the possibility that the American rescuers from the "Land of the Free" might commit such an ungodly injustice. But now he was a changed man. The vehicle jolted to a stop.

A soldier helped him out of the truck-bed and removed his blindfold. The June sun was blinding, and Thamer's eyes needed time to adjust to the extreme light. After a few moments, he realized he was standing in front of a large, unfamiliar complex of buildings. He wondered about the fate of the comrades who had been arrested with him but knew better than to ask. The guard removed his cuffs, and Thamer closed his eyes at the sudden abrasive pain, followed by the tingling of blessed release. The plastic cuffs had been cinched so tight the bands left deep red marks in his wrists.

The guard led him inside the building to a desk manned by a soldier. Thamer tried looking around, but the desk-sergeant screamed, "Don't turn your head! Look straight ahead!"

Careful not to turn his head again, Thamer studied the room with his peripheral vision. He stood at the edge of a big hall with several metal tables, chairs scattered about, several file cabinets, and a bed in one corner. A female soldier sat at one of the tables, writing in what looked like a logbook.

"Take your shirt off and stand against the wall," the familiar soldier ordered him.

Thamer slowly and painfully removed his shirt. Every movement sent pain ricocheting through his muscle, bone, and flesh.

The sergeant grabbed a camera and snapped photos of Thamer, asking him to turn this way and that.

The female soldier stopped writing, looked up, and gasped, "Oh my God!" then turned away.

Startled, he looked down to see what had upset her. The beatings had left his entire upper body covered with bruises, a patchwork of sickening colors announcing the varying ages of the injuries: yellow, green, blue, purple, red, black. For the first time in days, he felt self-conscious about his ruined body, this proof of his weakness, this reminder that he would be so easy to kill.

The sergeant set down the camera and scribbled a note in his record. "From this point forward, you are number 200091," he told Thamer, "or ninety-one for short."

"Ninety-one," Thamer repeated.

Then the sergeant called another guard to escort Thamer through the prison, past closed doors, down hallways, and eventually into a large hall lined with cots.

"Thamer! Thamer!" a voice called out.

He didn't dare turn his head, though his eyes searched eagerly for the source of the voice. Someone here knew him!

"Thamer! Thamer!"

He turned his head ever so slightly until he saw a man waving to him from a doorway. It was Sinan, one of his colleagues from the Directorate who had been arrested with him two weeks earlier. Tears filled Thamer's eyes, and he couldn't help smiling at the sight of Sinan, apparently well and safe. He not only felt relieved for his friend but for the realization that maybe he wasn't going to die here.

"Okay, let's keep moving," the guard ordered.

Thamer snapped his head to attention and tried to pick up the pace, but every step sent pain shooting through him. All he wanted to do was lie down.

They walked past another metal door into a hall that appeared to be makeshift barracks, filled with neat rows of cots. Stepping inside, he saw it was full of other Iraqi prisoners. Their expressions echoed that of the female soldier who had gasped at the sight of him. A few faces were familiar, and he knew that those people would recognize even more the extent of the damage he'd suffered: the lost weight; his taped nose, crooked from the break; and his once easy smile, now strained and weak.

The guard pointed out his cot and left. Then the other prisoners rushed forward to greet Thamer. Those he didn't know introduced themselves. The Minister of Higher Education, Minister of Trade, Director of Military Intelligence, and other high-ranking Ba'ath party members welcomed him with gentle hugs, pats on the back, and well wishes that he was safe. Through a fog, he heard more names and titles than he could keep track of. Thamer guessed that there were around twenty people housed in this hall.

STEPHEN PHILLIP MONTEIRO   67

He later learned that there were several other halls like his in the facility, all of them housing Iraqi prisoners. One hall next to his held Saddam Hussein's two brothers, a cousin, and officials with close ties to Hussein, including Thamer's former boss at the National Monitoring Directorate.

Thamer didn't realize it yet, but he had undergone almost two weeks of interrogations, beatings, food- and water-deprivation, and sleep deprivation. He didn't know exactly where he was, but given the time it had taken to transport him, he guessed he was still close to Baghdad. He would later learn that while the Americans had decided to give up interrogating him, he was now a prisoner of war in the largest US detention facility in Iraq: Camp Cropper.

On that first day, several dormmates offered to share food and water with him. Thamer thanked them but said all he needed was rest. Sinan gently shooed everyone away, "Let's leave our friend alone," and everyone courteously shuffled back to their previous conversations or their own naps. Thamer sat on his bunk, and once he was certain the other men's eyes were averted, he put his head in his hands and cried. He cried for his family, surely sick with fear. He cried because he didn't know if they were safe and because he could do nothing to protect them. He cried for his broken body. He cried for his broken country. He cried that his country's saviors had betrayed and brutalized him. He cried for his colleagues who were still unaccounted for. And he cried with relief that for what had felt like an entire day, no one had beaten him.

After a few minutes, he took deep breaths, wiped away his tears, and vowed that he would stay strong. He would stay strong for his family.

EMAN STEPPED OUT OF THE DIM, hot kitchen into the bright, hot garden. She flipped the switch on the generator, which rattled into noisy, smelly action. The acrid odor of the diesel fuel gave her a constant headache, but the family needed power. Because of the constant bombings, Baghdad had taken to cutting each household's power down to a few hours a day and sometimes to none at all. The generator kept her and the kids from total darkness, it kept the refrigerator going, and it gave them a small measure of relief from the oppressive heat. Weeks had passed without a word from Thamer, or from anyone who had any idea where he was, or even if he was alive. She glanced at the phone on the kitchen wall, willing it to ring, but the only sound she heard was the roar of the generator.

She grabbed the pitcher of cold tea from the refrigerator, poured two glasses, and carried them into the living room. There, her father and her sister, Leda, sat fanning themselves with magazines. She had scolded them for risking the trip from their neighborhood to pay her this visit. It was only two miles away, but it meant exposing themselves to the shifting pockets of violence plaguing Baghdad streets. Foreign troops, local insurgents, black marketeers, and ordinary troublemakers jockeyed for control of the city in the wake of the invasion. But the truth was, she was grateful they made the effort. Seeing her family comforted her, even though it was getting harder to laugh over the lighthearted things they used to talk about. The conversation quickly fell into its new wartime pattern.

"Everyone says it's the scientists they're after," Eman said.

Her father shook his head, the way he used to when she was a girl afraid of the dark.

"Eman, trust me, the Americans are interested in the leaders. Why would they want Thamer?"

"If they haven't captured him, where is he?"

"Maybe in hiding."

"Why would he hide if they're only interested in the leaders?"

"Because he's a worrier like you."

Now Eman shook her head. "He would have contacted me."

"If they're capturing scientists, then he is someplace safe and will be released shortly. Surely, they will not have reason to keep a man whose specific job has been to work with the UN to keep peace," her father insisted.

"Many people are missing," Leda said. "Many people are in the jails, and no relatives have been informed, at least none that we know of."

Eman had no idea if her sister's observation was meant to bolster her argument or her father's. Perhaps that ambiguity was what Leda intended, hoping to avoid a family quarrel. Eman flinched at a sound out front. Footsteps. Voices. She held her breath and listened. Was it Thamer finally coming home? Someone coming to inform her that he was dead? Maybe she had imagined it; it was difficult to hear anything over the generator.

"Eman," Leda's voice startled her. "I think someone's knocking."

The two sisters looked from each other to their father. The back of Eman's neck prickled. She couldn't bring herself to move.

"I'll go see," Leda volunteered. Eman resisted the urge to hold her back.

The banging got so loud it sounded as if someone was trying to break down the door. "Please wait," Leda shouted. "I'm coming!"

Eman heard the door open, then a man's angry voice speaking a foreign language—English maybe. She ran to the door where Leda faced several armed men, eyes fixed on the barrel of what looked like an automatic weapon pointed at her shaking her head in terror, mouth opened wide as if to scream but nothing coming out. Another thundering sound added to the escalating terror shooting through Eman's body: a helicopter hovered overhead, rotors beating the air. It created a hot wind that boxed her ears.

Eman was too terrified to speak, lest she say the wrong thing and the man with the rifle pull the trigger. She didn't speak English. She was pretty sure these were Americans. One of the soldiers behind him spoke up, in Arabic. He was Iraqi, a translator, she supposed. "We're here to inspect your home. You must cooperate."

Eman and Leda backed away from the door to make way. The soldiers pushed past them and rushed inside. Her father stiffened in his chair, not wanting to make any movements that might be thought of as a threat by these men with guns. He didn't move a muscle, just stared at the guns.

The interpreter was still talking. "We're here to inspect your house for any evidence of biological agents or any papers or other items involving your husband's work."

Eman was confused. She knew some of Thamer's work, but he never brought home anything like they described. The only thing she could think to say were the words that had been on her mind for weeks now, "Where is my husband?"

The Iraqi soldier translated this for the apparent leader, but he and the other men ignored the question. A few of them fanned out through the house, opening drawers and cupboard doors, knocking things over and tossing items on the floor. Her heart slammed in her chest, but she didn't dare speak against the armed men. Three men remained in the living room: the translator, a man in civilian clothes, and a soldier who pointed his high-tech-looking rifle in the general direction of her father, her sister, and her.

"It's important that you cooperate and help us or you'll be in a lot of trouble," the translator said. His eyes were kind but his voice was firm.

Without taking her eyes off the weapon, Eman lowered herself into a chair beside her father, nodding her understanding.

The civilian showed her several small vials and asked her something in English that she didn't understand. She looked from him to the translator.

"Has your husband ever brought home anything that looked like this?" the translator asked.

Eman shook her head rapidly. "No, I've never seen anything like this."

The other men continued searching. For what? What was in those vials? Nothing good, it seemed. But Thamer would never have brought home anything dangerous. They had children.

Eman looked from Leda to her father, and voiced her thought out loud, "What could Thamer possibly have that they would want?"

Her father shook his head. "There's nothing we can do except wait."

For more than an hour they waited. They listened to the sounds of the men opening and emptying every drawer, yanking hangers from closets, raiding the refrigerator and cupboards, breaking glasses. Later, she was stunned to see they had gone through all their personal belongings: toiletries, underwear, jewelry, family photos, books. They even inspected the water tanks and uprooted the garden.

When they left, they took Thamer's briefcase and many of his papers, along with a handgun he owned to protect against looters. Eman didn't care anymore. She wanted only one thing at this point, the answer to her single question.

"Please, *where* is my husband?" she begged, running after them as they strode out of the house and down the walk.

She got no response.

"What is it you are taking?" she asked.

Again, no response.

Eman learned later that the soldiers had gone to a neighbor's house first by mistake. That mistake would be costly to her family. Soon rumors spread all over the neighborhood: Thamer was a spy, Thamer was wanted by the Americans, Thamer was cooperating with the insurgents.

It didn't matter whether the rumors were true or false; that kind of attention put her whole family in danger. Three days after the search, Eman packed up her belongings and those of her children. She locked the doors of the house she and Thamer loved and fled to her father's home.

Chapter 9

CAMP CROPPER PRISON, IRAQ—JULY 2003

AT LEAST I'M NO LONGER IN ISOLATION, Thamer thought as he sat on his cot listening to murmured conversations up and down the multiple lines of cots filling the men's dorm. Their meals, if you could call them that, were brought to them—brown bags with sandwiches and other cold items, maybe some crackers. At first they weren't permitted to exercise, write letters, or make any contact with the outside world. None of his jailers had yet told him why he'd been arrested or even that he was under arrest, though the yellow jumpsuits they all wore and the barbed wire atop the camp walls made it clear that he was a prisoner. Since the closing of Abu Ghraib prison, the population of Camp Cropper prison had increased dramatically, and the prison was roundly criticized for its abuses of detainees. Word of the abuses made it out of the prison to the insurgent groups and became a tool for recruitment.

If he hadn't been certain before about why he was here, it was obvious now. The "hall" that was now Thamer's home was practically riddled with people from Iraq's Ministry of Science and

Technology. The Western military coalition had rounded up every government employee they thought might have the slightest idea where Iraq had stored weapons of mass destruction.

Thamer knew that most of the men held in his hall were neither combatants nor criminals. They were scientists and scholars, men of honor. Through brief whispered conversations, he learned they had all been through a similar experience: arrested without warning, imprisoned without being told the charges, interrogated without access to attorneys or advocates of any kind, beaten, abused, asked endlessly about WMDs—these were other common threads that ran through the stories he picked up. All seemed surprised that the military they thought had come to free them from the repressive regime of Hussein, had instead imprisoned them without cause. They were dismayed that their innocence, cooperation, and honest lack of information about the existence of WMDs had not led to their release. None had been allowed contact of any kind with anyone outside the prison, certainly not their families.

Despite the lack of outside contact, rumors circulated about what was happening in Baghdad. None of it was good. He heard that armed gangs roamed the streets. They stopped and executed right then and there anyone they thought was of a different tribe from theirs, or from a different religious sect, or working with the Americans, or for almost any reason at all. Worse, an organized armed resistance against the coalition forces was growing in strength. The possibility of victory or peace was dimming and seemed further away than ever.

Despite repeated pleas to his captors, no one would give Thamer any information about his family or how long he would be held. He begged them to at least get word to his family that he was alive. They didn't even pretend to consider this request, just flat-out told him, "No."

Every night, he lay down on his squeaky cot, but he knew from experience that sleep would not come. He dreaded those hours most of all, when the halls were quiet and he was alone with his thoughts. The silence his captors demanded at night made the place feel as eerie as a tomb full of sleeping ghosts.

He spent his first nights terrified that his interrogators would return, once again drag him away, strip off his clothes, blindfold him, and scream questions for which he had no answers. Or maybe this time they'd kill him. Wondering what had become of Eman and the children led him down mental labyrinths almost impossible to bear. And why were his captors so bent on keeping his family ignorant of his whereabouts or well-being, unless they planned to make him disappear? Even after weeks went by without his tormentors returning, he remained jumpy throughout the interminable nights. Fear was a familiar companion in the silent dark, darkness filled with nothing but the shared breathing of men awaiting their fate.

"MARK MY WORDS," SA'IB SAID after a guard passed by, "The Americans will tire of this fight. They will go home."

"They never stay in other countries," Daaneesh agreed. "They like to attack, declare victory, then leave."

Thamer found it difficult to talk to his colleagues. There were so many rumors, so many opinions, and so many scenarios being battered around.

"We will be set free soon."

"They must give us a trial."

"What will happen to our families?"

It never stopped. It felt as if, trapped in this place, they were no longer the men they had been and now had little in common other than proximity and circumstances. Each of them had their own problems and perhaps weren't inclined to hear and deal with anyone else's. And he found the other prisoners an odd assortment. Some were quiet, while others never seemed to shut up. Most of them repeated the opinions and rumors spread by other prisoners, often continuing the rumors they started—as if a rumor coming full circle somehow proved its veracity.

Thamer became close friends with a prisoner he hadn't met before the war. Adeeb was a former Iraqi journalist, and he and Thamer found comfort commiserating about "this damn war."

"Mark my words," Adeeb told Thamer. "The Americans are not going away anytime soon. They do not understand what they are getting into and they never think ahead about how they will get out." Adeeb seemed more realistic than Thamer's fellow scientists whose powers of reason and deduction seemed to have stop functioning.

Thamer sometimes felt betrayed by his own gifts. Blessed with intelligence, he had worked hard to become educated, believing it was the key to a brighter future. Yet, it had led to the career that landed him in this prison.

After six months, Thamer forged an unlikely friendship with a young American soldier named John. He knew he couldn't afford to draw the attention of fellow Iraqis to this unlikely friendship he'd forged in the strange crucible of prison, so whenever John walked into the men's dorm and stood in the far corner, Thamer took his time about making his way to that part of the hall. He thought of John as "the good American," a friendly soldier with bright blue eyes who had a kind word for everyone, and who seemed concerned about Thamer's well-being. John asked Thamer plenty of questions about his family and his past.

At first, Thamer feared John was trying to earn his trust so he could milk him for information. But over time it became clear John was an idealistic, young soldier who genuinely wanted to connect with someone, who missed his own family as much as Thamer missed his. Thamer got the impression the young man saw him as a father figure.

"Here," John would say and secretly press into Thamer's hand an orange or other piece of fruit. "I thought you might like something fresh."

"Thank you, my good friend." Thamer had come to accept John's offerings with gratitude rather than suspicion.

"You're getting some visitors today," John said, "from Washington. I think you've worked with some of them before?"

Thamer felt an uplifting of his whole countenance, but quickly his joy gave way to apprehension. Although he had worked alongside UN inspectors on nonproliferation of weapons of mass destruction, would they still see him as an ally after all these years?

John patted his shoulder. "It's something good. I promise."

A few hours later, the guards escorted Thamer to a room he hadn't been in before. He walked in to find several Americans who introduced themselves as being from the Department of Homeland Security and the Department of Justice. As Thamer shook each of their hands it was easy to imagine this wasn't a prison, but that they were meeting somewhere civilized as colleagues and equals. They explained that the purpose of the visit was to determine whether he had information of value to the US government. Although Thamer had come to associate words like "interview" and "information" with pain and fear, he felt no threat in their intent. It felt like a real interview, not an interrogation. What's more, these men understood science and asked the kind of mentally stimulating questions Thamer enjoyed answering.

"You have knowledge and experience that would be very useful to us," one of them said. "In particular, your work in microbiology is something that we would be very interested in."

Thamer wasn't sure where all this was heading, but he gladly obliged as they plowed further into his background and work, particularly his work at the bio production plant at Al Hakam.

"How would you feel if we let you out of here, then moved you to the United States with your family so you could come work with us?" one of his visitors said.

Thamer was flabbergasted at the offer. These hot and cold Americans confused him.

"Yes," he said, making no effort to disguise his enthusiasm for the country of his childhood fantasies. "I would be very much interested in doing that."

Back in the hall, Thamer's head began to spin with doubt. Was this a ploy to continue down the same WMD path, he wondered. Could he trust these Americans? He also didn't know whether he could trust his fellow prisoners; he didn't know their true sympathies and loyalties, and he realized that rumors of his cooperating with the United States could get him and his family killed.

In bed that night, sleep once again eluded him, but this time for a new reason. He could think of nothing else but his sudden change in fortune. These people who had arrested him, beaten him, and imprisoned him were now offering him a new life in the land he had always dreamed of living in. He lay awake planning his children's educations at the stellar American universities he had read so much about. Was it possible something so good could come out of the worst experience of his life?

He tempered his elation by looking on the other side of this shiny new coin. He had spent all of his more than fifty years living in Iraq, and it was a country he loved. And what about his extended family? Could he move so far away from them without feeling he had abandoned them, without fearing he had given up some vital piece of himself? All to live in a culture that seemed to become more of a mystery every day? Which of the many different Americans he had come in contact with in the past year were the typical Americans? The suspicious, easily-enraged thugs who used their uniforms and power as an excuse to take pleasure in torturing him or the open-handed Americans who gave him oranges, asked for stories about his childhood, and offered him asylum?

Thamer reminded himself that Iraqis, too, came in many different personalities. Certainly, it could be just as big a risk to trust whichever Iraqis came to power once the Americans left. His spinning thoughts kept returning to one constant: in Iraq he had no future. Yes, he thought as he drifted off to sleep, he would be happy to move to America, very happy indeed.

A couple of weeks after the meeting with US officials, Thamer was visited by the FBI. They administered a polygraph examination. Mostly, they wanted to make sure he was who he said he was, and that he didn't have ulterior motives for cooperating. They told him he passed.

Thamer took comfort in recalling their firm handshakes and reassuring smiles. He began to allow himself the excitement about building a new life in America, a safe haven where his wife and children would be welcomed and would experience all the wonders of *the land of the free*. He thought, how thrilling it will be to tell Eman!

The US government officials promised to return, and when they did, Thamer would make clear *his* promise to share all of his scientific knowledge with the United States. He gave them earnest assurance that he was eager to work with the US and pumped their hands with enthusiasm, gratitude, and relief. He knew fairness was an important value to Americans—it was in all their movies. This gave him the hope he needed to bear yet another night in the dark. And another.

Days passed. Then weeks passed. Then months passed. And every day, Thamer's hopes faded more and more. He had no idea how long he would be held in prison, or how long it would take the Americans to keep their promise. Did they forget? Did they change their minds? These thoughts weighed on Thamer like an anchor.

After being held for six months, Thamer was given permission to write a letter to his wife, to tell her he was alive and well—relatively speaking—but he had no idea if it reached her because he received no response. Maybe she had moved in with extended family or fled Baghdad. Maybe she had sent a reply, and maybe the Americans refused to deliver it to him because they still wanted to punish him for failing to tell them what they wanted to hear about the WMDs. Nothing was clear anymore. In the absence of truth, very little made sense and all he could do was continue to wait to hear from his wife and from the Americans.

ON DECEMBER 13, 2003, AT 8:26 P.M., six months after Thamer's arrest, US forces concluded one of the most intense manhunts in history without firing a single shot. News of Saddam Hussein's capture quickly spread throughout the prison, but it would be several days before Thamer dared believe it wasn't just another of the many, whispered rumors. Maybe the devil had been captured, but decent men still sat in prison paying for his crimes while evil ran rampant in the streets. The only news Thamer craved now was word that his wife and children were still alive.

The long slow days of Thamer's prison life became regimented. There were set hours for rising and eating, lights on and lights out. Showering was limited, and they rarely stepped outside for fresh air or to look at the sky. Thamer passed the terribly long days making conversation with the twenty other prisoners in the hall. Day after day, they pondered why they were being held captive, how long they'd remain imprisoned, and most of all, what was happening to their families. Frequently, individual prisoners were removed for questioning. About what, Thamer didn't know. It was better not to ask. But given that this was a prison, Thamer didn't think it was all that bad, nothing like the gritty, angry, violent, filthy institutions Thamer had seen in so many American films. Then again, this holding facility wasn't pleasant either. The cots were squeaky and the mattresses so thin he could feel their metal coils pressed against his back as he lay awake every night replaying the horrors of his abduction and his countless worries about his family and their future. The food was tasteless American fare, on cardboard-like bread, chewy boiled meats, overcooked vegetables, and dry potatoes or watery rice. Their primary daily activities were pacing, reading, talking, and praying.

The Americans allowed the Muslims to observe their prayer times in the hall, and Thamer requested a rug so he could join in. He hadn't prayed much before, but now it comforted him. Again and again, he prayed for Allah to reunite him with his wife and children. Thamer went through the same motions day after day, a man hypnotized.

FOR SEVEN MONTHS, EMAN DIDN'T know if her husband was dead or alive. Then one day she opened their mailbox and found a letter addressed to her and with no return address but showing the markings of the Red Cross, the intermediary between those held in custody and their families. The handwriting looked fragile and the letters shaky, as if scribbled by a child, but Eman recognized her husband's unmistakable handwriting, and the awareness sent a jolt through her body. Her fingers trembled as she opened the letter, the pages wrinkled as if she weren't the first person to read it. Her starving eyes gobbled up the words like great helpings of food, then going back for seconds and then thirds. She smiled as she traced a finger over the words.

Thamer wrote that he was alive but in prison. He couldn't tell her where, but he said she shouldn't worry. He was safe but desperate to hear news of her and their family. He missed them all and prayed every day that Allah would reunite them. She cherished the words that spoke of his love for her. Although he was a caring man, he rarely spoke such sentiments aloud.

He was alive.

She closed her eyes and gave thanks to God. She also gave thanks to the Red Cross, for it was they who had managed to get this letter from wherever Thamer was being held to her father's house. Thamer was safe and she prayed to Allah to give her husband the strength to make it through. By the end of the day, she knew the letter by heart, and it offered as much confusion as comfort. Where was he? How long would he be there? And most confusing of all, *why* was he in prison?

She remembered how she and Thamer had welcomed the arrival of the Americans, so happy to be free from the dictatorship that strangled their country. They were sure these Americans would bring with them a better life, a life defined by democracy, justice, and fairness and replacing the tyranny of a despot with the rule of law. But she knew beyond a doubt that her husband had never, *would* never, do anything criminal, so how could such an upright man deserve such a fate? She had always envisioned America as a heroic country that championed the downtrodden, but now that image was very tarnished.

Then she looked again at the letter, reread Thamer's reassurance that he was safe, and felt her anger subside. It was not time to indulge in resentment over the broken promise of the American arrival, or her fear over the unknown future, it was time to write back to her husband, who she was sure was desperately waiting for news of his family. She took out a pen and stationery and began.

ABOUT A MONTH AFTER WRITING to Eman, her return letter arrived, and Thamer was ecstatic to read that his relatives were all alive and relatively well. Over the next several months, Thamer exchanged many letters with Eman and the children, and kept every last one he received under his pillow, until the lump grew uncomfortable. Even though he could not read them after lights out, reaching under the pillow to touch the letters made him feel closer to his family.

After a year had passed since his capture, the prison administrators granted permission for Thamer's family to visit. He cried when he got the news. The days dragged on as he awaited word on when the visit would take place, and eventually, he gave in to a depression even worse than in those early days when he feared his captors might kill him. To be so close to his heart's desire and not be allowed touch it felt like the cruelest blow of all, greater than any physical torture his jailors could have concocted. He wished they had never promised him a family visit at all.

Weeks passed and no one came, not his family nor the government officials who had promised to help him. Thamer worried about what all these broken promises might mean. Losing the promise of America was not what concerned him—that had always seemed more dream than reality. What frightened him was that he had agreed to cooperate with the invaders at a time when they were becoming increasingly unpopular. What if word leaked out to those in the insurgency and they labeled him as a collaborator? Even in jail, this could be dangerous for him. But he'd gone too far to turn back now. It was a gamble he would have to take.

Then one day he was escorted into a room and told to wait.

"You're going to have a visitor, your wife," the guard told him.

"Thank you, thank you!" Thamer burst out. His prayers had been answered and at that moment he had renewed hope that eventually the nightmare would come to an end.

Eman and Thamer had to agree to a long list of rules in return for permission to have the visit. They couldn't mention where the prison was located to anyone, anywhere, ever. Eman could bring nothing for him, no food, no clothes, no blanket, no photos, no care-package of any kind. They weren't allowed to hug. Finally, after all the dos and don'ts had been explained, the door opened and Eman entered. The only contact permitted was a brief handshake in the presence of an American guard.

Smiling at each other, holding back tears, Eman and Thamer shook hands in one long slow movement, until the guard announced, "That's enough."

They could barely keep their emotions in check, but they fought the urge to cry and to wrap their arms around each other. Eman looked the same to him, beautiful and demure. But he knew he didn't look well.

He had more questions for Eman than she had time to answer. Where was she living? Who was supporting her? How were all their relatives? She told him he looked thin. He didn't tell her she looked more beautiful than ever; there were too many people around, and he didn't want to cry in front of them. She stared at his hair, and he knew that was because it had turned white. But there was no mistaking the feeling conveyed by their mutual gaze: never before had they felt so overwhelmed with joy to see each other.

An unspoken thought hung between them all like a portcullis: he was still in prison and no one knew how much longer the separation would last.

They'd been talking only a few minutes when the guard told Thamer it was time to leave. This time nobody could stop the tears from falling, and they said their goodbyes. Eman and the children continued to write and from time to time were allowed to visit. This kept him going.

Like any man with nothing to look forward to but the passage of time, Thamer counted the days of his captivity. He did this until they added up to 930.

Chapter 10

BAGHDAD, IRAQ—DECEMBER 2005

ON DECEMBER 16, 2005, TWO YEARS, six months, and sixteen days since Thamer's arrest, John, the friendly guard with the bright blue eyes, waved him over. John was tall, and he leaned down, closer to Thamer's ear, so he could say quietly, "Tomorrow will be your last day in prison. You're going to be released!"

Thamer's knees threatened to give way underneath him, and he slumped back against the wall so he wouldn't fall.

"Are you certain of this?" he whispered.

"Positive!" John's cheerful tone was that of a parent telling an orphan his real parents had been found. "You're on the list."

Thamer's eyes teared. He closed them tightly and leaning against the wall, giving silent thanks. He tried telling himself that he would soon be free, would soon hug his children without fear of punishment, and would soon sleep with his arms around his wife. He wiped his tears and tried to calm himself. The day he prayed for was finally here.

"Will my family be notified?"

"I'm not sure if they will contact your family directly, but I know they put out a list to the public of prisoners to be released."

Thamer gasped. "My name is on a public list?"

John patted his shoulder. "They just make it public so the families will know."

The rumors of what happens to released prisoners immediately flooded his brain. The latest headline circulating throughout the prison was that the Iraqi insurgents were hunting down any prisoners being released and executing them on sight. But why? The perverted explanation was that such prisoners had surely been turned into American spies—why else would they be released? Another rumor, another worry.

If these rumors were true would his family be in danger, he thought? He tried to stop thinking about who else might see his name on such a list. But he couldn't get the word out of his head: list, a list, you're on a list.

"Congratulations," John said.

"Thank you!" Thamer said, but that word kept repeating: a list, a list, a list. He looked at John, then away, then back again. "What about the Americans?"

"They're letting you go!"

"No, not *those* Americans. The ones who came to see me here, who told me that in return for my cooperation they would bring me and my family to the United States—to safety."

John shrugged. "I don't know about that. I just heard you were going to be released. You and about twenty others."

Though his tone was not unkind, John looked uncomfortable with the turn this was taking. Clearly, he'd expected Thamer to be more grateful for the news. Thamer nodded and forced himself to smile. He was ecstatic and thankful to Allah over his release but at the same time worried. He felt guilty about dampening John's happiness for his Iraqi friend. The young soldier had been kind to him. But Thamer's head was crowded with thoughts of being reunited with his family as well as question about what would happen next. He'd been behind walls and locked doors for two and a half years, and all that time the war had raged on with no end in sight, and he could see the uncertainty in the lines of tension in Eman's face during their few brief visits. He could see his wife conveying that life in the new Iraq was bleak.

Thamer was one of twenty-one Iraqi prisoners scheduled to be released on the same day, and during their final twenty-four hours of captivity, their lives miraculously changed for the better. Thamer and the other twenty men were segregated from the larger group that would remain behind. He and his new dorm mates were treated to better food, and they were allowed to take longer showers.

A guard gave him a thick stack of forms to sign. Thamer could read some English, but most of this was in legalese he did not understand. He signed anyway, wherever the guard pointed. He hoped he wasn't signing anything that confessed his guilt for something he hadn't done, but he wasn't about to question the guard about the forms, and he wouldn't have dreamed of refusing to sign. He felt certain that signing whatever anyone placed in front of him was his only option if he wanted out of here. His hand shook as he signed the last page and pushed it back toward the guard. He sighed so loudly, it struck him that he must have been holding his breath.

At this point, everything moved fast. A guard handed him the personal property they had seized when he was captured: his flip-phone, stray coins, keys, the clothes he'd been wearing the day he was arrested. They kept his pocket knife. The guard also gave him new street clothes to wear instead, but in an act of defiance, Thamer put on the same shirt and pants he'd worn when he'd arrived. It felt great to take off the yellow jumpsuit. Glancing down at his own clothes, he saw no evidence that anything bad had happened to him when he last wore them. They were unstained—no sign of blood, sweat, or grime. For a moment, it all seemed to have been a dream.

"This is for you," said the processing guard as he handed a cell phone to Thamer. "It's programmed with a number to the US Embassy."

To Thamer, the gesture implied that the Americans would keep their promise to bring him to the US to work with the government there and that the months that had passed since their visit had been only a delay. After all they were fighting a war; this is what he told himself. He clutched the phone as if it were a lifeline, a single tenuous strand tethering him to a new existence. Then he walked out of the processing hall.

On his way out, he passed a mirror and felt compelled to pause and stare. He hadn't seen a glass mirror since his imprisonment, only metal ones that offered blurred reflections of himself. Looking at his clear outlines in the bright glass brought him back to reality. He was a shriveled version of the man he used to be, now gaunt, with a hunched posture, creases on his face, and dark bags under his eyes. His muscles had so atrophied that the skin of his arms sagged, and his legs sometimes felt barely able to carry his frame. He ran a hand through his hair, which had gone completely white.

Others were waiting behind him, so he continued shuffling past the mirror, shocked at how slowly his form retreated, his movements small and shaky as a man twenty-years older.

A guard hit a button, and the prison gate slowly opened in front of Thamer and the other twenty prisoners leaving with him. He walked through the gate, but instead of feeling joy in the open air, he felt the weight of fear pressing in on him. He flinched at the final slam of the gate shutting behind him and took a deep breath, inhaling a silent prayer of gratitude to Allah for helping him survive this far. Then he exhaled a prayer that Allah would continue to do so.

"Line up for the bus!" a guard ordered.

All twenty-one men shuffled to obey as fast as they could.

It was around 6:30 in the evening when he boarded a bus that took all the prisoners to a rallying point where relatives were waiting. The night was already dark, and inside the bus, the atmosphere was even darker. The windows had been blackened to prevent the men on board from seeing out and to keep anyone outside from seeing in. He guessed it was for the prisoners' safety.

He closed his eyes and wondered if things would be different with Eman. In the years of marriage leading up to his imprisonment, they'd never been apart for more than a few days. After spending most of the past two and a half years apart, would she still love him the same way? She had always stood by him, but how much could she bear without detaching from the past and allowing her mind and heart to move on? The bus finally stopped.

Thamer listened intently as a guard stood in the doorway of the bus and called out each prisoner's number.

"Ninety-one, step off the bus!"

Thamer jumped to his feet, almost as used to his number as he was to his name. The moment he stepped off the bus, he recognized that he was near the Baghdad Airport. Thamer's heart pounded, this time with excitement. He didn't realize until this moment how afraid he'd been to trust that this wasn't a trick. For the first time, he believed he was about to be reunited with his wife and children.

Despite his eagerness, he stood still for a moment, feeling the ground beneath his feet. Although the new shoes the guards had given him were too tight, it felt good to stand there an almost free man. The air was cool and dry, a welcome change from the stifling heat of the bus.

He walked a few steps from the bus and surveyed the parked cars where the guard had said that his family would be waiting. He saw a small, silent group of people standing huddled but saw no familiar faces. The prisoner who had gotten off the bus before him was already out of sight. A couple of cars slowly inched away from the lot, the gravel under their tires crunching loudly in the quiet.

Thamer stepped a few paces closer to the group of waiting families but still saw no one he knew. Had nobody come for him? Had something happened to his family? Had they not been informed of his release? Would he have to cross the city alone on foot?

"Thamer! Thamer!" There was no mistaking his wife's clear, strong voice. He turned and spotted her with their sons, Mustafa and Usama, standing by his old car, the car he had driven to his last day at work. He half-ran toward them. It was as fast as he could go.

They ran at him and all four crashed into each other in a tight embrace, laughing, crying, and thanking Allah. All that had happened to him, all that his family had endured evaporated into the night, at least for now. They clung together as if he might vanish again should they let go. What joy to embrace his wife, to feel the reassuring pressure of her lips on his cheek, to inhale the scent of garden flowers and cooking spices that surrounded her like a cloud, and to feel the flesh-and-blood reality of them all.

They didn't let go until an American soldier startled them into leaping apart.

"You need to leave the area," he warned.

But Thamer said to Eman, "Wait one moment."

He scanned the parking area, hoping to spot any of the US government officials who visited him in prison. He saw no one. He waved Eman toward the car, "We must hurry and get out of here. It's not safe."

Once they felt secure in the privacy of the car, the boys began to chatter with excitement, trying to catch their father up on all that had happened. Much had changed while he was in prison. Although they had exchanged letters and shared some brief visits, there was still so much to tell, and Thamer wanted to hear every word of it. He was on his way home, and his heart was full.

After 930 days in prison, Thamer was no longer locked up, but with no money, no job, no future, and a target on his back, he was far from free. He'd simply been transferred from one prison to another. Unless he found someone who could help him flee Baghdad, his odds of staying alive weren't good.

Chapter 11

BAGHDAD, IRAQ—JANUARY 2006

THAMER STARED OUT THE WINDOW of his father-in-law's house and told himself not to worry that someone might be watching from the street but took care to stay back in the shadows. During his imprisonment, he'd desperately missed evidence of nature, and now just the sight of the date palm tree in the front yard nearly brought him to tears. Despite that, he couldn't help chuckling to himself. How often had the old man said, "Iraq has more than 400 varieties of dates, you know," and had then done his best to name them all?

His in-laws' house stood near the main road in the neighborhood of Al-Bunouk. It was a typical Iraqi home—small, clean, crowded—though maybe not so typical anymore, now that he'd moved back in a marked man.

For the first nine years of their marriage, Thamer and Eman had lived with her father. During that time, Thamer saved enough money to build his family a home of their own. Now here he was, back again, and starting over. He sighed and told himself to be grateful that he was inside a house at all. Still, it was a bit crowded now that Thamer's family had moved in. Farah, now lived with her husband's family. He was sad she was gone, but it was just as well. There was no room for them here.

Living with relatives while saving money to venture out on your own was common for young Iraqi couples, but Thamer was now a fifty-year-old man. Under the circumstances, he knew there was no shame in it, regressing from head of his own house to dependence on his wife's father. Thamer had long been a good provider, and wartime was hard on everyone; it was only right that family stick together in hard times. But Thamer's presence posed an added risk.

The thought that he was putting his entire extended family in danger simply by remaining alive distressed him. His family had already been through enough. Eman was a paler, slimmer version of the woman he had left behind, the sparkle in her eyes now dimmed by more than two years of living in a country at war. Though both his sons seemed older, they hadn't matured through personal growth so much as through the burden of excess responsibility, deprivation, and worry. Mustafa was still a teenager but looked so much older. Farah's husband, Mahmoud, was a nice young man from a good family, and Thamer had known and liked Mahmoud before his imprisonment, but every time he saw them, he felt the sting of having missed his own daughter's wedding.

In prison he had learned some of what was happening to scientists in Iraq. Now on the outside, he quickly learned that they hadn't been rumors. There was a concerted effort targeting him and his colleagues. His biggest fear was the safety of his family. He refused to make his family more vulnerable by staying with any of them and making them a target.

But where else could he go? He had nowhere to turn. He'd lost his job and his home. He did have something else though, he reminded himself, reaching into his pocket and taking out the cell phone that had been given to him when he was released. He hoped it would ring soon, and that the long-awaited caller would tell him that his promised escape to the United States had been arranged.

Thamer's father-in law walked up behind him and followed his distracted gaze out the window. "The garden looks good, doesn't it?"

"It looks beautiful," Thamer agreed. "The date tree grew a lot while I was gone."

"It did. You know, we have over 400 kinds of dates in Iraq."

"Really?" Thamer suppressed a laugh.

"At least we used to." The older man's voice grew thoughtful. "I wonder how many are left, how many have been destroyed."

As they stood together, staring out the window, it seemed to Thamer the date tree looked skinny and weak. And much too tall, too easy a target.

"Talk to me, Thamer." The old man beckoned to two chairs and sat down in one of them. "Tell me what happened to you."

Thamer hesitated. He felt tremendous affection for this proud, honorable Iraqi who had always been generous with both his home and his love, but he didn't want to share his troubles with him. He had caused him enough worry. Besides Thamer hadn't even told his own wife the details of his arrest and imprisonment. He couldn't very well tell her father what he wouldn't tell her.

"Better left buried," he said softly, and lowered himself into the empty chair. "Better to forget it."

His father-in-law didn't let up. "Buried does not work that way," the old man said, "That makes it harder to forget, not easier."

Thamer looked into the face of this second father and decided to tell him the truth. He needed to tell someone, especially those details he could never bear to reveal to Eman or the children. The shame ran too deep, and he couldn't bear the idea of his wife or children looking at him with pity or shame. But it seemed to him this wise older man could shoulder some of the weight of his experience without making it a greater burden, that between them they could make it lighter.

Thamer stared down at the flowered rug beneath their feet, focused on its intricate designs, and began his halting tale of the day of his arrest, his torture, his months reduced from a free man to a caged enemy, from a man of honor to a man filled with doubt and fear. When he looked up, he saw tears filling his father-in-law's eyes. At the sight of those tears, Thamer sensed the depth of what he had lost.

That afternoon, he lay alone in the bed he usually shared with Eman, trying to take the nap she had advised, but he couldn't sleep. His mind raced to figure out how he and his family might escape the danger he knew was making its way toward them. Then, a burst of tinny music made him jump. It was the cell phone the Americans had given him, ringing and buzzing, vibrating its way across the nightstand. At last! He grabbed the phone, fumbled the buttons, and struggled to answer in a calm tone, "Hello?"

"Is this Thamer Abdul Rahman Imran?"

He hesitated, hand to his thumping heart. "Yes. This is he. To whom am I speaking?"

"Thamer, it's important that you listen carefully," the still-unidentified man said. "You must avoid any government offices or contact with any Iraqi officials and avoid the police at all costs. We've received new information that they're looking to arrest you."

The room, already dimmed for his nap, seemed to grow darker. "Why would they want to arrest me?"

"We don't know. The only information we have is that they're all looking for you. Thamer quickly surmised that his relationship to the previous regime might be why the new Iraq government wanted to arrest him. "The insurgents too. They're kidnapping scientists. We'll tell you more when we know more."

"Who is this?" demanded Thamer.

But the man had already hung up.

Thamer had already been warned that this very thing might happen. In prison, he learned that the "new" Shia controlled Iraqi government was arresting former regime personnel. However, to have it confirmed, in such a jarring way, only intensified his heightened fear for himself and his family. He knew if he was arrested that the best scenario would have him spending more years in prison, a much grimmer prison than the one he'd just left. The worst, he didn't want to think about.

He kept the bad news to himself as he walked into the kitchen to watch his wife and her sister, Leda, prepare lunch.

"Did you have a good nap?" Eman asked.

"Fine, just fine."

Her worried look said he could never fool her.

"We're making a nice meal for you," Leda said.

"Rice and stew," Eman chimed in, "You'll love it, and you need to eat a lot of it. You've lost so much weight!"

"Much too thin." Leda shook her head.

He appreciated their loving concern, but food was the last thing on his mind. He sat at the kitchen table anyway because it comforted him to watch the two sisters cook, to listen to their feminine murmurs. It seemed forever since he'd heard the voices of women. It troubled him to know how dramatically those soft tones would change if someone came pounding at the front door to take him away.

Thamer ate a few bites of the stew under the watchful eye of Eman, then pushed his plate away, walked to the stairway, and called out so that the entire family might hear, "Everyone, please come into the living room! I need to tell you all something."

The adults and older children walked in while the younger children continued playing in the garden or running in and out. He was grateful they were so easily distracted.

He stood and solemnly surveyed the expectant faces around him.

"I've been told there's a warrant for my arrest."

"By whom!"

"For what?"

"They already arrested you!"

Thamer held up his hand for quiet. "Also, I've been told that the Jihadi's might be looking for me too. They're kidnapping scientists. I'm telling you this because my being here makes this house unsafe for all of you, and I cannot let that happen."

"This is my house," said his father-in-law. "And I decide who stays in my house. I'm not afraid to have you live with us. I'm more afraid of what might happen if you move out!"

"I agree completely," said his brother-in-law, Saad. "What is family for if not to support each other in bad times as well as good times?"

"I'm not afraid," Leda said, looking around for agreement.

"I'm not either!"

"Me either!"

Thamer backed into a chair and sat down, still and silent, swallowing the lump in his throat. More than a dozen people, from teenagers to senior citizens, all nodded at each other, eyes fierce, stances determined. For a moment, he was too overwhelmed to speak. Then, he thanked them for the sacrifice they were prepared to make. Yet their kindness made him only more determined, as a man of honor, to refuse to put them in jeopardy. Regardless of what they said, he would find someplace else to go and would stay on the move from place to place until the situation changed. For the moment though, he let the sad truth sink in: even now, sitting in this familiar home, surrounded by loving family, he was not a free man.

There might never be a safe place for him in Baghdad. He would have to find a way out. Alone.

The next day, he was still at the house in Al Bunouk when one of Eman's brothers slaughtered a sheep, an Iraqi tradition for celebrating the return of a loved one from a trip, a wedding, or, in Thamer's case, prison. More relatives came over for the feast. The crowd overflowed into the kitchen, along the stairs, out the garden, and into the road, and all he could think was: no, no, no, now all these people might be in harm's way just for coming to see him.

All around him the crowd laughed, applauded, and talked, everyone jostling for their moment with the guest of honor. He sat quietly, saying little, listening to the women gathered in clusters around him, clucking over his pallor, his lost weight, his white hair.

"Look how thin he is," one cousin murmured as if Thamer weren't sitting just a few seats away. "More than twenty-five pounds he lost!"

"It's more than his weight," another cousin murmured. "Thamer was always joking, always the lighthearted one."

He knew it was true. Every mirror he passed told him he had withered. His shoulders sagged. His cheeks hung down as if too fatigued to hang onto the bone. And yes, his eyes looked empty, as if his spirit no longer lived within him.

"Oh, now, give him time," someone else said. "He's been in prison, after all. Surely his spirit will recover."

There were many sighs. No one seemed certain it would.

After his second sleepless night, he got up late and took breakfast with Eman in the kitchen. He sipped his tea, lit a cigarette, and waited until her eyes met his. "It's the children, Eman, that's what keeps me up all night. I can't stay here. My life is one thing, theirs is another."

"But nobody knows you are here!"

He took her hand in his. "It won't take them long to figure it out. All those relatives came to see me yesterday, and all it takes is one wrong word to one wrong person."

"They wouldn't do that."

He shook his head. "Even if they don't, this is where you have been living for the last two years. This is where we lived before we had our own house. This is where they will look."

She clutched his hand to her heart. "Where will you go?"

"To other relatives. More distant ones. I'll keep moving around until the Americans call and tell me they're ready to take us to the United States as they promised."

She started to protest but he held up a hand to stop her. "I've made up my mind, Eman."

Eman nodded and nothing else was said.

That night Thamer packed only what he could carry in the backpack he borrowed from Mustafa. He felt too weak to carry much beyond a couple of changes of clothes, some toiletries, and his wallet. Like his cousins had said, prison had left him weak. Saad arranged for a neighbor with a car to pick him up just before dawn.

Before five a.m., his family lined up outside to bid him farewell. His father-in-law stepped forward first and pressed an envelope into his palm. "Thamer, please take this."

Thamer opened it and found 50,000 Iraqi Dinar inside. Thamer thrust it back at him. "I cannot accept—"

His father-in-law threw his hands in the air and stepped away, refusing to take it back. "It is done. No more word of this. You will need money."

It was true. Many Iraqi government officials were corrupt. If he came across someone who recognized him, a bribe could come in very handy. Because of the war, even the highest-placed officials didn't have much money and could probably be bought off, if it came to that. But there was no guarantee, of course; he'd heard that some corrupt police would accept a bribe and arrest you anyway or kill you and take the rest. But having money was better than not having it. He couldn't argue with that.

Thamer thanked them all profusely for everything they'd done for him, and with that, he silently embraced his children one by one, and finally Eman, who trembled. Then, for only the second time in his life, he left his family behind.

At five a.m., Thamer's brother-in-law gave him a ride to his sister's house in Baquba, thirty miles north of Baghdad. He stayed with her for about two weeks. For the next several months, Thamer moved from one location to another, to the homes of friends, family, and wherever else he thought he might be safe. He was worried about the safety of those he stayed with, so he never stayed long. Considering every possibility to keep from being discovered, he decided to change his appearance. He found a barber, dyed his gray and white hair black, and started wearing glasses.

It was a lonely, painful time for Thamer, as lurking, hiding, and moving became the focus of his existence. Mere existence was all it was. His life, it seemed, would never again belong to him. His family would never again be safe. He would never again be able to claim his true place as father, husband, brother, friend, not even as a man who could earn his own way. And if he wasn't any of those things, who was he? What value could a fugitive have in the world?

At times he thought about giving himself up to the government. It would finally end his nightmare. But the thought of returning to prison seemed more unbearable than being on the run, so he hung on, tethered to this new underground life by only one thing, the love of his family.

Every other day or so, Thamer would call the programmed number, but his calls bore no fruit. He always heard the same answer, "No news." On one of these occasions, a different embassy official answered, and the change unnerved him. Thamer had to explain who he was, which made him fear he'd been forgotten, that this man was only reading from some script of what was to be recited to all desperate Iraqis who called.

"Sorry, but there is nothing new to report," the man said.

"When *will* there be?" Thamer asked.

"Look," the man said, "when there's something to tell you, we'll tell you."

It was not until that moment that Thamer discovered something buried underneath the depression that had been suffocating him for months: rage. At that moment, it burst to the surface, and he exploded at the American stranger on the phone. "How long do you expect me to wait? Do you *realize* how I've been living? How I've suffered from this American inaction? Your people made promises to me! Those promises *need to be fulfilled*!"

There was a silence on the other end for a moment and then, "We'll call you if something changes." The man hung up.

Over the next two days, Thamer felt increasing regret over venting his anger at the American stranger. He felt guilty as he realized that the guy on the phone probably knew nothing about Thamer's situation. More than that, he feared he might have antagonized someone who would now say negative things about him to others in the embassy, maybe poison them against him, make them less likely to help. Who knew how important the stranger might be? Had he just burned a bridge?

Thamer debated over the next couple of days whether to call back and apologize. Would that seem pushy? Might that irritate the guy even more? He decided to risk it. Hand shaking, Thamer picked up the phone and dialed the number again while silently rehearsing his brief but heartfelt apology. He dialed the number but heard only a series of steady beeps. He kept trying, thinking maybe he was doing something wrong. Several tries later, the same thing. He knew that communications could be shaky, so over the next couple of days he continued to try to reach the Americans. Eventually, he realized that his phone had been cut off. The US government had no further use for him, no plan for relocation. Their promises had added up to nothing. His heart sank, and he cursed himself for losing his temper.

Chapter 12

WASHINGTON, DC—MAY 2007

IT WAS FIVE YEARS AFTER 9/11, and day by day, Thamer Imran's file was growing thicker in my hands. With each new piece of his story, it occurred to me that all my training, experience, and commitment to this mission now came down to this one man—a man who seemed less and less of a threat every day. The mission hadn't changed. But I was changing. In a strange way, I started to think that I, or we, owed him. Exactly what, I didn't know. But we didn't owe just him. There were many like him, many Thamers whose lives were shattered in a country turned inside out. I couldn't put my finger on it but I started to feel differently about my so-called enemy.

The US military at Camp Cropper had released Thamer into a hostile environment. It was like sending a lamb into a pit of hungry wolves. Al-Qaeda was still calling on all of Iraq's scientists and technicians: "Either use your skills to help fight the infidels or die!" Thamer was in extreme danger, so I was constantly thinking about where he might be and what he might be thinking. Was he safe? Was he confused? Was he feeling desperate? His plight occupied my thoughts like no other assignment had ever done.

I had questions. If our government wanted to work with him, why had they cut him loose? Did he have a change of heart? Was he not who he seemed?

Meanwhile, the war dragged on, and our reasons for being in Iraq became fuzzy. By then I knew what most Americans knew, that the threat posed by Saddam Hussein's purported weapons of mass destruction was based on faulty intelligence. Hussein had been an evil dictator, but the world had those aplenty and America rarely intervened. Worse, our military had been flung into this conflict with no long-term strategy. I was now disillusioned with the fight I had once thought of as a righteous effort to protect America from another violent threat in the Middle East. In this new frame of mind, it wasn't lost on me that the deadly environment Thamer now faced was created unintentionally by the United States. It was the US-led invasion, after all, that had made good people, innocent people of science into targets. An unintended consequence perhaps, but our fault nonetheless.

I bounced from disillusionment to frustration as every bureaucrat I encountered demonstrated a cavalier attitude about the injustice I'd uncovered. It was now plain to me that Thamer wasn't our enemy. He was, according to the information I uncovered, someone who had put his faith in the salvation he thought the United States had brought, only to be cast aside and erased like a pencil mark on a piece of paper.

I had numerous meetings with Dr. McCarthy to explain this truth that my exhaustive research had uncovered. Yet despite all of our protestations, we couldn't get a green light from the Homeland Security Council to let me go to Iraq and bring this man in. Why were they holding us back?

"They, uh, found another scientist dead over there," my contact at the State Department told me over the phone. Her voice was always polite to the point of childlike, and it never failed to irritate me.

I sat up abruptly in my office chair. "Who was the scientist?"

"We don't know if it's your guy yet. The body just turned up. We should know soon."

"I'll be right over."

I left my office in a hurry, walked to the metro station, took the red line to Foggy Bottom, and walked the few blocks to the State Department. It was another hot, humid, spring day in DC, but I was drenched in more sweat than the weather could account for. By now I felt I knew Thamer, maybe even better than I knew some of my friends. Each day he was out there increased the odds of something bad happening.

The State Department had never looked so much like a prison as it did to me that day, a vast utilitarian concrete gray block with rows of anonymous square windows, a place where it seemed easy to slip through a crack into a void and get lost. In the lobby, I fought to calm my breathing as I waited in the long line for my turn to walk through the metal detector, show my ID, and be cleared by the guards. I thought about all the visits I'd made to the State Department in recent weeks trying to get their help to move closer to a course of action, *some* course of action. Maybe another dead scientist would finally kick the higher ups right in their complacency.

I walked into the office of my counterpart at State. She was the liaison for the IICSI program. She was bright but naive or else very good at projecting naivete; either way, I'd come to think she'd been told to keep our group at arm's length. The State Department was leery about our involvement in "foreign affairs" and wanted to keep a tight leash on things. She told me the name of the latest victim. It wasn't Thamer. I heaved a sigh of relief.

"The victim was apparently . . . " she glanced at her notes, " . . . the Deputy Director of The Iraqi Interim Center for Science and Industry."

I snapped to attention. "So, he probably had a list or at the very least knows the names and perhaps contact information of those in the IICSI program, including Thamer's!"

"If he did, I don't think he shared the list with anyone." She wrinkled her nose as if such concerns were silly.

I clenched my jaw. "What would they be after, if not the list?"

"Even if they wanted a list of names," she said, "his body was examined, and it showed no signs of torture, which leads us to believe he didn't give up any information."

I made no effort to hide my dismay at her credulity. "Really? If a guy takes a gun and holds it up to your head or threatens to kill your whole family, would you give up the list? You don't need to pull fingernails to get information! People resisting massive amounts of torture for 'the cause' are what happens in movies; in the *real* world, most people will give up all they have long before the really mean stuff starts. It's called self-preservation."

She cocked her head. I'd hit a nerve. "Meaning what, exactly?"

"Meaning, if the IICSI has been compromised, none of its members are safe."

Although it grated on me to explain to this misinformed messenger the perils that Thamer now faced, in a perverse sense, I welcomed the bad news she'd delivered. Surely, *now* the State Department would draft a plan to relocate the remaining scientists.

Then she said, "We need to wait and see what else transpires."

"Are you kidding me? The strategy is *to wait*? That's *it*? Wait for the murders of more scientists?"

She looked down at the floor and said nothing. One thought kept repeating: I had a problem I needed to solve, that problem was in Iraq, and I was sitting on my ass in Washington, DC trying to use a 6,000-mile-long screwdriver to fix it. I knew my gung-ho team of Kevin and Jim were just as anxious for our handcuffs to be removed, but it was damned unlikely anybody else would be excited for this mission to really take off—not the State Department, not the Homeland Security Council, and certainly not my wife. Even I worried it might be the craziest idea I'd ever had. I wanted to go on a search-and-rescue mission for a wanted man in a country at war. Yeah, it sounded ridiculous to me too. And there was no doubt that the Homeland Security Council was deliberately stonewalling us, so I was going to need to build one hell of a good case to convince them to let me go.

My office phone rang, and I grabbed it fast. "Come again?" I shouted into the telephone as I bolted upright in my chair, "He did what?"

"Well, apparently your Iraqi scientist was really upset about what he called 'the American inaction,'" my contact at the State Department said in her irritating, emotionless tone. "The embassy official who took the call found him threatening. I mean, it frightened him. So, uh . . . "

"So? So *what*?"

"So, he did what he felt was the safest thing to do under the circumstances. He disconnected the cell phone we'd given him."

I gasped in disbelief. "He intentionally cut off communication with the very person we've been working all this time to bring over here?"

"Hey, Steve, look, the guy at the embassy felt threatened."

I wanted to reach through the phone and strangle her, to say, I'll show you what threatened feels like. Instead, I sank into my chair and shook my head. "Threatened by a phone call? Come on. Exactly when did this happen?"

"A month ago. I don't know. Maybe longer."

I closed my eyes. An unknown official in the US embassy in Baghdad had now made things a lot more difficult, and dangerous, for Thamer. Nothing my contact told me gave me reason to believe that anything about Thamer's call had been materially threatening. Yes, he was frustrated, but could anyone blame him? In his calls to the embassy, Thamer never gave up his location. He was careful. Now any chance of using that connection to find him was gone. *Dammit*, if a government employee in a war-zone couldn't understand what fear sounded like, he had no business there. But there was no point in arguing any of this with my State Department contact. She was the messenger, not the one to blame, and there was nothing she could do about it anyway.

I was deeply unsettled to realize how much power some low-level embassy employee had to throw away an innocent man's life. That Thamer had been deemed a valuable American asset and that the cell phone he carried might be our only link to him had apparently never occurred to the bozo who disconnected Thamer's phone. I was furious. And I was getting even more scared for Thamer.

What concerned me now was that it had been a month between when Thamer was left out in the cold when I heard about it. That made me more certain than ever that someone, maybe everyone, wanted me to fail at the task of finding Thamer Imran. He was out there somewhere, and I was more determined than ever to find him.

Project Zebra, with all its setbacks, got deeper and deeper under my skin. One night I left work early, slamming my office door behind me, and even the ride home hadn't been long enough to calm me down. At dinner, I silently rotated pasta on a fork and shoveled it into my mouth without paying attention to it until I looked up to find Carmela staring at me across the table.

"You look like you're a million miles away," Carmela said as she passed me more linguini with clams, one of her specialties. I always asked for seconds, but this time I didn't dig in; I just sat there looking at the beautiful meal as it got colder. "What are you thinking?" she asked.

"I'm thinking the years have been good to you," I said, mustering a smile. "Just thinking back . . . wondering where all the time went."

The way she stared me down as she picked up her wine glass, I knew she wasn't buying it. My wife wasn't one for nostalgia. She once told me that sentimental reminiscing about days gone by just made her sad.

"You're right," she said after a while. "There have been a lot of years. So, I know when something's bothering you."

"Nah, I'm fine." I wasn't trying to evade her. I just had no idea how to untangle the ball of frustration inside me and explain it.

She didn't give up. "I don't need to be a detective to figure out you haven't been fine in a while." I suspect that most wives have a sixth sense. My wife has a tenth sense. Nothing gets past her.

"Meetings, briefings, more meetings, more bullshit, and nothing ever gets done." I shook my head. "Nobody cares."

Carmela gave a knowing nod. She'd heard all that before. She waited in patient silence with a look that said she'd wait all night if that's what it took. I'd already told her I was looking for a man named Thamer, and she asked hopefully, "They located him?"

"No. No one has heard from Thamer in over a month. He could be anywhere." I swallowed. "Or he could be dead."

She quietly waited for me to work through my thoughts. This patient understanding was one of the qualities that made me fall for her. But tonight, it just made me feel more impatient.

"If he's alive," I said, "Time isn't on his side. We're losing the race. There are bad people over there who will catch up to him, and if they do, it won't turn out well for him."

"If this is so important, I don't understand why the government doesn't go get him instead of just putting it on a contractor."

My throat tightened. "What's that supposed to mean? *Just* putting it on a contractor? Do you think I take it any less seriously because I'm a contractor?"

"You know what I mean. It's their issue. You're there to help them, not take it on all by yourself."

"You don't get it," I said in the booming voice my wife can't stand. This was my usual retort when I knew she was right. Truth is, I *was* "just a contractor." The government had given me an assignment without giving me the authority to make the commitments necessary to carry it out. But that was only one of the things that made this job frustrating.

I ran my finger around the top of my wine glass, thinking. I wanted to clarify for both of us what was bothering me most.

"I keep getting this feeling I'm going up against more than the bad guys in Iraq or even the idiots in the US Embassy who cut off Thamer's cell phone. I know in my gut that this case is bothering officials right here in Washington. They all give me those big fake smiles and handshakes and 'good luck' and 'wish I could help,' but I see it in their eyes, and their actions or really their inactions never match their words. It's obvious the higher-ups have hidden political reasons for not wanting to find this scientist." I took a breath. "I think this goes pretty damned high up."

"Why would they give you an assignment they didn't want you to carry out?" she asked.

I shrugged. "I haven't figured that out yet. That's what I keep asking myself. *What* are they afraid of? *Why* do they want this project to disappear?"

I must have looked desperate for an answer. But all she said was, "You're too involved."

I gave her a look that admitted what I couldn't say aloud, I know. Carmela let it go, and we finished dinner in silence.

Lying in bed that night, I muttered an apology to Carmela for taking my frustrations out on her. She forgave me as she always does and fell asleep with my arm thrown over her in our usual peacemaking gesture. Still, I couldn't sleep.

Carmela was right again. I had personalized this assignment more than any other in my life. A bond had developed between me and a man I'd never met. I had seen Thamer only in a small black and white photo stuck in the middle of a thick stack of files piled on my desk, but I felt connected to him. I felt like I'd taken on responsibility for him. I'd come to care about him. He was a person to me now. I looked at that small grainy print wondering where he was, what he was doing, whether we'd ever meet—whether I'd ever be able to get this thing unstuck.

Recognizing how emotionally involved I was only made me feel worse. I worried that it might cause me to lose perspective or miss an important lead. I feared that, in my passion to rescue an innocent man from God knows what, I might make a fatal mistake.

I also had an inexplicable feeling that I should help Thamer simply because it was the *right* thing to do. I thought about Thamer, surely more alone than I, separated from his wife and kids, hiding underground, waiting anxiously for someone to show up and give him the help he'd been promised. I pictured him lying awake in the dark like me, and this image gnawed at me like my never-ending back pain. I wanted badly to complete my mission and help him but the forces against us were strong and I was getting very tired.

Chapter 13

DAMASCUS, SYRIA—MARCH 2006

THE YEAR 2006 TURNED OUT TO BE one of the worst of the war. The insurgency was in full force and foreign fighters continued to flood Iraq. Thamer's passport had been confiscated when the Americans arrested him, yet he, Eman, and their two sons needed passports if they were to have any chance of getting out of Iraq. His country's interim government was still in thrall to the US, and the US was still not giving him the time of day. Thamer's only hope of getting replacement passports quickly would be through bribery, and Eman's brother, Saad, said he might know an inside man who could help. It wouldn't be cheap. Thamer reached out to family and friends to help him put together the money.

Saad made all the arrangements. Thamer rarely ventured out in public anymore, but he decided to risk going with Saad to pick up the documents that he hoped would lead to getting out of Iraq. Thamer didn't want to let Saad face the danger alone, and he also wanted to be there to personally inspect the documents that could be their ticket to freedom or a giveaway that would seal their demise. They parked Saad's car downtown, a couple of blocks from the agreed upon meeting place a coffee shop near the University of

Baghdad, not far from the Al Jadriyah Bridge. Thamer reached into his pocket to reassure himself that his folded dinar was still there, enough to pay the insider plus a bit more just in case.

Thamer walked differently in public now—face down, striding fast, moving with purpose—to neither draw attention nor make himself easy prey. But even with his face down, he took in the surroundings. Since his arrest some three years earlier, his city had become almost unrecognizable to him. Once-vibrant streets were now lined with at least as many bombed-out ruins and piles of rubble as actual buildings. Even among the buildings that still stood, there seemed to be little going on in the way of legitimate commerce. In some places men stood in small groups, idly talking, as if waiting for something. He had the impression that, like him, they'd been waiting a long time. Other men walked past, but he didn't meet their eyes, and he didn't get the impression they tried to meet his. There had always been fewer women than men around Baghdad, except in the marketplaces, but now he saw almost none.

They drew closer to the meeting place, and his heart began to race. He tensed as a stranger approached, and they eyed each other just long enough for Thamer to see fear in his eyes. Oddly that comforted him. Maybe the stranger was on the run too. Then Saad turned into the alley with Thamer following, and the stranger turned with them. Saad nodded to the man.

"Do you have the money?" the insider asked.

Thamer reached into his pocket and this time pulled out the cash, handing it over with shaking hands, embarrassed to realize the bills were damp with his sweat.

Without hesitation, the contact pocketed the soggy bills. He then handed Thamer the "official" Iraqi passports for him and his family. Thamer carefully examined the passports. Satisfied, he nodded to Saad, and the men went their separate ways. That was it. Thamer followed Saad back the way they'd come, breathing hard as if he'd just conversed with death.

Thamer had already decided where to let this passport take him.

"I need to get to Syria," he had told Eman. "From there, I'll find a way out."

It wouldn't be easy. So many Iraqis had fled to Syria that the country was overwhelmed. Syrians had at first welcomed their fellow Arabs with open arms, but as the refugee population surged, many Syrians grew weary. Their border seethed with refugee camps, while many hungry, desperate people seeped into the cities wandering homeless with nowhere to go. Saad helped Thamer arrange for a driver to take him across the border. He decided to bring Eman with him to Syria, which might make him appear less suspicious than if he traveled alone. It was a risk to their safety making the crossing. He prayed to Allah he was making the right choice.

ON MARCH 27, 2006, THREE WEEKS after getting the new passports, he and Eman stepped into the old, rented hunk of metal that pretended to be a car and headed to the border of Syria. He tasted the metallic adrenaline of a condemned man set free, but he admonished himself not to count his blessings just yet. A lot could still go wrong.

His driver was reputed to have experience getting people across the border which meant he was good at bribery. The drive to the Syrian border took five hours. For five hours, Thamer, Eman, and their hired driver sweated out every checkpoint, every passing vehicle, every turn in the road. Mini convoys of armed men in pickups drove past, perhaps heading to battle with the coalition forces, Thamer thought. At any point they might run into militia groups, insurgents, bandits, or kidnappers. In case any of that did happen, they carried bribe money, but they knew the money might not be enough to get through every shakedown between them and the border. They held each other's hand tightly as they continued the dangerous trek to the border.

Four hours went by and nobody stopped them. Then the car slowed as traffic became heavier with people crossing between Iraq and Syria. There was no turning back now. After an hour spent inching through the line, their car pulled up to the checkpoint. The driver turned to Thamer.

"Let me have both of your passports and the 10,000 dinar."

Thamer handed over the cash without hesitation. The driver had told him that bribing border guards was standard operating procedure and that this was the standard price. Thamer tried to breathe evenly, trying to exude an air of calm. It seemed the sour smell of his fear permeated the car, but there was nothing he could do about that. It's normal to sweat, he told himself, and maybe they won't even check the car.

The driver walked up to a group of Iraqi border guards, and Thamer and Eman watched the men hunker in a circle as the guards and his driver occasionally raised their heads to look back at their car. Then his driver slightly tipped his head, once again gesturing toward the car, and handed over the money. Thamer thought that would end the conversation, but on and on the men went talking, talking. Sweat beaded on Thamer's forehead and neck as he watched in nervous silence. Then the mood of the guards changed, their shoulders relaxing as they and the driver burst into laughter. Thamer and Eman looked at each other and sighed in relief.

It occurred to Thamer that the driver and the guards all had a lucrative deal going. They were all making a killing thanks to this war. His own countrymen—profiting from the extreme suffering of fellow Iraqis. It was despicable, but Thamer told himself to stay focused; all that mattered was getting out of Iraq alive.

The driver came back grinning and tossed him his passport. "They didn't even look at it," he said.

Thamer replied with a tense smile and nod. The driver inched the car through the checkpoint, and a few minutes later the guard shack was in the rear-view mirror. Thamer heaved an explosive sigh of relief. They had crossed out of Iraq. But he still had to cross into Syria.

The driver assured Thamer that getting into Syria would be the easy part. So as soon as they passed the Iraqi border guards, they pulled over to call Saad and let him know they had successfully left Iraq. Then the driver paid off the Syrian border guards, this time using Syrian liras. And with that, Thamer and Eman entered Syria.

About ten hours after leaving Baghdad, Thamer's driver pulled to a stop at an apartment building in a Damascus neighborhood called Al-Husseinia. This was the home of Thamer's niece Sanaa. She wasn't expecting Thamer and Eman. It wouldn't have been safe to send word ahead. He climbed to the second floor, paused on the landing to catch his breath, and knocked at the door. The door sprang open and he was greeted by an unexpected face, albeit a beloved one: that of another niece, Rajaa. At first, she looked shocked to see Thamer and Eman, then overjoyed. They hugged and kissed with the kind of excitement people share when war has ended, although it had not.

Thamer didn't know that Sanaa had left for Spain on business with her husband. He was relieved that Rajaa had temporarily moved in, or he would have found an empty apartment forcing him to use what little money he had on a place to stay.

The next day, Rajaa showed Thamer and Eman around Damascus. The beauty of the city stunned Thamer, and given the dismal wreckage he'd left behind, it was wonderful to see a city standing so grand and pristine. They visited the Umayyad Mosque and the old city and spent time at the Souq-al-hamidiyyeh, a vibrant shopping district. They visited the Damascus Opera House and the Saladin Mausoleum. For the first time in a long time Thamer felt at peace.

Many believe Damascus to be the oldest continuously-inhabited city in the world, dating back to the third millennium, BC. Thamer and Eman wandered the ancient city, and Thamer tried to imagine himself being just another tourist on holiday. He was enthralled by the Roman City walls and Temple of Jupiter, the Great Mosque of the Umayyad Caliphate, and the winding streets of the Souks. They comfortably strolled the large covered markets where friendly merchants plied him with herbal teas as he perused their colorful wares, everything from mouthwatering spices and nuts, to rich silks and perfumes.

Despite the peace they found in Syria, Thamer and Eman worried constantly about their children, who were being cared for by Eman's brother and father. They would call as often as they could to check on them and reassure them that they were doing everything to keep them safe and find a way out of Iraq. Their time away from their children was difficult. To Thamer and Eman, it was another hardship in an ocean full of them.

Thamer and Eman realized that despite this break from the turmoil in Iraq, none of the beautiful sights could make them forget the seriousness of Thamer's real purpose in Damascus. He and Eman spent the bulk of their days wandering from one foreign embassy to another, petitioning for asylum, and pleading for his family's future.

They waited three hours for an interview at the British Embassy, and the embassy official who interviewed him showed no interest in promises made to Thamer by the US. He acted unmoved by his arguments that the Americans considered Thamer a man of some importance, and in fact seemed to be giving him the brush-off.

"Yes, yes, I understand your predicament," the official said. "The problem is there are so many Iraqis who share your problems. We simply can't grant visas to everyone."

"But I am a scientist. I can speak English. Surely I have a profession that might be—"

"I'm so sorry," the man cut in, standing up to indicate the session was over. "I sympathize completely with what you and your family are going through, but there is simply nothing I can do at the moment." He held the door open.

Each day, they headed to another of the European embassies or consulates on his list, armed with all the paperwork required to apply for asylum in that country. And each day, he requested an audience with someone in authority, but he ended up speaking to no more than low-ranking diplomatic employees. They all responded with some version of the speech he'd heard from the man at the British Embassy. Each lacked the personnel, the time, or the authority to help him. Everyone addressed him with sympathy, expressing regret that they couldn't help.

The polite brush-offs were the most positive responses. In most cases, he waited hours, only to be turned away with no explanation and told not to return at all. Every day for months Thamer and Eman knocked on doors, and not once did they leave the meetings with any real hope that they'd be able to make it to freedom through Syria. So, on February 25, 2007, eleven months after arriving in Syria and with no other options, Thamer and Eman returned to Iraq.

Chapter 14

WASHINGTON, DC—FEBRUARY 2007

"HE'S BACK IN IRAQ, JIM!" I SHOUTED into the telephone. Jim and Kevin had been patiently waiting for any new word on the status of Project Zebra. Finally, I had something positive to tell them.

"How do you know?" Jim asked.

I got a call from my State Department contact with the IICSI. She told me that one of Thamer's colleagues contacted the IICSI staff, and that Thamer was trying to set up a meeting at IICSI.

"That's great news."

"Listen," I said, "Let Kevin know, I gotta run, call you later." I ran to Dr. McCarthy's office.

"We need the interview, we know where he is, and now have a connection to contact him. We need to move now before he disappears again," I urged.

"I know Steve, I'm doing everything I can."

"I'm having a hard time keeping Kevin and Jim onboard, given all the delays."

She nodded, and I walked out of her office even more frustrated than normal because we were so close. But I knew Dr.

McCarthy was a fighter, and she would do everything possible to get approval for our team to find Thamer.

Kevin called frequently asking what the holdup was, insisting "We're running out of time. He'll only stay still for so long. Then we'll lose him again and who knows for how long?"

Weeks went by, and still we received no approval to move in and pick up Thamer. Meanwhile, more scientists went missing. I kept in contact with the embassy in Baghdad through my IICSI contact at state to keep loose tabs on Thamer. He was being careful and hadn't given up his location. Pondering my next move, I thought back to how puzzled I'd been by the lack of support we'd gotten from the Homeland Security Council during my initial White House briefing in February of 2006, when they told us we were wasting our time trying to talk to Thamer. I didn't understand this position. Thamer was deemed to be important, yet I kept receiving mixed messages: keep looking for him, but not really.

By 2007, there was no doubt in my mind something wasn't right, and I was no longer going to sit quietly. I knew that the Bush administration had taken a lot of heat over the WMD issue, and in response, unleashed holy hell of an effort to find any trace of WMDs. This was the reason Thamer was abused and imprisoned. The press was brutal: America is involved in a nasty war with no end in sight, and American soldiers are dying for no good reason. Eventually, with nothing to show for their efforts, the US government let go of the idea of locating WMDs as a justification for the invasion and came up with another.

America's new justification was the evil of Saddam Hussein—getting rid of Hussein at all costs and freeing the Iraqi people had become the rallying call. It had been an embarrassment to the administration that the initial intelligence had been so wrong, and the press kept hounding Bush, so Vice President Dick Cheney had been given the task of point man for the new campaign. Cheney was fairly effective in his messaging and eventually, as with most political scandals, the public turned its focus elsewhere, a shift the administration welcomed. Things were beginning to cool down.

The intelligence community, on the other hand, had been stung right where they lived. They couldn't afford any more mistakes, or for any revelations to come to light that might kick up the WMD fiasco. The faulty intelligence had been laid at their feet, and they grudgingly accepted it. Time to move on. Then it hit me like a migraine headache, the answer for why we were being blocked: with the WMD catastrophe fading, the last thing the HSC and the White House Administration wanted was to bring it back into focus. Then along comes our team, wanting unfettered access to a WMD scientist, trying to bring him to the US, a non-hostile environment where he'd feel free to talk about *everything* he knew.

What embarrassing information might that yield? Could he tell us something they didn't know? Could he reveal information about WMDs? Could there be any still in Iraq? Was he going to talk about his imprisonment and harsh treatment? Apparently, certain people in our government didn't want to find out, so they slow-rolled us, hoping we'd lose interest and go away. They wanted no more discussion of WMDs—period.

The problem was, burying the truth wasn't the mission I'd accepted. So, my team and I pressed on, trying to stay focused and not let Project Zebra get derailed. By the spring of 2007, we became desperate to execute our order to bring in Thamer and obtain his cooperation, which by all accounts he was eager to deliver, so we continued to hold meetings at the White House to discuss this project and the larger issue of what to do with all the displaced scientists in Iraq. But still no progress.

Keeping up the morale of my team became a challenge. Kevin and Jim kept ribbing me about my "failure to launch," but none of us could bring ourselves to laugh about it anymore. And they had other work to do that they couldn't continue to put aside while standing by for the final phase of our mission. They'd simply stopped believing that our moment would ever come. I tried to hide from them that I no longer believed it either, and I kept telling them we were on the cusp of getting the green light. They responded with blank stares and silence.

In October of 2007, Dr. McCarthy and I returned to her office after yet another HSC meeting that featured more delay tactics. Then, in the midst of my extreme frustration, it occurred to me that we needed to change strategies.

"We need to convince them beyond any doubt that we're not interested in anything they're worried about," I said.

"Explain," Dr. McCarthy said.

"We need to promise them that our questioning of Thamer won't touch on anything but the forensics of low-level bio production techniques. We won't ask him about anything else, nothing related to the location of WMDs in any way—nothing about anything but bio production. And we tell them that we'll discourage him from offering information about anything else. They know what we're after; we just need to convince them that we won't go beyond strict parameters."

Her faint smile told me that I might be on to something.

"We have to give them our absolute commitment on this," I said. "And we have to come back with a proffer of his value."

I went on to explain that we had to make it clear what the HSC stood to gain by our asking those questions and those questions alone, what they had to lose by not letting us ask those questions, and what we should offer Thamer as a return on that value.

Although I said all those things outright, I privately thought the strategy was bullshit. The incompleteness of it went against my training. As an experienced investigator, I held it as my professional standard to never cut off a line of questioning or discourage someone from offering intelligence, even what might seem like insignificant details. You never knew where even the most mundane information might lead. But I knew if we didn't get off the dime and make our move soon, nothing good would come of these endless meetings.

My feeling about Dr. McCarthy was that she was a single-minded, driven person who was all business. But in that moment, even I was unnerved by the severity of her stare, I knew her mind was in overdrive, calculating how we would best build our case.

Finally, she uttered only one word: "Allies."

"Excuse me?"

"We need allies. We need to stop fighting this alone. We need others, if not to support our cause, at least not to stand in the way."

"Yes. The council will never become our allies on their own. They're afraid we'll find out something they don't want us to know."

Dr. McCarthy gave me another serious look, and I knew we were mentally listing everything the council feared we might discover once we had unfettered access to a WMD scientist from Iraq.

Then she said what I was thinking, "What if he told us there were WMDs stockpiled after all? What if he told us where they were stashed? What if he told us something their two-and-a-half years of incarceration and interrogation failed to find out? What if they had to admit to the president that the initial call on WMDs *was* correct but that Thamer and his colleagues had fooled them into thinking it wasn't? It would be another embarrassment, not just to the intelligence community—"

"—but to the president himself."

So those blocking us at every turn had a motive. It wasn't a complicated one, but it was an important one, at least to them: they didn't want to be wrong again. Reputations could be ruined, and careers could be at stake. I could just imagine the conversations:

"There are weapons of mass destruction in Iraq, and we're certain enough to go to war. No, wait, there are no weapons of mass destruction, we made a mistake. No, wait, we just learned that there *are* weapons of mass destruction in Iraq." The press would go nuts!

I'm not naive. I know how DC works. But it really pissed me off to realize that some public servants protect their careers at the expense of protecting our country, that to save their reputations, they'd cast aside the importance of obtaining as much information from Thamer as we could, that their track records were more important to them than the intelligence we might learn about the threat of bioweapons. It was all about self-preservation. Nothing more.

Angry as I was about all the closed doors, this new perspective was energizing. I was starting to feel optimistic again.

"We've been working this from the wrong perspective," I said. "It's about them, not us."

"So what do we do?"

"We do what you said—find allies. And we do what I said, reassure them we won't hunt for information that might make them look bad."

She continued, "And after they approve our plan. . ."

". . .we find out the truth."

"Whether it makes them look bad or not."

Now, we were getting somewhere.

OVER THE NEXT FEW WEEKS, we methodically swayed people from every vital national security and law enforcement branch of the federal government to our side. Relying on one-on-one visits rather than on meetings with leadership teams proved effective. It allowed us to talk freely and didn't put anyone on the spot in a public forum. In our search for allies, Dr. McCarthy and I made the rounds of the State Department, the FBI, and the CIA. We reassured every one of them that if they would expedite our request to pick up Thamer Imran, take him into protective custody, fly him to America, and interview him, we would ask him only about the forensics of bioweapons—and nothing else. More importantly, we promised to come back with a proffer to let them know what value Thamer could be to the US.

We had to work the Justice Department the hardest, because they seemed to harbor the greatest misgivings about our plan. The Justice Department said it was about law and order, and that their concern was that Thamer was wanted by the Iraqis. They argued that they were trying to establish the rule of law in Iraq, and that smuggling a wanted man out of Iraq ran counter to that. If we got caught, our government would face yet another embarrassing scandal over this messy war. Never mind that corruption in Iraq—which included Iraq's American-approved leaders siphoning off millions in American taxpayer dollars—was rampant or that the Justice Department made little effort to enforce "rule of law" to get the money back.

I suggested to Dr. McCarthy that our attempt to protect America and its allies against a potential biological attack trumped the law-and-order issue. "The needs of the many outweighed the needs of the few" and all that. But it was her call. At her suggestion, we pulled our request for Justice to throw its support behind us with direct involvement. Instead, we merely asked them not to stand in the way. We explained that we wanted to visit Thamer in Iraq and get a sense of the value he proffered, and we offered to not bring him back until we could present the HSC with a good argument for doing so. We promised not to seek one iota of intelligence about anything other than the forensics of biological weapons. This was the compromise.

The way the HSC was run, if just one agency objected, it would send Project Zebra all the way back to square one. We couldn't afford to present our official request to the HSC until we knew we had every last department on board. We were on a roll, and success was in sight. We were *this* close to getting approval to send the mission to Iraq.

Chapter 15

BAGHDAD, IRAQ—OCTOBER 2007

I SAT AT MY DESK TAPPING THE PHONE number I'd circled multiple times amid the frantic scribbles that filled my notepad. We had tracked Thamer down through various contacts in Baghdad, and now I sat with phone in hand, staring at his cell phone number. Now that it came down to it, I was afraid to make the call. I worried that calling Thamer directly would scare him off. Thamer had no idea who I was. There had to be a softer approach.

I picked up my desk phone and, instead of punching the numbers on the pad, called my contact at State. We'd barely said hello before I blurted with sarcasm, "Are there any other scientists still alive in Iraq?"

"What do you mean?"

"Look, I'm sorry for the smart-ass comment, but could you find me someone, say, at IICSI who is still in the program and knows Thamer?"

"I can try."

IN THE MIDST OF YET ANOTHER LISTLESS afternoon trapped indoors, this time at his father-in- laws home, Thamer's personal cell phone rang. It was a sound so unfamiliar to him that it caused his heart to thunder. Should he drop to the kitchen floor or run for his life? Did this ring signal the approach of kidnappers or bullets, or may be its just one of his relatives? What a way to react to a ringing phone, he thought.

He scrambled to grab the phone as it vibrated across the table, then picked it up and hit the button to accept the call. He said nothing, just held it to his ear, listening. Waiting. His pounding heart told him it was the end. But the end of what?

"Thamer?" It was a familiar voice; one he had never expected to hear again.

"Jassim!" Thamer rose to his feet, stunned nearly to tears. They hadn't spoken since Thamer's arrest four years earlier, and Thamer had assumed that Jassim was dead. "Yes, it's me, Jassim. How are you? It's so very good to hear from you, my friend."

"I'm fine. Listen, we can catch up later, but I have a message for you. The Americans want to talk to you."

Thamer's body chilled. He flopped down into the nearest chair. "Why? To arrest me?"

"No, no. I think it's for a good reason. It's Americans in Washington who want to talk to you, not Americans in Baghdad. They contacted me because they thought I might have your number. They asked me to ask you if it's all right to give it to them. . . so they can call you."

Thamer paused. How could he be sure this wasn't a trick? "Let me think about it, Jassim," and hung up.

I RUSHED TO PICK UP MY OFFICE PHONE, thinking it was my contact in Baghdad calling with news about Thamer. It wasn't. It was Kevin. He was in a panic.

"Dude, listen. I'm getting a lot of crap from my bosses over the idea of going to Baghdad and picking up this guy. You have no idea. I can't take any more. I'm out. I'm sick of fighting them. Man, it's over. I'm done."

"What happened?"

"I don't know, dude. They say it's taking too much of my time, that kind of argument. Somebody got to them."

Kevin's panic infected me. Perhaps someone from the HSC had heard we were closing in on our target and was trying to prevent us from talking to Thamer. The more Kevin talked, the more I felt like a man who climbs a cliff face only to reach the top and encounter a villain who one by one peels your fingers from the rock.

"But damn, Kevin, we're so close to pulling this thing off! Can you set up another meeting? I can have Dr. McCarthy come over to square things away."

"No, man, that won't work. This is causing them too much grief. It's over!"

I tried to think of new arguments to keep him, then I remembered his tendency toward the dramatic. I decided to call his bluff. "Okay. I don't want you to get jammed up. You've done a lot for me on this, and I appreciate it. I understand, okay?"

"Okay." He sounded puzzled.

"I'll contact Dr. McCarthy and fill her in, tell her your bosses want you out, and Jim and I will carry out the mission without you. I'll arrange to have you debriefed out of the project. We should have you out by tomorrow."

There was silence on the other end. I smiled. "Kevin? You there? Hello?"

"So, I'll be debriefed out?"

"Yeah."

"And you and Jim will go?"

"Right."

"And I'm done right?"

"Yup."

"Wait a minute, man. Wait a minute. Let me make a call. I'll call right back. Dude, don't do anything yet."

"Ok."

Five minutes later my phone rang. "Steve, this is Kevin. I'm in. I'm back in."

"What happened?"

"I don't know. I'm back in, that's all I know."

I couldn't help laughing as I hung up. I knew the thought of Jim and me finishing off this assignment without him would drive Kevin nuts. I couldn't wait to act out the conversation for Jim, sure it would give him a good laugh, too. But Kevin's frustration was a clear sign of the damage all the delays were causing. We'd been stuck in this holding pattern way too long, full of pent-up energy and ready to burst.

IN JUNE OF 2007, TWO WEEKS AFTER Jassim called him, Thamer picked up his cell phone and returned the call.

"Jassim, give the Americans my number." He hoped he'd made the right decision. I already knew Thamer's number but wanted him to feel he was in control and comfortable.

A few days later his cell phone rang. He picked it up but once again waited for the other party to speak first.

"Hello. May I speak to Thamer Imran?"

The man who answered took a breath that sounded extremely shaky to me. It was loud and had a fearful tone to it.

"This is he."

"Hello, Mr. Imran," I said, "My name is Steve Monteiro."

"May I call you Thamer?" I asked, "Or do you prefer Mr. Imran?" I tried to maintain a professional tone, but my nervousness was causing cartwheels in my stomach. I was finally speaking with Thamer Imran, the man I'd begun to worry just might be a ghost.

"You may call me Thamer, thank you."

"Great. Please call me Steve. I'm assigned to the Department of Homeland Security, and we'd like to talk with you. I'm calling from Washington, and I can't say too much over the phone, but do you remember when the Americans came to see you while you were in prison"

Silence . . .

"Hello? Are you there?"

"Yes."

"I know some time has passed, but it's important that we meet and continue that conversation. I'm calling from Washington. First, are you ok?"

More silence.

"Hello? Can you hear me?"

"Yes."

"Are you ok?"

"Yes."

I gave him my contact information but didn't get much in return. It was clear Thamer didn't trust me. And why should he? My goals for our first call were simple—most of all I didn't want to scare him off. I would just keep it simple and tell the truth. I kept the call short, under five minutes, and I wrapped up by telling him I'd reach out again when I had more information. I was elated. After all this time, I was finally talking to the man I'd been pursuing for so long. Thamer! Of course, I had no idea if he'd take another of my calls. But he hadn't hung up on me, and that gave me hope.

Dr. McCarthy was thrilled when I told her about the call. Over the coming weeks, she continued her valiant fight with the HSC to move the project to the next level, while I periodically called Thamer to keep him on the hook. It wasn't easy. My infrequent calls started to sound the same: "We're working on arrangements to meet with you, blah blah blah. There's a lot of red tape, blah blah blah . . ."

I filled the time between our calls with obsessive worry. Would he change his mind? Would he go back into deep hiding? Would he get captured or killed? I didn't dare tell him the United States government hadn't even given me permission to go to Iraq and meet him. No point in darkening this new ray of hope.

The HSC roadblocks continued, though we kept up our steady efforts to wear the resistors down instead of the other way around. My relationship with Jim and Kevin wasn't faring much better, as now they were both threatening to pull out because of my failure to get permission to execute our mission. Here we were now five months after my first call to Thamer and still we didn't have permission to take the next steps. It was maddening.

It was then that Dr. McCarthy decided to drop the bomb. She had arranged a meeting with Secretary Chertoff and his Deputy Secretary Michael Jackson. We were going *directly* to a member of the president's cabinet. I'm sure this blew up the HSC but my boss was determined. Dr. McCarthy and I drove from our downtown office to DHS headquarters on Nebraska Ave. We got to the secure room first and anxiously awaited. About ten minutes later Secretary Chertoff and Deputy Jackson walked in alone. After introducing me, Dr. McCarthy laid out our plan. Briefing materials had been sent ahead so Secretary Chertoff was aware of the details, some of which I was not privy to. Both men listened intently as Dr. McCarthy used her limited time to get their support. With that, everything we could think of had been done. As the briefing came to a close, Dr. McCarthy and I had hoped that we had presented a convincing case. We needed the Secretary's support. As Secretary Chertoff began to rise from his chair, he looked at Dr. McCarthy and then me and said, "Okay go get him." Secretary Chertoff and Secretary Jackson then shook my hand and wished me luck. To say that Dr. McCarthy and I were pleased would be an understatement.

FINALLY, IN NOVEMBER OF 2007, OUR persistence as well as our new strategy paid off. The HSC granted our team permission to go to Baghdad—only to get a proffer; that is, to find out whether Thamer actually had valuable information to offer. This would not, could not, be a thorough debrief, which was the kind of interview that would require more time, more expert interviewers, and a more secure location. But for now, we'd take what we could get.

After months of beating my head against the wall, we were finally moving in the right direction. I called my team to share the news.

"Hey, Kevin!"

"Yeah?"

"Are you ready?"

"Ready for what?"

"We're going to see our guy."

"Are you shitting me?"

"No."

"Seriously?"

"Seriously."

"Well, it's about fucking time!"

"Ya think?"

"Call Jim! We're going to Iraq!"

Now that we had the green light and plans for our trip were underway, I could take a moment to sit back and exhale. *We were doing this.* I was headed to the Middle East. My thoughts dashed ahead to all the protocols we'd have to prepare for relative to a Middle East assignment. First, we'd need Department of Defense Common Access Cards (CACs) to give us the access and support we'd need. Then we'd need this and then that, I thought as I prepared a mental list of everything we'd have to get before we could go. It was a dangerous part of the world, and thinking about that sent my mind back to what happened to me on my first trip to that part of the world—Saudi Arabia.

In 1991, I was part of a group of agents sent ahead to prepare for the visit of President Bush to Saudi Arabia. The president was making the trip to obtain Saudi cooperation regarding the upcoming conflict with Iraq. Saddam had invaded his neighbor Kuwait and President Bush put together a coalition to kick him out. It was the start of Operation Desert Shield. The Saudis were interesting to me because they played both sides of the fence; they were allies with the US when it was in their interests to be but were a major sponsor of terrorism around the world. And, in no way did they want democracy. The two thousand or so members of the extended Saudi royal family that held the real power and wealth have no interest in giving it up, so elections are out of the question. The evidence is clear that Saudi Arabia is the world's largest source of funds to and promoter of Salafist Jihadism, an ideology rooted in the principle that only the Sunni sect represents "true Islam." Years later it was still a major concern when Secretary of State, Hillary Clinton wrote, "Donors in Saudi Arabia constitute the most significant source of funding to Sunni terrorist groups worldwide." As I said they played both sides.

The meeting took place in Jeddah, a beautiful city on the coast of the Red Sea, and my assignment was to assist the lead intelligence advance agent in amassing any intelligence information that might affect the president's visit. This would involve cooperating with the Saudi military, Saudi intelligence, and Saudi National Police. It was a dangerous part of the world, and we took nothing for granted.

A police escort took us to the King Faisal Palace on the prestigious Boulevard Al-Andalus. Built in the 1960s as a royal palace for the late King Faisal, it then served as a guest-palace for official visitors. Talk about opulent guest quarters!

Although my luxurious sleeping quarters were fit for a king, I was too wired to rest, and I wanted to stretch my legs. I knew I'd be busy for the rest of my time in Saudi Arabia and that this might be my only chance to get time to myself. I put on a track suit and left the palace for a late afternoon run. My run took me along the city's main road parallel to the Red Sea. It was a beautiful sight as the setting sun's rays danced off low rolling waves toward a long, beautiful stretch of sand. The scenery was so stunning, I practically forgot why I was there, in that place, at that time.

As I ran, it took me a few minutes to notice something bizarre: every Saudi I passed gaped at me as if I were naked.

My line of work took me to far-flung locales, and I was used to receiving stares as a foreigner in other people's lands, but this felt different. I was eerily conscious of the feeling of being watched. Then the unmistakable sound of screeching tires broke through the quiet. It took me a second to recognize that those tires belonged to police vehicles, at least four of them. A slew of police officers leaped out and advanced toward me, shouting, semi-circling, and moving closer as they leveled their machine guns at me. My experiences as a Secret Service agent told me what to do next if I wanted to survive: not a thing.

I raised my arms above my head, kept my empty hands visible, and took care not to make any unpredictable movements that would give any of them an excuse to pull the trigger. Stay calm, I told myself.

When I used to interview victims of armed robbery, they always told me they'd fixated on the gun, not on the person brandishing it. That's why getting a good description of the person was sometimes difficult. I've heard this described as a complicated psychological phenomenon, but to me it seems pretty simple: the gun holds the bullets that can come out at a speed of thousands of feet per second, tear into you, and end your life. At that moment, I was like all those other victims I had always felt sorry for, fixated on the machine guns and without a clue how to deal with the guys attached to them.

A policeman approached me, speaking hard and fast in Arabic. He sounded extremely pissed off. This only made it harder to look away from the gun. Passersby started to gather but kept their distance.

"I'm an American," I blurted, motioning at the passport in my rear pocket. I didn't dare reach for it. Then I forced myself to lift my head to face the cop who was talking to me.

His eyes had a frightened look, and I had the distinct feeling he'd been following me for most of my run. I looked from his face to the others. All of them looked from me to each other, every glance and movement rapid, jerky, and furtive told me they were scared. Maybe they thought I was a suicide bomber.

The head officer and another member of his team made their way toward me. They patted me down as if afraid to touch me, as if I might blow up on contact. I nodded at the officer in charge and tipped my head toward my hip pocket. He nodded and pointed at the pocket with his chin, giving me his nonverbal okay to take out my passport. I slowly pulled it out and held it up, both hands again above my head. A second officer snatched it from my hand.

Then the pair broke away and started a tense dialogue with a third. The others kept their guns trained on me. The language barrier prevented me from explaining who I was and why I was in their country, that I was, in a way, one of them. I held my hands over my head for I don't know how long—maybe ten minutes at that point—and by now pain shot through my shoulders and arms. It was my first time experiencing the fear and pain I'd subjected so many suspects to through the years. I understood that these guys were doing their jobs, but I still had no idea why they'd come after me.

The trio of officers wrapped up their discussion. And with a wave of his hand, the officer in charge motioned for the others to lower their weapons. I dropped my arms with relief. The tension started to evaporate and my heartrate began to slow to normal.

"Where are you going in such a hurry?" the officer in charge asked me in heavily accented English.

"Jogging . . . running . . . exercise." I kept trying different answers, none of which seemed to please them.

They continued to question me in their broken English about my "odd" behavior. I learned at that moment that in a country on the verge of war, running was seen as the action of a bomber or saboteur or at least someone with bad intentions. It took a while to convince them I was an American here on peaceful business, not a bad actor with a fake passport who was here to stir trouble. Although they never said anything to me, they must have figured out that I was there because of the upcoming visit of the president of the United States. If I'd told them this information, that might have eased the situation a bit, so I'm not sure why I didn't. Just one of those things.

I worked up quite a sweat by the time they handed me back my passport and allowed me to go free. The Saudi's knew war was coming to their region and they were edgy. I couldn't blame them. I walked slowly back to the palace. The Saudis, I learned that day, took their security very seriously. The beauty of the Red Sea would remain forever vivid in my memory, as would the memory of almost getting shot and killed as a suspected Middle Eastern terrorist.

Chapter 16

BAGHDAD, IRAQ—NOVEMBER 2007

THAMER TOOK A DRAG OF HIS CIGARETTE and watched his wife cook. He admired Eman's energy and purpose as she moved from cutting board to stove to sink. He wished he had a task to keep him busy.

Time went by slowly when there was nothing to do. He considered returning to the Iraqi Interim Center for Science and Industry, but traveling to and from the center was dangerous.

Iraq's scientists were still being targeted, all the more if they worked at a place associated with Americans. Any trip outside the house would be dangerous for him and would necessitate traveling the streets in disguise. But he had let his hair go gray again. He was tired of disguises.

Thamer sipped his tea, rolling the precious liquid around on his tongue before swallowing it. Tea was expensive now, and they drank it sparingly. He limited himself to one cup a day to make sure there was enough for his in-laws to enjoy. This kitchen had two wide windows, one overlooking the garden, the other offering a view of the street. He gazed out at the steady flow of traffic visible over the short fence in the front yard and thanked Allah for the kindness of all the relatives who had selflessly taken turns hosting his family, several months here, several months there for the five years since the invasion. Five years of fear and boredom, living in endless limbo, waiting for something to change.

IN NOVEMBER 2007, WE FINALLY completed the mountain of paperwork that would allow us to travel to Iraq. We left Dulles Airport in route to Doha Qatar because going directly to Iraq was not an option. Flying to a staging area was normal. It allowed the military to account for personnel, verify their orders, and be prepared to support them when they arrived in Iraq. Also, it allowed the military to add supplies onto any aircraft that wasn't full. Jim, Kevin, and Dustin were all younger than I, but after several hours of flying, they looked beat. Every part of my body ached, and I didn't know how my back could stand any more of this trip. Dr. Dustin Razsi, Chief, WMD and Health Intelligence for DHS was our microbiologist, the lone scientist who would translate Thamer's specialized knowledge and bring back to the HSC the proffer of Thamer's value. The grueling hours of travel and the seriousness of our mission had already forged a bond between the new guy and us. Dustin was one of us now.

Our jet landed in Doha, Qatar, and we all blinked at each other in a daze, sharing the unspoken thought, *can you believe we're still not there?* We loaded into the military SUV for the drive to the US air base.

I was amazed at the onslaught of development rolling through the city of Doha. I lost count of the cranes tilting over high-rises in various phases of construction, government buildings, commercial office space, hotels, housing. The number of luxury automobiles sharing the road with us seemed over the top—everywhere there were high-end Mercedes and BMWs. I learned later that Qatar has quite the car culture and can afford it. Everything in the city seemed brand new, as though Qatar had just been created.

Al Udeid Air Base was a massive roaring swirl of noise, motion, and dust. The facility was a way station for military personnel and equipment from several coalition countries, including the US, UK, and of course Qatar. In theory, it should take us only two hours to fly from there to Iraq. That was, if we could get a plane.

I had chosen Qatar as a jumping off point for our team. It seemed like a logical choice given that our military flew that route all the time. But the destination's popularity turned out to be a problem. We were scheduled on a space-available status, and right now there wasn't any space available.

We sat for hours on hard metal folding chairs in the holding room, shifting from one uncomfortable position to another. Every time the flight coordinator told us it looked like there would be room on the next flight, we'd be bumped last minute, replaced by personnel or cargo considered more "essential" than we were. Shipping toilet paper into Iraq was apparently a higher priority than getting us in.

Each time we were bumped we headed to the "transit" tents, so we could sleep only to be awakened and told to hurry to the holding room for a departure. A circular pattern emerged: grab our gear, run to the terminal, wait a few hours, get bumped, go back to the tent, repeat.

At one point Kevin struck up a conversation with a young Air Force officer who was also on standby. She told Kevin she'd now been waiting to get a flight out *for three days*. In response, Kevin slid down in his seat as if to pour himself onto the floor in a puddle. "Jesus, if the Air Force can't make room for one of their own, what chance do we have?"

During one of our waiting sessions, we received a stark reminder that, however many Americans surrounded us, we were about to enter a foreign culture. A group of soldiers had just arrived from Iraq for some R&R, and they stood at attention listening to a sergeant instruct them in their code of conduct while in Qatar. He laid out an intimidating series of dos and don'ts, with many more don'ts than dos: You're allowed a two-drink maximum per day. You must wear modest attire that covers legs and shoulders regardless of how hot you get. You can't go here and you can't go there, can't do this and can't do that. Our team was already in agreement on one thing: R&R in Qatar sounded depressing. These were active-duty service members who had seen action, but their downtime had so many rules how could they possibly rest and recuperate? I had to hand it to those kids, though. They made no complaints, not one despairing grimace but instead stood tall, listened earnestly, and sounded off respectfully, "Sir, yes sir!" I was moved by their decorum.

When we were called to actually board—three days after arriving—we had to "kit" up in helmets, body armor, and other safety equipment. The roar of a massive engine nearly deafened us as we entered the cavernous guts of the C130 transport. The aircraft was full to capacity, and you couldn't have slid a sheet of paper between my body and that of the young soldier with shaved head sitting ramrod straight to my left. Our "seats" were benches made of canvas and metal, with sling straps to hold us in—built not for comfort but efficiency, to carry as many troops as possible.

My seatmate was a soldier who looked about nineteen, not much older than my youngest son. The same age I was when I joined the military. So young to be responsible for life-and-death, I thought. But then war is always about young men paying the tab for old men's decisions.

Once we were airborne, my team and I began talking with my young seatmate, screaming to be heard over the engines, and we learned he was with the 101st Airborne Division. His father had passed away, and soon he was negotiating with Jim about the possibility of fixing Jim up with his mother. Jim, who was always interested in meeting "the right person," appeared genuinely interested.

At one point, the soldier leaned close to my ear and bellowed, "You know sir, I really admire you!" I could barely hear him over the noise of the engines.

"Thanks! But what for?" I was honestly confused. We'd just met.

"For being out here, doing this sort of stuff—at your age!"

My age? I gave my seatmate an amused look, which I hoped conveyed that I didn't know whether to thank him or throw him out the window. I muttered a thank you for the backhanded compliment and expressed my admiration for his service. I had to laugh because most of my life people had teased me about looking too young for whatever I was doing. When I was hired by the Concord Police Department, I looked like I was a teenager, and I remember one sergeant calling out as I walked past him, "Look, it's so bad now, we're hiring boy scouts!" But now "*my age*"? Although I laughed, my young soldier was right. I wasn't eighteen anymore.

I didn't realize I had fallen asleep until I jolted awake a couple of hours later to the sound of a voice announcing over a loud speaker, "We are approaching Ali Al Salem in Kuwait."

Wait, What? Kuwait?! What happened to landing in Iraq?

"Shit, Jim," I yelled to my tough Marine comrade who was supposed to be our logistics expert, "you can't even get us to the right country!" I was only half-joking.

Jim held up his hands in a "don't blame me" gesture.

Apparently ever-shifting military priorities had again changed our travel plans. We got off the plane in Kuwait to once again wait several hours for another transport plane with sufficient available space. Then we got off the ground again, finally headed to Baghdad.

As we approached Baghdad International Airport, we were told the flight was going to get a little rough due to the diversionary maneuvers the pilots had to take to avoid being hit by rockets. In this instance, pilots didn't want to go slow and low, which was typically a safer way to land a plane. The corkscrew maneuvering our pilot used was called "Khe Sanh-ing," a tactic developed by pilots in Vietnam to avoid being downed by enemy fire from the ground. Upon approach, to avoid missiles the pilot takes a steeper dive as opposed to a low and slow descent. The pilot does the reverse with a steep ascent upon leaving. Although a couple of guys lost their lunches, better that than losing body parts. We arrived unscathed, and I sent up a silent prayer of thanks.

Stepping off the aircraft into the Iraqi heat was like stepping in front of a blast furnace. It wasn't the hottest part of the year but Christ it was hot that day. The dry desert heat sucked the breath out of me, the sun hitting me in the face with an intensity that made me feel that my skin might peel from the flesh. The sun was so blinding, I stopped walking to wait for my eyes to adjust.

Once the world came into focus, the next thing I noticed was the brown hue of the fine sand that coated everything as far as I could see. Before I knew what was happening, it was stinging my eyes, crunching between my teeth, creeping into my clothes. I would soon come to feel like I was twenty pounds heavier in Iraq just from the sand I carried around. Sand got into everything. We couldn't keep it off us, and we couldn't get away from it.

That initial blast of heat and sand was nothing compared to the intensity of the mistrust that pervaded Baghdad, a city both at the center of an armed conflict with a foreign army and embroiled in a fight against itself; the Shia were fighting the Sunni, the Sunni were fighting back, and the Kurds hating both of them. Everywhere, there were tribal rivalries, Iranian fighters, Al-Qaeda splinter groups, insurgent groups, and armed gangs. It was a city saturated with violence, suspicion, and secret operations, and this is where we had to search for Thamer.

Our SUV driver took us across the airport to check in with base operations at Camp Victory. We were assigned sleeping quarters, a portable unit that looked like a small tractor-trailer and doubled as our team's war room. We arranged for the use of two armored SUVs, along with sufficient weapons and ammunition to protect ourselves. We grabbed food from the chow hall, and headed back to our quarters to make plans.

In addition to crawling with members of the US military, Camp Victory was also home to a sizable federal law-enforcement presence. The FBI, Secret Service, ICE, Customs, and other US entities kept agents in country for the purpose of investigating fraud and other criminal activity. Counterfeiting was one such activity. The US government brought plenty of US currency into Iraq, and its policy allowed Iraqis to exchange dinar for US dollars. Enterprising Iraqis took to counterfeiting Iraqi money to turn it in for US dollars. The Secret Service was brought in to put a stop to that thievery. In addition, thefts of gasoline and other goods from our bases kept our guys busy, and we needed to put a stop to these thefts that could aid the enemy. US law enforcement was also on hand to obtain intelligence on criminal gangs as our country sought to help Iraq establish rule of law.

Kevin had connections at Camp Victory, and he quickly recruited two new members to our team: Joel, an ICE agent; and Don, a Secret Service agent. Joel and Don had been in the country awhile and knew their way around. After briefing our new team members, the six of us crowded outside my trailer. It was time to contact Thamer.

Kevin took his mobile phone out of his pocket. My phone was supposed to be set up for international calls, but it didn't work. It was pretty much useless. I reached into my hip pouch for a slip of paper with Thamer's number on it and handed it to Kevin. We all exchanged a look and leaned in close, heads almost touching so we could all hear the call. The others had yet to hear the voice of our "target." Even though I had spoken to him from DC, part of me felt like we were on a quest for some mythical figure. Another part of me felt like we were calling a long-lost friend: Hey buddy, long time no see. We're just passing through town. Mind if we drop in?

I nodded to Kevin. He nodded back and punched in the number. I watched him push the keys in what seemed like slow motion as I held my breath. I'd barely slept in days, and the drone of the trailer's air conditioner outside exacerbated my already throbbing headache. It sounded as if Kevin had punched twenty numbers, and he was still going.

"What are you *doing*?" I snapped. "How many numbers are you dialing? We've got to make contact today!"

"Come on, dude, give me a break," Kevin said.

Nothing was happening on the line. Kevin pressed "end" and started punching numbers all over again.

"What kind of phone system do these people have?" I muttered. "Are you sure you're doing it right?"

Kevin stared me down. "This is the number you gave me," he said in a tone that conveyed, *Get off my back*.

Keep your cool, Steve, I told myself, take a breath. After a grueling wait, Kevin stopped dialing and held the phone to his ear. Putting it on speaker would only decrease our chances of decent reception, so the rest of us waited through a long silence. I couldn't hear the rings, but I imagined them in my head: . . . five, six, seven, no answer.

"I don't know, dude. This isn't good," Kevin said, stating the obvious.

"Let it ring," I said. "Maybe he doesn't have his phone nearby."

But Kevin had gotten into my head. Three possibilities hammered my brain: Thamer doesn't want to cooperate. Thamer has been kidnapped. Thamer is dead.

So much was riding on this call. Two years of hard work, our reputations, and my personal commitment to see it through. Did Thamer really have anything of value to tell us? I thought about the naysayers back in Washington who insisted we were wasting our time. Were they right?

Then Kevin spoke into the phone, "Hello, my friend."

Relief washed over me. Thamer was still among us and apparently still willing to cooperate. I had to temper my desire to hug Kevin. Though much was left to be done, I felt good for the first time in a very long time.

IT WAS ONLY WHEN THAMER FOLDED the cell phone closed in the palm of his hand that he noticed he was trembling.

Eman sat next to him at the kitchen table. "Was it an American?"

He shrugged. "Yes, an American."

"What did the man say, Thamer?"

"He said his name was Kevin, and he and Mr. Steve from Washington are here and they want to meet with me." He took a deep breath. "I'm still worried maybe the Americans want to arrest me again."

Eman took the phone from his hand and replaced it with her own hand. They sat in mutual silence until she said, "The Americans at the Center for Science and Industry have contact with you. If they wanted to arrest you, they could have set you up by now."

He looked up at her, wanting to hope. "That's true . . . "

"What did you tell him?"

"Maybe in the next few days, we shall see" Thamer answered. "I told him I would have to arrange for transportation, and that might be difficult. He said the people in Washington needed to meet me as soon as possible. I don't know if that's true or if they're trying to pressure me. He said he'd call me back in an hour."

Eman looked up at the clock, and a thought sparkled in her eye. "My brother will be home from work soon. We'll get his opinion. If Saad thinks it's safe, he can drive you to the meeting."

Eman's optimism was infectious, and Thamer couldn't help smiling back at her. Maybe this was the meeting he'd been hoping for.

"I want to make the right decision" he said, walking to the bedroom to be alone to think. Eman is right, he thought. If the Americans wanted to arrest me they could have done it already. He knew in his heart that this could be his one chance, albeit it a risky one. After much thought he came to a decision, and called out to Eman. "If I'm really being invited to a serious meeting with serious men, proper dress is required. I'll wear a suit and tie."

Chapter 17

CAMP LIBERTY, IRAQ—NOVEMBER 2007

DAYS HAD PASSED AND THAMER finally agreed to meet us, but that didn't stop my worrying. A lot could go wrong. We would pick him up at an agreed upon location in Baghdad, bring him to Camp Victory for our interview, then take him back. So much could go wrong at any point, mostly anywhere outside the perimeter of Camp Victory. Just driving through the wrong area could get Thamer killed. It could get us all killed, which is why excursions outside the base were usually made via military convoy. Although it wasn't a requirement, a convoy was recommended for safety. But our operation wasn't a military one, and arranging a convoy or even a small combat team to back us up in case of attack would have required a herculean effort and countless approvals. We had neither the energy nor the time. So, we would be off base with only a handful of support personnel armed with minimal firepower, in two so-called armored vehicles that were little more than glorified SUVs. Should we come under concerted attack, it would be game over.

I gathered the team to cobble together a plan in hopes that Thamer would agree to it. The six of us crowded into "the coffin," our nickname for our sleeping quarters, which we also used as our war room, now crammed to capacity with people and equipment. It looked and smelled like crap, typical of a man cave with shit thrown everywhere. Everyone in it looked disheveled with one exception: Lieutenant Colonel Jim Elseth wore his marine battle dress uniform and, with his John Wayne haircut and clean shave, he looked like a perfect Marine. The rest of us looked as if we hadn't bathed, shaved, or changed clothes for weeks.

The room was quiet, except for the drone of the air conditioner, which struggled overtime to beat back the relentless Iraqi heat. I looked at our assembled team and worried that I was risking all six of our lives. Most of us were used to jobs that entailed risk, but this was danger of another order. We weren't going on a routine patrol or interviewing suspects; seeking out a potential high-value asset with a target on his back was one form of begging for trouble. I'd spent many months promising myself I wouldn't stop until I found Thamer and safely brought him in, but now I seriously questioned whether we should proceed. Being off base with no military support and with our own resources limited, I thought, what the hell are we doing? Thamer had struggled to stay alive all these months. Could meeting us be his downfall? Shit, I thought. Wouldn't that be a fucked-up end to this whole thing?

For one suspended moment, as I thought about the danger of what we were about to do, the five faces before me became one face, the face of Nick Berg. Much as it pained me, I owed it to these guys to keep in mind what had happened to Nick.

Nicholas Evan Berg was twenty-six, a native of West Chester, Pennsylvania, and the owner of a company that rebuilt communications antennae. Like many contractors, he'd gone to Iraq in the wake of the invasion, hoping to secure a contract for his company. He arrived in Baghdad late in December, 2003. For the next several months, he traveled the country assessing the communications needs of businesses and government agencies seeking to rebuild and foreign military organizations seeking to keep order. During his time in Iraq, Nick stayed in constant touch with family—his parents, brother, and sister—via video calls, phone calls, and emails.

One day in March of 2004, Nick's communications stopped. His family grew worried something had happened to him, and after several days they began a series of calls that led them to a US State Department investigator who began an official inquiry into Nick's disappearance. The inquiry went on for two months but produced no leads.

Then, on May 8, 2004, a routine US military patrol in Baghdad found Nick's body on the side of a freeway overpass. The army's official public statement said his body showed "signs of trauma." At the time it wasn't disclosed that Nick had been decapitated.

On May 11, 2004, the website of the militant group Muntada al-Ansar posted a video with the opening title, "Abu Musa'b as-Zarqawi slaughters an American." I was sitting at my desk at Secret Service headquarters when one of my colleagues sent me an email with a link to the video, which broadcast Nick's decapitation in vivid detail. The message also contained the audio. I wish I had never opened it.

At the beginning of the video, Nick is very much alive. He's wearing an orange jumpsuit, kneeling before five men in ski masks. He looks into the camera and says in a shaky voice, "My name is Nick Berg, my father's name is Michael, my mother's name is Suzanne. I have a brother and sister, David and Sara. I live in West Chester, Pennsylvania, near Philadelphia." Then he reads a lengthy prepared statement from a paper he held in his trembling hands. According to the statement, Nick is about to die in retaliation for the abuse of prisoners at Abu Ghraib prison. The men in ski masks then converge on Nick and decapitate him with a large knife. It is not a fast murder. It is slow and utterly excruciating to witness. Nick's gurgling death sounds will never leave me. After cutting his head off, the masked men placed it on top of his body. I don't know why they did it, maybe for shock value. If so, it worked.

As I tried not to imagine the worst happening during this current mission, Nick Berg's face loomed in my mind. And the more I tried not to think about him, the more vivid his image became. I tried to change the channel in my mind, so I thought back to my first day on the president's Secret Service detail and the sign hanging above the entrance that read, "Everything Is Your Problem." I learned quickly that as Secret Service agents, we all had the mission of keeping the president safe; regardless of our individual assignment and set of duties, our goal was always the same, which meant that we needed to always work as a team. The problem of one became the problem of all. It was about working together to achieve our common goal. I was inspired by the "Everything Is Your Problem" way of looking at things. I really loved it. The sign also contained a hidden message and everyone in the Secret Service knew it but seldom discussed it openly. Our lives were expendable, and if need be, would be given up for the greater good of keeping the president alive. Mission before self. Country before self.

I also remembered the advice the agent in charge of the president's detail gave me when I first arrived: "Steve, I can't tell you what to do in every circumstance. Too many different things can happen, too many variables. But what I can tell you is this, *do something.* Don't be afraid to make a decision." Overthinking a problem to the point of delaying action can be deadly. The bottom line: if you're afraid to make a decision, you shouldn't be in a position to make one. Leave it to those who can make the call under pressure.

I scanned the faces gathered around me now, all of them now waiting for just that, for me to do something, to make a decision, to give the instructions. Jim, Kevin, and I had developed a rapport over the previous few months grounded in our sense of mission, and I knew they'd do whatever I asked. Our other three team members had the determined looks of men who were equally committed. I knew that these five men would follow me and put themselves in harm's way and this idea rattled me.

I thought about why we'd come this far: we believed Thamer could help protect our fellow Americans from future threats. But at the moment all that was only an idea, while the men in front of me were very real. Sooner or later when those who vow to serve their country find themselves in the field, this moment always arrives, the moment when we have to accept that putting our lives on the line for our country really means putting our lives on the line for the buddies by our side.

I silently pledged to do everything possible to keep us all safe and minimize our exposure, but if things didn't go our way, I promised myself I'd fight until I died. I wouldn't allow my family to go through what Nick's family had gone through.

I glanced around the room to see if I could pick up any dissension. But every face reflected my determination.

"All right," I said. "Fuck it. Let's go get him!"

This declaration was greeted by smiles and approval from every man in the coffin. They then picked up their armored vests, weapons, and ammo, and walked—or should I say sauntered out —single file, mission in hand, ready to go. It reminded me of the movie, "The Magnificent 7" minus one. I was the last one out the door, and I said a silent prayer.

Only once we'd loaded the gear and were ready to go, wheels up, did Kevin call Thamer again. Thamer gave us the location where his brother-in-law wanted to drop him off. Kevin agreed. Our plan was to get there ahead of him to make sure the area was safe.

"If you don't see us, don't leave," Kevin instructed him. "If there's a problem, we'll call you."

Thamer said he would be in a small white sedan driven by a relative. Because of the language barrier we didn't get more of a description than that before he hung up.

The pickup point we'd agreed to was about ten miles from base, but our two local guys, Joel and Don, assured us it was about as secure as we could hope for. It was a basic grab and go operation. One vehicle for transport and one for security. Drivers stay with the vehicles ready to go, others are assigned to get out and make the grab, and others provide a perimeter of security. You go in quick and get out quick. That was the plan. But as Mike Tyson said, "We all have a plan till we get punched in the face." Communication was essential. If we sensed it wasn't safe, even just a hunch that something was off, I'd yell "abort" and we'd abandon the pickup and beat feet back to the base.

Although we planned to arrive before Thamer, we didn't want to beat him by much. Hanging around might draw attention we didn't need.

Joel led our micro-convoy of two armored SUVs. He was a very capable ICE agent, but that day he had a bad case of kidney stones and was suffering intense pain. He was supposed to return to the States for treatment, but had stayed on instead to help us. He was that kind of guy, mission before self. The concrete barriers and sand-filled drums that had been positioned to prevent enemies from getting in made getting out laborious and nerve-racking. We passed through the final checkpoint, and Camp Victory and the Baghdad International Airport shrank in our rear-view mirror.

We now had to traverse Route Irish, once dubbed the most dangerous road on earth. It had been said that if you could survive the ten mile stretch of road from the airport to the center of Baghdad you could survive anything. The road was a magnet for insurgents who knew that all coalition forces had to drive it sooner or later. Bullets, rockets, hidden improvised explosive devices and car bombs were the norm. The soldiers called it IED alley. Suicide bombers in cars packed with explosives would lurk at on-ramps waiting for American convoys or other targets. Insurgents in cars with darkened windows mingled in traffic, would lower their windows to let loose bursts of machine-gun fire. Insurgents disguised as members of a road crew would bury daisy-chained artillery shells beneath the roadway, then trigger them with garage-door openers and cellphones. In 2004, the dangers were so extreme that State Department personnel were forbidden from using it. By 2007, the security of Route Irish was better, but it was still considered highly dangerous.

Every minute of the drive revealed a reality nothing could have prepared me for, despite all the reports I'd read about this corner of the world. Baghdad was no longer a city. It was a post-apocalyptic war zone that vividly reminded me of Ground Zero. Few people roamed the streets, and the few who did move quickly without smiling; they kept their distance and stared as we passed, as if accustomed to vehicles like ours and the possibility that we might bring trouble.

For a brief second, I thought about Scott Helvenston and what happened to him. It was all over the news. On March 31, 2004, Scott, a former Navy Seal turned contractor, along with three other security personnel, were ambushed escorting a convoy in Fallujah. They were raked with automatic weapons while still in their vehicles. They had no chance. They were then lit on fire and their blackened bodies were hung from a bridge over the Euphrates. The act was so barbaric that it led to the first battle of Fallujah, code-named Operation Vigilant. The operation was launched in part to find those responsible for the gruesome deaths. I had to clear my mind of that horrible vision and fast.

It took about thirty minutes to reach our meeting point.

We spotted the white vehicle, but as we approached, the driver took off. Had Thamer changed his mind? Was he too scared to meet us? We took off in pursuit, the driver sped up, and then we were on a mad dash through city streets. I was in the rear vehicle, and both the white car and our lead SUV kicked up so much sand, I could barely see in front of me. All we could do was follow the dust cloud. We caught up to the white car, and our lead car sped around to cut it off while we blocked it from the rear so they couldn't drive off again.

We got out and approached the vehicle carefully, weapons drawn. We were concerned our aggressive stop of the vehicle could draw unwanted attention, so Kevin and I slid up along the driver's side, heads pivoting to look out for any signs of furtive movements. We raised our weapons to the ready position and pounced, both of us facing the driver whose eyes were filled with terror. He held the steering wheel in a white-knuckle grip. I looked at the passenger seat. There was nobody there. I looked back at the driver. He wasn't Thamer. He was an older man, yes, but I'd been studying Thamer's face for two years, and it was seared into my memory. This guy wasn't Thamer.

I carefully peered through the window, at the backseat, down at the floor. Thamer was nowhere to be seen. We had the wrong white car. Fuck me, I thought, slowly lowering my weapon as we uttered a "sorry man" apology to a scared to death driver and exited as quickly as possible.

We got Thamer back on the phone. He wasn't even at the pickup point yet, and this time we kept him on the line as we vectored back to the pickup location. Narrow streets are death traps and they needed to be avoided. We had to make sure we didn't chase him around and get ourselves lost. One wrong turn, that's all it takes for you to be in deep trouble. Despite the initial snafu, we arrived back at the designated point at the same time he did. We now had the right vehicle and drove up fast, sliding to a stop and kicking up more dust.

Jim jumped out of our armored SUV, opened the passenger door of the old, dented, white economy car, grabbed a man I hoped was Thamer—though I saw only a doubled-over man with white hair—ran with him the few steps to our vehicle, and shoved him into the backseat. With the grab and go complete, we sped back to the base. Conversation was almost non-existent. Everyone needed to focus.

I turned the rear-view mirror to glimpse the man I'd been getting to know for two years. His hair held my attention. It looked much whiter than it had in his photos.

I scanned the streets, which had seemed almost empty less than an hour earlier but now struck me as crowded. I felt the burning stares of hundreds of black eyes with bad intentions. Or maybe they had no bad intentions but were just scared and sick of the violence and chaos that was Baghdad. I couldn't get off those streets fast enough.

Driving out of the city and back toward the base, we approached the first of several checkpoints leading into the controlled area. A guard approached the vehicle Joel was driving. He looked like an Iraqi.

"You must empty your weapons of all ammunition." He barked out. The Iraqi guards demanded we clear our weapons before proceeding, meaning they wanted us to empty our guns of ammunition. They were none too polite about it.

Under an agreement, the outer perimeters of some of our military installations were protected by Iraqis, and the loyalties of some of them were questionable. I was aware at the time that several US soldiers had been murdered by insiders, so-called friendly forces. Sometimes Iraqi police and Iraqi military pretended to be on our side only to later carry out suicide attacks. I found it safest to assume that any Iraqi I ran into unexpectedly might be bad news.

My SUV idled behind Joel's, and I heard him reply to one of the guards, "No, sorry chief, we don't do that. We're all federal agents, and we don't empty our weapons of ammunition when on duty." He was so adamant I heard every word loud and clear.

The guard shouted, "You cannot go further! You must empty your weapons."

More guards approached and began a slow circle around our cars. The voices got louder. Joel's anger was getting a lot of attention, and attention was the opposite of what we needed, but having empty weapons in a war zone is like having an empty gas tank at Indy—useless until loaded. On the bright side, I thought, if these men were the insiders we feared, they'd have killed us already.

Joel wasn't giving in. We weren't clearing our weapons, and they weren't letting us go. The guards moved closer, and then they spotted Thamer in the backseat. They requested his ID. Shit, I thought. Thamer had no ID that would allow him to have access to the base.

The fact that they spotted Thamer upped the game a lot. Now we had two battles to fight. As my anxiety increased, I eased the M-4 rifle from the seat next to me onto my lap, and I saw the tension notch up in the eyes of the two guards closest to me. It was clear they had no intention of backing down, and they had the force to back up their demand.

The guard commander walked out to join the fray, a swarthy fellow with a black mustache, black eyes, and a dark demeanor to match. Why the fuck did it seem like every Iraqi officer I encountered had a mustache like Saddam's? Coincidence?

The presence of their commander seemed to have given his men more confidence, and they moved even closer. Now that they'd seen Thamer, we had no choice but to resist. If he was taken into custody, it was all over. I couldn't believe we'd made it unscathed through what was supposed to be the tough part only to wind up having to take Thamer back or run the risk of a serious altercation with the guards if we forced the issue.

While Joel and the guard commander kept yelling over each other, I was trying to figure a way out. Joel was in front of me with guards in front of his vehicle effectively blocking him in, so I couldn't go forward, and backing up wasn't going to happen with the serpentine barriers. We were in a tough spot. I thought, okay. . . radio to Joel to go around the guards and try and make it through the serpentine concrete barriers. Hope the SUVs armor holds if they open fire, and keep going until we reach a checkpoint guarded by Americans. Nope, that idea evaporated as quickly as it appeared. Too dangerous and unnecessary. Joel's window was down anyway, so if I radioed him, they might hear, and most of them spoke some English, so that might not work. I moved the M-4 rifle across my lap.

Just when I thought the tension had neared explosion, the head honcho of the guards apparently realized we weren't going to capitulate to his authority and decided this wasn't a battle he wanted to continue. He probably figured that getting into a gun fight with Americans whose base he's assigned to protect might not be good for his future in the guard business. His shoulders dropped, and in a formal, respectful tone that belied everything that had transpired up to that moment, he said, "Okay, go."

His expression and words revealed that we'd caused him deep personal embarrassment by forcing him to give ground in front of his men, but we didn't spend one second lingering to revel in our victory. We sped the hell out of there as fast as we could.

As soon as we arrived on base, we drove Thamer straight to a safe house arranged by one of Joel's contacts. We got out of the vehicles, and I stalked over to Joel.

I was still pissed off and feeling the surging aftermath of adrenaline, so it was a struggle to maintain my cool as I said, "Jesus, Joel! What the fuck was that all about?"

"What?" Joel said, his face a blank.

"The guards, dude. You know, the guys that just had their fucking guns pointed right at us and were ready to smoke us? You remember *those* guys, right?"

Joel only looked more puzzled. "What?"

"Never mind. Must be your fucking kidney stones."

I walked away to join my team. Joel did the right thing, no doubt. You don't carry empty weapons in a war but I was pissed because I thought he should have been perhaps . . . a little less confrontational. That shit almost escalated into a disaster. But in the end, he was right and I was glad he was with us.

Chapter 18

CAMP LIBERTY, IRAQ—NOVEMBER 2007

OUR SUPPORT TEAM WAITED OUTSIDE the safe house while Dustin and I escorted Thamer inside for his interview. The moment Thamer stepped inside, he took one look around and dropped his frightened gaze to the floor as if he couldn't bear the sight of the room before him, as if he knew what a room like this meant he was in for. I could imagine what was on his terrified mind, that maybe this interrogation would make his original arrest feel like a dress rehearsal, that maybe he'd been wrong to trust us. "Safe house" was a polite term for this dismal place, a bare room devoid of furnishings besides a rectangular wood table and three metal folding chairs. The floor was a concrete slab, the walls gray concrete blocks. There were no windows. A mere glimmer of light buzzed from an overhead fixture. It reminded me of a vintage thriller with detectives wearing white shirts, suspenders, and fedoras, leaning over some sweaty slob who insists, "I swear I don't know nothin'!"

Given all my interrogation experience, I knew this was a perfect place for our goal, a peaceful, straightforward question-and-answer session. With nothing to catch the eye or encourage the mind to wander, it was precisely the type of environment I liked for coaxing information from reluctant subjects. And at this point, Thamer had to be viewed as a reluctant subject. But I knew why, and I felt confident that my team and I could change his perspective. At this point, that would be up to Dustin, chosen because he was a microbiologist like Thamer, and me, an investigator trained in the art of obtaining the truth. I knew instinctively that all Thamer needed to coax him to share information of value was to talk to people committed to the truth, and I was deeply committed to the truth. Kevin, Jim, Joel, and Don stayed outside to keep away any unwanted visitors.

Thamer stood with his back against one of the walls. Dustin handed him a bottle of water and made small talk to reassure him but then stopped when his chatter seemed to make Thamer more nervous.

We had only this one afternoon to obtain the proffer. A thorough debrief would take weeks or months, but all we needed today was a glimpse of the kind of information a debrief might reveal, just enough to make our case to bring Thamer to the US. Dustin would determine the value of Thamer's scientific knowledge, and I'd determine whether he was a good guy or a bad one.

Dustin and I arranged the table with our laptops and notebooks and sat next to each other, then I gestured for Thamer to sit in the single chair on the other side.

"Please have a seat."

Thamer sat down, looking from my face to Dustin's. Then his eyes returned to study mine intently. He began to shift back and forth ever so slightly as I broke the silence.

I began. "Please tell me your name."

"I am Thamer Abdul Rahman Imran."

I knew that of course, but asking it was protocol. Then it hit me. I was sitting only a few feet from a man I had come to think of almost as my friend. But I warned myself that for two years, he had also been my prey and that he still might turn out to be my enemy. His white hair made a fine contrast to his dark complexion, reminding me of an old Cary Grant, minus the thick glasses. There had been so much chaos when we picked him up that I hadn't noticed until now that he was nattily dressed in a fine if slightly dated black suit, white shirt, and gray tie. Although he was covered with fine Iraqi dust, he looked more put together and professional than any of us, definitely out of place on a base full of soldiers wearing BDUs and carrying guns.

"Do you have any identification?" I asked him.

He reached into his pocket and produced a new Iraqi passport. I opened the black booklet bearing the crest of Iraq and flipped to its recent photo of the man before me.

"Where did you get this?"

He didn't answer but gave me a faint smile that made me feel embarrassed I'd asked. I knew it had come from the black market, and his face said he knew I knew and wasn't about to say so out loud if he could help it. It was a legitimate passport, and how he got his hands on it given that the Iraqi government had a warrant out for his arrest warrant wasn't my immediate concern, so I dropped the subject but was nonetheless impressed. He was resourceful.

The tired, worn look on his face told me he was struggling to navigate what might be the most important interview of his life. Thamer had a choice to make. He could continue to live as a recluse, hoping he wouldn't be captured or killed, or he could cast his lot with these new Americans, who for all he knew might be no different from the Americans who had captured him, beaten him, and released him into a hostile environment. I didn't envy his choices.

I made clear to Thamer how high the stakes were from my perspective: "One lie and it's all over, and I don't care what happens to you then."

Then Dustin jumped in. "Tell us about your background, where you went to school and your formal training."

"The Americans who came to see me before asked me all these questions. Did they not give you this information?" Thamer asked.

"Well, to make sure we have the correct information, why don't you tell us?"

Carefully and methodically, with some pauses because of his limitations in English, Thamer told us an abbreviated, impersonal version of his story. He outlined his formal education, his work in the military, and his later research as a microbiologist, up to his last assignment before the start of the war. Some of the information we already knew, some we didn't. With that ice-breaker out of the way, Dustin launched into the technical questions that would become the deciding factors about Thamer's value to the United States.

Dustin launched questions about Thamer's background, his specific involvement in production of biological agents, his understanding of low-level production, and many other issues that fell within Dustin's expertise. I didn't mind that most of the technical details went over my head; I was here not to learn the science but to measure the man. Because we had limited time, I was unable to follow my usual pattern of interrogation, which involved working my way through questions that would slowly build on each other to create a trusting relationship with the subject. When Dustin needed a break to review his notes, I jumped in and my questions came fast and furious. Did *anyone* ever contact you about using your skills? Did anyone direct you to meet with us? Do you know of any scientists that are working against the Americans? I kept launching questions, and he kept his composure.

It was important to have a read on whether he might be misleading us, hiding hostile intentions or ulterior motives. Was he a good guy, a bad guy, or both? Although I had spent a lot of time studying his case, my feelings about Thamer remained mixed. American soldiers were being killed by Iraqis every day, and here was an Iraqi sitting across from me. Although I believed he had been treated unfairly by our government, that didn't mean

I felt sure he was a good guy. Did I know what drove him, what he wanted, which side he was on? No.

I sensed Thamer felt the same hesitation about me. Yet his eyes now looked straight into mine, casting a piercing, determined look, as if he'd been waiting a long time for this conversation, this chance to prove he really wanted to help us. He sat up straight and proud, unlike most people I'd interrogated over the years who typically slumped and squirmed in their chairs, desperate to keep track of the lies they told me.

One sign I looked for in evaluating the veracity of every individual I interrogated was their level of emotion when answering questions. Trying to fake emotion is difficult to pull off, even for the most skilled liars, so genuine emotion is a telltale sign of veracity. There are also telltale signs of deceit: small changes in a story, answers that sound scripted, hesitation in answers that should come easily. With Thamer, there was no room for error; I had to be completely alert for any indication that he was playing us. We were sticking our necks out, and Thamer had to be squeaky clean—no criminal activity, no human rights violations, and no ulterior motives. I didn't have much time to study him for signs, for any evidence of activities or slips or lies, and for every minute of the interview I was acutely aware that whatever transpired in that room would determine the future relationship between Thamer Imran and the United States of America.

At every opportunity I made it clear that I meant what I'd said at the start: one misrepresentation, one white lie, one exaggeration and we'd pack up and leave. Those were the rules, and there would be no negotiations, no do-overs, no reprieve. Thamer held up under the challenge. I was impressed that he never looked away from me except to answer a question from Dustin. He maintained a tone of respect and projected a poise and confidence that surprised me for a man in his situation. He answered questions directly and convincingly. To some of our questions he answered, "I don't know," which was important to me because that, too, is an indicator of truthfulness. I could see that he was an intelligent man who clearly understood the risk of cooperating with a foreign government, the risk associated with helping Americans. I admired him for his willingness to take these risks with no guarantees.

I'd need a private discussion with Dustin to determine the value of Thamer's scientific information, but every now and then Dustin gave me a couple of glances that suggested Thamer knew things worth pursuing. For my part, our hours with Thamer convinced me that he'd been forthcoming. The question was, would he hold up to the rigors of an extensive debriefing outside of Iraq?

The United States had gone down this path with him before and hadn't kept its end of the bargain. But I could tell by looking at him that he had come to believe this meeting was different, so I silently vowed to make sure the results would be different. This time we would follow through on our word.

We had to keep track of the time, and more important, the daylight, which was easy to forget about in a windowless room. It wasn't safe to travel at night in Baghdad, and Kevin and Jim interrupted us a couple of times to remind us of that. We were losing light fast, and we were all growing tired and hoarse. We concluded the debriefing, piled into our armored vehicles, and headed off base to meet Thamer's driver, his brother-in-law, at a different location from where we'd met them in the morning.

We scouted the area, and when we thought it was safe, we rendezvoused with his brother-in-law. I looked around to make sure nobody appeared to be lying in wait to follow them, then we hustled Thamer to the white car, shook his hand, and told him we would come back for him soon. In that brief moment, as I gripped Thamer's hand in mine, my gut told me he was everything he seemed, an honest man who had somehow managed to hold onto his self-respect and dignity against all odds.

I watched the white car fade into its own dust cloud as it drove off into an actual sunset. Dustin had already hinted that

Thamer's proffer was valuable, which was excellent news for our mission. But my focus now went beyond that fact. After what he'd been through in the past few years, the least America could do was to keep its promise to him. I would try to make good on America's promise, and I expected things to go quickly now that we had the proffer. I didn't know at the time, but it would be many months before I saw Thamer again.

"IT'S ALL RIGHT," THAMER SAID AS his wife threw her arms around him, rejoicing at having him back alive and unharmed. "It was the Americans, just as they said they were. Very nice Americans."

She laughed as she pointed to the package in his hands. "What's this? Did they did give you a gift?"

Thamer looked down to the carton of cigarettes he was holding. "Yes. Mr. Steve, the one in charge, gave me a box of Marlboro cigarettes. He said it was from the American government." He took Eman's hands, led her to the couch, and sat down next to her. "And a better gift—this Mr. Steve told me he would come back for me very soon. I asked him if it was possible to meet in another place instead of Baghdad because it is so dangerous for me to be seen here talking to any American, and he agreed. Next time, he said, we'll meet in Erbil province in the north."

Eman smiled. "You see? I was right to hope."

Thamer nodded. "You were right to hope. I should know by now that you are always right."

He kept one thought to himself: he was certain Mr. Steve represented his last chance to get out of this war alive. He hoped Mr. Steve was all he seemed to be because he didn't think he could run anymore.

Chapter 19

KUWAIT CITY, KUWAIT—MAY 2008

"THIRTY DAYS. THAT'S IT. THAT'S ALL you have. You go to Iraq, get him, bring him to DC to debrief him, and get him back to Iraq." Before deciding on the plan to bring Thamer to the US we discussed the possibility of conducting the in-depth debriefing of Thamer in the northern province of Erbil. Northern Iraq was under the control of the Kurds and was a safer environment than the rest of Iraq, and the Kurds were still our friends. In the end it was decided it was much safer to bring one man out than a whole bunch in. Erbil was nixed.

Thirty days was the final word from the Homeland Security Council after Dustin briefed them on our mission in Baghdad and explained the value of Thamer Imran's proffer. Dustin had convinced them that Thamer possessed scientific intelligence about low level production techniques and he had learned enough to determine that it was worth talking to Thamer at greater length to learn those details.

Seven months passed. I had called Thamer periodically since then, sweating bullets when he failed to pick up the phone fast enough. Every time one of my calls went unanswered, I wondered, is he still alive? Is he still going to cooperate? When he did pick up, the sighs he uttered when I told him I had no new news made it clear to me that his own doubts about me, about all of us Americans, were on the rise again.

I knew I should be excited that we'd gotten the okay from the HSC to bring Thamer over for a debriefing, but instead I returned to my cubicle at DHS headquarters and slumped in my seat. It nagged at me why those in charge were so adamant about having us stick to narrow parameters: get in, get him out, then in thirty days, take him back! Thirty days wasn't nearly enough time, and they knew it. They wanted to limit our time with Thamer. More important, I wondered what would happen to Thamer after we finished with him and sent him back to Iraq. But I didn't dare voice my uneasiness out loud, fearing if I pushed too hard the HSC might reverse their approval. If the other team members had similar concerns, they kept quiet too. Instead, we all focused on developing our plan to extract Thamer from Baghdad.

"Steve," Dr. McCarthy was standing in my doorway.

I jumped out of my slump, and answered with military briskness, "Yes?"

"You guys are all set! Let me know when the logistics are worked out." An ear-to-ear smile lit up her face.

I forced myself to smile back. "Absolutely. I'll let you know."

I watched my gutsy boss walk away, head held high as if she'd won a marathon. I admired her perseverance. That same see-it-through-to-the-end quality lived within me too, but now after months of beating my head against walls for this mission, I could hardly remember where that quality was hiding.

Although we had permission to get Thamer out of the country, that didn't mean we knew how to do it. The fact that the Iraqi government had a warrant out for his arrest added to the long list of problems we faced. The warrant made it too risky to fly him out via Baghdad International Airport because the Iraqis controlled the airport, so there would be passport checks. If we put his name in the system, it was liable to set off a red flag to security who might call police to arrest him right then. Even if his name wasn't flagged or if we used a fake name and passport, there still might be trouble. If any Iraqis picked him up it was all over.

In general, Iraqis were suspicious of other Iraqis leaving the country. What's more, not everyone who might swoop in to grab Thamer would necessarily be a legitimate cop doing their job; at the airport, there were bad guys posing as good guys. Although the US government was working with the Iraqis to establish rule of law, up until then such a thing hadn't existed—at least not under Saddam Hussein—and the Iraqi form of justice was still big on brutality, small on fairness. I didn't know what would happen to Thamer if he were taken into custody, but I was sure it would be very, very bad. Using the civilian side of the airport posed too many risks.

Flying Thamer out on a military plane was an option, but the US has strict regulations governing the transport of foreign nationals on military aircraft. Thamer would need official military orders to board, so I contacted an Army liaison who took my appeal up the chain of command to General George W. Casey, who was the senior coalition commander in Iraq. They agreed to facilitate transport. But I soon received a second call from the liaison to say the Army was rescinding their support. The liaison explained that the General was involved in delicate negotiations with the Iraqis and that putting an Iraqi national wanted by the Iraqis on an American military plane could present an obstacle. The liaison said that the US had a team of DOJ lawyers in-country trying to establish rule of law, so it was the worst possible time to circumvent their laws. I told him I understood their concern. Plan B.

My only other option was to get help from friends in the CIA. The CIA "owned" part of the airport, and they had the aircraft. Dustin took the lead in trying to convince them this was a critical intelligence matter and that they therefore had a stake in helping us. This sort of black ops stuff is what they do, so I felt sure this would be our answer. But despite our assurances that the Homeland Security Council itself had approved our mission, in the end the CIA went the way of everyone else: "Sorry, our hands are full fighting an insurgency."

This went on for months, and I could still find no reasonable explanation for why everyone wanted to put up roadblocks to something so obviously in the best interests of our country. I really wanted to quit, and at that point quitting would have been relatively simple. Time has a way of wearing people down, and if enough time passes, even the most dedicated will eventually move on, including me. But I couldn't quit on Thamer.

Despite my deep, burning desire to honor my promise to Thamer, a giant shadow of doom hung over the entire operation. I was out of solutions. Then one day, Jim called me with an idea. While taking another stab at our travel logistics, he learned that a British company called Gryphon Airlines had started offering flights from Iraq to Kuwait. Their target was the contractor's market. Contractors were finding it difficult to get in and out of Iraq on military planes, what with all the restrictions about when people could fly and why, and the "space available" bullshit, which led to the endless waiting that cost everyone time and money. Gryphon saw this as a niche that needed filling, and Jim was excited about the possibility of using them.

Still feeling hopeless, I asked, "What good will that do? We'd still need to deal with the Iraqis at the airport."

"No, no, that's what I'm trying to tell you! They operate from the military side of the airport. No Iraqis to deal with!" Jim hadn't sounded this excited in months.

"Christ, is something finally going our way?" I said, only mildly excited given our record of success.

This new plan would still require finagling. We still had to find a way to get Thamer onto the base. We also had to operate out of Kuwait as our new staging area for getting our team into Iraq, getting Thamer out of Iraq, and then getting all of us to the US.

Still, with this new flight option, we had renewed hope. Jim, Kevin, and I met to throw around ideas and then made calls to Iraq to line up whatever help we could muster in the way of personnel and equipment for a Kuwait-based operation. Kuwait was a large staging area for the US military with many military flights coming and going, it looked like a better option than returning to Qatar.

To our amazement, all the approvals for traveling to Kuwait fell into place quickly. We didn't know how long this window would remain open, so we dove through it. Before we knew it, the three of us were on a flight bound for Kuwait International Airport, fifteen miles outside Kuwait City and about one hour from Baghdad by air.

The plan to get Thamer out of Baghdad, however, was still a work in progress.

Jim, Kevin, and I arrived in Kuwait at the Ali Al Salem Air Base and quickly set up our operation's staging area in a small, hot, windowless room piled with gear and lined with cots. We didn't stop to rest or eat, just grabbed a few bottles of water to stave off thirst in yet another hot, dry desert, and immediately made our plans to extract Thamer.

I called the DHS attaché in Baghdad and told him that what we needed first and foremost was a US visa for Thamer. Everyone entering the country regardless of the means of entry needs legal documentation to do so. Thamer was no exception. While I worked on the visa, Kevin contacted his ICE counterparts in Iraq to line up assistance on the ground. We had already signed up for the first available military flight out of Kuwait.

Kevin sent an unclassified update to Dr. McCarthy in DC using his Blackberry. Then we sat down and looked at each other, all of us worn out but still to wound up to sleep. We'd gone through so much to get to this point, I wanted to stay focused. We couldn't afford to let anything go wrong. On the other hand, I knew some stress relief was in order. So we headed into Kuwait City to unwind.

Flush with oil profits, Kuwait seemed to be doing very well. Kuwait City was modern and brimming with places to blow money. In my travels with the Secret Service, I tried to bring back a souvenir for my wife from every place I visited, and the guys were happy to head out with me to accomplish that side mission.

My favorite spot in Kuwait City was the Souq, or street market—a lovely, colorful place where I bought Carmela a hand-embroidered tote bag and where the guys found a couple of souvenirs of their own. That done, we still had hours of down-time on our hands.

We headed to a posh outdoor hookah bar with huge comfortable chairs, laid back music playing overhead, and a great view of Kuwait Bay. It was a perfect night, balmy with a little breeze, and the bar was a perfect place to relax. We settled into our seats and enjoyed people-watching. About a half hour after we sat down, a small group of attractive Japanese women sat nearby. They said they were in town on business, and I suppose, like us, wanted to chill out. They were friendly, and although there were language barriers, we had a good time talking. Afternoon burned into evening, and I sensed Jim and Kevin's muscles un-knotting thread by thread. But there was an edge to my relaxation, feeling the busy next day barreling toward me with all its demands. It was getting late, so I announced we should call it a night. My teammates had other ideas.

"Come on, man," Jim wheedled me. "Let's go to another place."

"What other place? No, I don't think so."

I looked over at Kevin and saw I'd be getting no help from him. He had a half-in-the- hookah bag grin on his face, and both guys were shifting their laughing eyes from me to the three pretty women. Shit, I thought, I think these guys want to take off with these women and then wind up God knows where.

Terrorist attacks have occurred in Kuwait including places visited by foreigners. Kuwait has also been accused of financing terrorist activity and Americans being targeted throughout the Middle East was not uncommon. I had a terrifying vision of worst-case scenarios: my comrades disappearing. They were both professionals, so it was probably my over active mind thinking crazy things, but nonetheless I was going to set this shit straight now.

I stood up too fast, sending hookah pipes flying, and shouted, "No fucking way are you guys going anywhere! There's too much riding on this, and I'm not getting up at four a.m. to go find your asses! This is bullshit! You're going to wind up rolled or in jail, and then what? I'll have to call DC and tell them the plan is off because you two went missing."

Everyone in our little party went silent. They all stared at me, and I knew I probably looked crazy to people in the bar and on the street, screaming at two huge, forty-something American guys at a hookah bar, while the three Japanese women gaped at me, but I didn't care. Jim and Kevin got the message that the party was over.

They rose to leave, Jim looking at the ground and Kevin chewing on words he wasn't saying. I knew they saw me as the bad guy right then, but I told myself they'd thank me later when they were clear headed enough to realize what they might have risked. They had poured so much of themselves into this mission, I knew they'd never forgive themselves if they did anything to botch it.

Still, I felt the sting when Kevin saluted me with a snap and said, "All right, General."

"Yeah, General Patton," Jim said.

The nickname stuck. The following morning, in the hotel lobby, Kevin said, "Jim wants to know how the General is feeling today."

"Tell Jim the General feels like shit, okay?" The hookah pipes gave me a raging headache.

"Yes, sir!" Kevin snapped back with a salute and his smart-ass grin.

"You know what? Both you guys can go fuck yourselves."

Jim tiptoed up to us, and he and Kevin snickered like kids. I shook my head and walked away. I loved those guys.

The next morning, we were back to work. After getting bumped only once, we caught a military flight from Kuwait to

Baghdad at 0930. But Kevin wasn't finished having fun at my expense. Soon enough, I'd find out that he'd arranged for a little surprise when we arrived.

We landed safely in Baghdad, debarked from the plane, and made the long walk across the Tarmac to the arrival area. As we approached the terminal, I noticed a man in military uniform moving in our direction, looking intently at us. As he drew closer, I could see an insignia on his collar that identified him as a major in the US Army, and then it became clear that he was actually looking intently at *me*.

He shook my hand, introduced himself, and very formally said, "Welcome to Baghdad, sir. We have your vehicle waiting."

What's this? I thought. This was supposed to be a small operation, sliding in and out under the radar. I glanced at Kevin. My vehicle? What vehicle?

"Just go with it man," he whispered.

"Go with what?"

"I'll tell you later."

The later came after the major, his driver, and an armed guard escorted our team via armored black sedans to the military's VIP guest quarters, a palatial guest home where they booked me into the ritzy Najaf suite. During Saddam's regime, the building served as a guest house reserved for high-level foreign dignitaries who visited Baghdad on official business. When our forces invaded Baghdad, the US military took control of the building for the same purpose, reserving it for VIPs visiting from the American government.

I waited for the major and our escort to leave, then went to Kevin's room to confront him. Kevin explained with pride that before we left the US, he sent a message ahead to his contacts that a high-level government official was on his way to Baghdad for a classified mission. He explained to them that we'd need their full cooperation. The army was up to the task. The "high-level government official" on this classified mission was me!

"Are you fucking *crazy*?" I hissed, trying to not be overheard. "We . . . I could get in serious trouble for this."

"No big deal, man." Kevin clapped my shoulder like he had it all taken care of.

"No big deal? It *is* a big fucking deal. Who am I supposed to be? I don't need this shit on my plate right now. The tents are fine."

"Well, we're here now, booked in. What do you want to do, tell them it's all bullshit? The military is in control of all this shit. Do you think we should piss them off now by telling them, 'Oh wait, I'm sorry we made a mistake, we don't have any high-level officials with us'?"

I shook my head "You're fucking unbelievable."

He had me. It would have been more trouble to fix it than play along, so I had little choice. Every time I walked into or out of the building, an enlisted soldier stood at attention. Soldiers held the door for me when I left my room in the morning to head down to breakfast. The soldier at the front desk snapped to attention as I passed, shouting, "Good morning, sir!"

Kevin had fun with it. When I approached him, he'd say, "Here comes General Patton."

"Fuck you, Kevin."

So for the next several days I played the part of an unknown, high-level official, from an unknown agency, on an unknown mission. I should have received a fucking Oscar!

It turned out that having a cushy room all to myself did make me feel more rested and able to focus on the demands of our mission. The morning after our arrival, my team members told me that they hadn't slept well having been woken by the sound and concussion of one of our 500 lb. bombs being dropped on some target, but I hadn't heard a thing. What's more, because of Kevin's little stunt, we had better support and assistance. Kevin had some first-rate qualities, and bullshitting was definitely one of them. But I wasn't about to admit that to him.

Chapter 20

BAGHDAD, IRAQ—MAY 2008

ONCE AGAIN, OBTAINING TRANSPORTATION and weapons was a priority. I had the others work on that. I needed to meet with the DHS attaché about Thamer's visa, which meant I had to get to the Green Zone where the US Embassy was located. The attaché hadn't called me back, and I was worried. This trip was complicated. We didn't come here just to talk with Thamer; Thamer was about to be exfiltrated out of his country, and I needed that damn visa!

The Green Zone was four square miles of Baghdad. It was the location of our embassy and of the new Iraq government, where only US military security and Iraqi government officials with security badges were allowed through the surrounding barricade of concrete walls. To get there, we'd hitch a ride with a military convoy that was making that day's trip up Route Irish. I had put in the request the day before but unfortunately, they'd already reached the allowed limit on personnel and vehicles, so it was a no go. But we weren't ready to give up. Next, we tried to hitch a ride on an army Blackhawk helicopter that was heading to the Green Zone, but that didn't pan out either. You don't just hop on a military aircraft; you needed to be manifested, and all the rides were full. We'd have to wait till next day.

I was frustrated at having to cool our heels. Then we heard it: the rumble and groan of a distant explosion. It wasn't close enough to put us in danger, but it signaled a bad day for somebody. There was a guard tower close by, and I ran to the top to see what had happened.

Looking out across from our base a few miles away, I saw a massive cloud of black smoke rising from the area of the main road to the Green Zone. Helicopters, always at the ready, sped overhead toward the site of the bombing. I had my camera-phone with me, and I lifted it and snapped a picture. I don't know why. Maybe I wanted to frame it, make it smaller— an image I could fit inside my brain. Something bad had happened, and there was no doubt in my mind that an IED or a car bomb had just been clicked off. I climbed down from the tower and told my guys what just happened. We exchanged looks that said we were glad we didn't make the convoy that day.

The Green Zone was a frequent target of the terrorists. In October of 2004, bombs exploded within moments of each other at a handicraft market and a popular café inside the supposed fortified zone. In December of that same year, two car bombs killed sixteen people and wounded thirty-eight when they exploded at an entrance to the Green Zone. It wasn't our time, but the attack was a sobering reminder of how quickly things can change. Due to increased security following the bombing, we wouldn't be going anywhere for a couple more days.

By and large, the base was safe, but "insider" attacks were always a concern. So many Iraqis worked on base that there was no way to tell the good from the bad. In December of 2004, a suicide bomber infiltrated a large military base in northern Iraq, walked into a very busy mess tent during their busiest time, and detonated explosives. The blast killed twenty-three people, fourteen of them US soldiers. So, security was always tight when we went to eat.

Sometimes explosions echoed from the edges of the base, where bad guys drove by in pickups mounted with mortars, lobbed small mortar rounds over the wall, and then hauled ass. Although the bases were big and our attackers didn't bother aiming, an occasional bomb landed on some unfortunate soul. I heard that a fellow from the Department of Homeland Security had been killed in one such attack. Alarms would go off when these attacks happened, and we'd all run for any of several sandbag blast shelters scattered around base. For the most part, though, as long as we stayed on base, we weren't concerned about coming under direct attack from outside. But inside attacks were always a possibility that kept us on edge. Leaving the base though, that was a much more dangerous story.

We finally finagled our way into a convoy, and despite the fact that convoys were often targets, I was glad to have those Bradleys and Humvees around. It felt a lot safer than going it alone in our so-called armored SUVs. We got to the Green Zone in one piece, and I told the team I needed to speak to the DHS attaché alone. The team headed for the chow hall while I headed for the attaché's office.

"It's finally nice to meet you in person," I said when he reached out to shake my hand.

But his unenthusiastic, "Yeah, nice to meet you as well" response told me I was in for bad news.

"What's going on with the visa for Thamer Imran?" I asked.

"I'm sorry, sir, but the consular officer screwed us and won't grant him a visa."

"How can that be? He's coming to the US at the specific request of the US Department of Homeland Security."

He said he didn't know and that there was nothing he could do about it even if he did. He seemed like a nice guy, but he came off like the unmotivated sort who gave up at the first sign of a challenge. He wasn't going to be much help, even though handling visas for assets like Thamer was one of his duties. According to State Department protocol, the consular officer on the ground has the final say on all visas and can't be overruled, not even by the Secretary of State.

The attaché politely agreed that the decision seemed crazy but said there was no option to appeal. I never learned the reason Thamer's visit was denied, but what I did know was that I now had a monumental problem on my hands. At that point, I'd lost count of all the meetings that turned out to be busts.

I caught up with the team and filled them in on my meeting with the attaché. Their faces dropped along with their appetites as they took in the news. My meeting with the DHS attaché made us miss the convoy so we had to drive our vehicles back to Camp Liberty without support. No visa meant more problems, which meant higher stakes. However, we weren't completely dead in the water. The possibility of Thamer not getting a visa was discussed and we had another avenue to pursue. It wasn't a sure thing but it was our last hope. But first, we had to get back to Liberty and we lost the daylight. It meant driving Route Irish at night.

We quickly moved out. In route we encountered a checkpoint manned by Americans. We stopped and showed our id's. I was riding with Jim. While they were verifying our id's, I noticed a red dot on my chest. I thought maybe it was a reflection from an interior light. Then it moved. It hit Jim and bounced over the dashboard and then back to me. Nope that's not an interior light, I thought. The red dot continued to bounce back and forth between us.

What the hell is this?

"Fuck, we're being lasered," I said. Someone in the guard tower had a rifle with a laser and was targeting us. Jim went ballistic as it moved across his chest and face area.

"Hey, tell that asshole to knock it off," he told the guard that had our id's. Better, Jim would do it himself. He stormed out of the vehicle, past the guard and right into the tower. Someone was about to get a serious beat down from a very pissed off Marine Lt. Colonel. I felt bad for the soldier who just might have been nervous about our two ramshackle SUVs that pulled up to his checkpoint on a dark night in dangerous Baghdad.

Jim came back to the vehicle got in and slammed the door with a "he won't be doing that shit again" look on his face. I can tell you it was not a good feeling to be targeted, knowing that a high-powered rifle is being pointed at you by a nervous, nineteen-year-old soldier. But hey, I'd be nervous too. The rest of the drive on the "highway of death" thank God was uneventful, but what to do about the visa situation was on my mind as we drove back to Liberty. We needed to find another way.

WE CAME UP WITH A PLAN B. It involved using a method of entry called Significant Public Benefit Parole (SPBP), used by the government to bring people into the US who would normally not qualify for a visa. An SPBP was usually reserved for criminal cases in which the prosecutor needed the testimony of a convicted drug dealer or terrorist, for example, who otherwise wasn't allowed to enter the US.

Kevin being an ICE agent would take the lead on plan B, but even if we made this happen quickly, we still had a problem. Although the SPBP would take the place of a visa once Thamer arrived in the US, it wouldn't help us get him out of Baghdad. We learned that Gryphon Airlines had a strict policy of checking the paperwork of all outgoing travelers leaving on flights from Camp Victory, and they wouldn't let anyone through security without official military orders or a visa. Thamer had neither.

Frustrated as I was, giving in to despair would only make things worse. I took a steadying breath and said to my team, "One problem at a time. That's how we've dealt with this for the last two years, and that's how we'll deal with it now. Right now, we need to contact Thamer, arrange to meet him, and get him back here."

Kevin and Jim worked on getting assistance to help us leave the base, head into the city and retrieve Thamer. We needed more people so Kevin once again enlisted a support team of two other federal agents.

I still hadn't figured out how to get Thamer on board without the right documentation, but our two-SUV convoy was ready to go grab him, daylight was limited, and our seats on Gryphon Airlines were booked. So, ready or not, we had to go. The plan to extract Thamer from the city went much as it had the year before, except this time we had a much better description on the car and we used a different pickup point in case Thamer was being watched. We made a worried but otherwise smooth cruise into the city, grabbed him, and headed back to the Victory Base Complex.

While in route to and from the base, I thought, Steve don't screw this up, get everyone back safely. With that, everything sped up like an old silent caper film, minus the comedy. First, we had to hide Thamer. It was important we keep it quiet that Thamer was on base at all because we'd never sought permission from the base commander to have him there. This was against regulations, and considering how hard it was to maintain security, if anyone caught us with Thamer there'd be hell to pay. But we did it this way because following the rules would have alerted a whole chain of people to his presence, and we just didn't need any more bureaucracy in this mission.

We decided to stash Thamer in the coffin. I hurried him inside the windowless room and told him to stand away from the door. With my M-4 rifle slung over my shoulder, I followed him as he moved to the back of the coffin. There was one way in and one way out, and I was standing in front of it. Thamer looked acutely aware of this fact as he turned toward me, his face a colorless mask of fear as his eyes locked with mine. Sweat dripped down his face and pasted his button-down shirt to his chest. He rocked in a rhythmic fashion, back and forth like a man regressing to his most primal instincts.

I became concerned about this sudden change in behavior. We had survived the most dangerous part of the day; we'd gotten him out of the city where he lived with a target on his back and into a protected zone surrounded by security. Yet the look in his eyes was worse than terror. It was resignation, as if he expected to die.

Our eyes locked until the door opened, Jim crashed inside, took one look at Thamer, and said softly, "Hey Steve, want me to take your weapon while you talk to Thamer?"

I looked from him to Thamer, whose expression changed as if he'd just received a reprieve. Thamer's reaction only puzzled me more. He was used to guns. He was living in a war zone and on a base with soldiers carrying guns. They were everywhere. When we picked him up both times, we were armed and none of that bothered him, so I was curious as to his change in demeanor.

"Sure, Jim," I said. "Here, take it." I lifted the sling over my head and held my M-4 out to Jim, still eyeing Thamer with concern.

"Please, Mr. Jim, take it!" Thamer yelled, more a plea than a request.

What was going on? I grew suspicious, worried that after all we'd gone through to get this far, Thamer had decided not to trust us after all. Was he going to back out?

Jim took my rifle and left. Then it was just Thamer and me, alone in that hooch, staring at each other. He stopped moving back and forth, the color returned to his face, and he appeared calmer. Then it hit me like a punch to the gut. He thought I'd brought him into this windowless space to kill him. I gaped at him in dismay, as I tried to grasp the stunning revelation that he'd seen a cold-blooded killer in me.

My mind raced for something to say to allay his fear, but instead I thought about something Kevin had told me when he attended an earlier HSC meeting. When discussing what to do about Thamer, an unnamed HSC member barked out, "Why don't we just take him out?" The room immediately fell silent as all eyes turned to face the person who just suggested that the HSC should sanction Thamer's death. The unnamed member immediately regretted his words as the entire room stared at him with incredulity. This was not the place, and these were not the people who would ever discuss such actions. The HSC member remained silent for the rest of the meeting. The fact that such an utterance was blurted out was shocking to me.

Thamer had good reason to be scared. In war, sometimes the innocent go down with the guilty. In his country under Saddam, a twenty-seven cent bullet is an efficient and cheap way to get rid of a problem. Thamer was a proliferation risk to us, so you pull the trigger and the risk disappears. Also, I realized that Thamer didn't know me as I felt I knew him. I'd spent more than two years getting to know Thamer through research and documents, but he didn't know me at all. We hadn't had the chance to build trust between us, although I often tried in our phone conversations to let him know that we were sympathetic to his situation and that it wasn't all business. But given all that had happened to him, I understood his fear. Perhaps to him, I was just another American with a gun.

I did my best to reassure Thamer we were armed to protect him, not to harm him.

"You're safe here with us," I said. "We won't let anyone hurt you."

He nervously chuckled.

It was difficult not to take his reaction personally. But I did get it. His decision to trust us this far took an enormous leap of faith. He knew that the American government was working with Iraq's new government, so it was only logical for him to wonder whether our government might make a deal with his government to turn him over.

For the rest of the afternoon, he remained jumpy and kept digging into the carton of cigarettes we bought him. Each of us took turns sitting with him, but the conversation was limited, both by the language barrier and by Thamer's obvious case of nerves.

Later that night our team got together and shared a laugh over Thamer's thinking I might shoot him.

"Hi, Dr. McCarthy this is Steve, uh, we won't be bringing Thamer back today or any other day. I had to shoot him." We laughed at the message we'd leave on Dr. McCarthy's phone. A jumpy, gray-haired scientist mistaking us for villains. Then I went to bed and guilt crept in. I regretted being so flippant about what had happened, about disregarding his feelings. That night I didn't get much sleep. I was not pleased with myself.

The next day we did our best to finalize our plans, which included giving Thamer cash for personal things he'd need once we got him out of the country. Giving him his own money prevented him from having to ask us to buy whatever he needed, including food. There were some stipulations on what he was to use the money for, and he'd have to keep receipts for items over a certain price. Although Thamer spoke some English, it was critical to make certain he understood the rules: no drinking, no drugs, no women, no sending money back home, etc. Being a Muslim and the kind of person he was, I wasn't concerned that Thamer would do any of those things, but we still had to explain the rules, and we needed a translator to help explain the details.

As the sun was setting, we jumped into our armored SUV and made a large dust trail as we hurried up the road to find a translator before the Iraqi liaison office closed for the evening. We got lucky and quickly found a young Arabic translator from Chicago who was assisting the coalition forces. She was a stunning young woman, and Kevin and Jim took immediate notice. They practically tripped over each other leading her to the SUV, opening her door, and introducing her to Thamer back at the hooch.

Kevin switched to all business, though, as we sat down with Thamer and the translator in the crowded coffin and got to work. We explained in detail the bureaucratic language regarding the use of the cash we were giving him, and the meaning of all of the forms he had to execute to account for it.

Thamer's eyes grew wide as we counted out the cash. The bills were all in one hundred-dollar denominations. It was a crazy scene, several of us crowded into one small trailer surrounding Thamer as we counted the money onto the bed, of all places. It was the only place in the room with sufficient space. I don't think Thamer had ever seen that many American dollars all at once. His hands shook as he gathered up the hundreds and signed all the forms.

"Make sure you don't lose it or get robbed," I joked. "I don't want to have to explain how you lost three thousand dollars."

The translator repeated my admonition in Arabic.

"You have my word, Mr. Steve," Thamer said directly to me in slow, deliberate English.

"This is just like the Sopranos!" the translator blurted as Thamer recounted the money and struggled to stuff the wad into his wallet, which clearly had been empty of cash until that moment. We all laughed. And so did Thamer as he always did, but I wasn't sure if he had any idea who Tony Soprano was. Thamer thanked Kevin and me repeatedly, saying it had been a long time since he had carried money of any kind.

We spent the next hour completing paperwork from the US Embassy to authorize the SPBP. With that, we had done all we could. It was now the day of reckoning. Time to see if we had wallpapered him with enough documentation to convince Gryphon Airlines to let him out of the country.

Chapter 21

MILITARY AIRPORT, IRAQ—MAY 2008

THE GRYPHON FLIGHT LEFT AT NIGHT. It was safer to fly in
the darkness that made planes less of a target for potential attack.
The enemy also used the cover of darkness to move about, so to
create fewer targets to shoot at by night, Camp Victory, Camp
Slayer, and all military installations in Iraq operated under virtual
black-out. Camp Victory was so dark, I couldn't see my hand in
front of my face as we walked Thamer from the coffin to the airport on the other side of camp. As a further precaution, we skirted
the base perimeter, and several times in the dark we narrowly
avoided tumbling into one of the ditches or canals surrounding
the base.

It wasn't just the darkness that tripped me up, but also my
distracted mind. We still had no idea whether Gryphon Airlines
would let Thamer board, a wanted man who had no visa but
instead a piece of paper that said SPBP. Even if military security
let him through and Gryphon let him board here, would Kuwait
allow him in when we arrived there? So much could still go wrong.

We walked to the small corner of the airport where Gryphon
Airlines operated and found ourselves at the end of a long line in
the midst of chaos—what seemed like hundreds of people were

crammed into one tiny room. Most were government contractors, many had clearly taken this flight before, and from listening to their conversations, we learned this was still a crapshoot. The line advanced at a painstaking pace, but although there was plenty of grumbling, everyone remained civilized. Clearly nobody wanted to irritate those with the power to decide who got out that night.

I stepped out of line to see what the holdup was. Nothing unusual, just a lone Gryphon representative at a small desk exercising utmost caution as he examined every travel order and passport. My palms began to sweat as we drew closer to the front. I felt like a smuggler. I was a master lie detector, trained to spot the slightest abnormal behavior, but that didn't make me an expert liar. I prayed the long wait would explain my jumpiness. Meanwhile, the Gryphon rep continued to move at a snail's pace and seemed eager to find any typo that would give him an excuse to turn someone away.

I leaned toward Jim. "Shit, look at this guy. He's taking this seriously."

"Yeah," Jim spoke in a monotone, as if he, too, feared attracting negative attention.

We were closing in when the Gryphon rep stepped away for a break. It sounded as if everyone in line sighed. I cursed to myself, son of a bitch!

Leave it to Kevin to recognize this not as a delay but an opportunity. Kevin beckoned me to follow him and hustled to intercept the Gryphon rep. They stepped out of the tiny room into the darkness of the tarmac outside. The rep wanted to take a smoke break, but Kevin was right on top of him. The rep gave Kevin a "what the fuck" look but Kevin was undeterred. I followed and saw Kevin display what looked like his wallet to the rep. They spoke in hushed tones as I approached, and I hung back to listen.

"We're on a highly sensitive mission," Kevin was saying, "and we have someone in our custody that absolutely needs to get on the plane."

The rep said something I couldn't hear.

"Listen, we have a ticket for him, and that's all you really need to worry about."

"As long as he has his proper orders and paperwork," the rep said.

"You don't understand. This is coming out of DC."

The rep said something about his supervisor.

"I don't think we need to go any higher with this."

Then, as if on cue, someone walked over to ask the rep a question.

Kevin grabbed my arm and pulled me aside. "Steve, do you have a badge?"

I knew he meant my Secret Service badge. "Yes, but it's no good. I'm retired."

"Take it out."

Kevin wanted me to play the role of "government official" again, but this time it wasn't to get me a better room. I refused to say anything to make the Gryphon rep believe I was a federal agent, but we were in a tight spot, and this was my shot to do something about it. I cast a glance at the rep and his supervisor, who were studying us and whispering. Their consultation ended, the supervisor left, and the rep walked back to where Kevin and I stood. It was decision time.

Kevin introduced me to the rep and told him I was part of the team. I took out my gold badge. With my finger over the lettering that read, "retired," I flashed the badge without a word. He looked at it. The words "Secret Service" always carried weight. His expression changed from irritable to dumbfounded. He straightened as if coming to attention. This could work. I began to believe I could get him to back off from examining Thamer's paperwork too closely but only if I was so convincing that he didn't call for military police or base officials to back my story.

I reminded myself that Thamer's life hung in the balance. With that, I conjured a mask of calm authority the kind that I was used to expressing.

"Okay," I said, "what are we going to do?" It was as direct a question as I could bring myself to make to the rep. So far, I hadn't told an outright lie, and I'd try to stay clean as long as I could.

The rep was still holding out when Jim joined us.

"Are we all set?" he asked in the most casual tone, as if the answer were a foregone conclusion. "What's the holdup?"

The rep looked up at Jim and took an involuntary step back. Jim was wearing his Marine fatigues. I could see on the rep's face that Jim's six-foot-three presence had sealed the deal.

"Okay," the rep relented, "you guys are on."

"Listen, dude," Kevin said, "this is a sensitive issue, so any chance we could board first?"

I clenched my jaw to keep it from falling open, willing Kevin to read my mind: don't push it!

But the rep shrugged, almost smiling. "Sure, no problem."

He led the way back inside as I said to Jim under my breath, "Okay, Jim, grab Thamer. Let's go now before this guy changes his mind."

But the Gryphon rep looked proud to lead us at this point, chest out, legs in full stride. We had him now, hook, line, and sinker. We grabbed Thamer and all our gear at top speed, then ran, I mean ran, to follow the rep as he escorted our entourage to the plane first, leaving behind the moans and groans of those who had waited in line ahead of us.

He left us at the door with an attendant who pointed us down the aisle. We took our seats, still panting for breath. My hands shook as I buckled in, impatient for takeoff. Kevin sat next to me, and gave me a nod, eyes wide.

"I can't believe that worked," I whispered. I began to relax.

After everyone else boarded, I saw the Gryphon rep at the front of the plane. He started down the aisle.

I turned to Jim, seated across the aisle with Thamer. "Shit, Jim, he's coming."

"Who?"

"The Gryphon guy."

Jim's head popped up. "Oh man, that's not good."

I looked past Jim at Thamer, but there was no way to read his expression as his eyes were closed tight. Probably praying. Nobody had to tell him we weren't out of danger yet.

My team and I followed the rep with our eyes as he closed in, his head pivoting back and forth, looking for someone as he slowly made his way down the aisle. I was sure the ruse was up, and I wracked my brain for how to talk my way out of this. He got to our row, and I craned my neck to look up at him, a casual question mark in my eyes. He gave me a nod of acknowledgment. He must have felt he was helping with an important case. I nodded back with a smile that I hoped conveyed, "You're part of the team!" To my relief, he continued past me down the aisle.

I sat there pondering what a poor representative of the Secret Service I made at that moment—retired or not: several days' growth of beard, sweat pouring down my face, tired, aching back and circles under my eyes. I didn't have a mirror but I'm sure I looked like hell. And the night wasn't over.

I'm no fan of flying, but right then I could barely wait for the pilot to get that damned thing off the ground. We taxied and taxied and taxied until, to my relief, the engines roared to life.

The cabin was in total darkness as the plane took off and climbed steeply, doing the Khe-Sanh maneuver in reverse. Although I traveled millions of miles as a Secret Service agent, I am not exactly a "happy flier" so I really, really, hated that fucking Khe-Sanh shit. All we could do was hang on and pray we didn't get hit.

The cabin lights finally came back on, signaling we were out of range of attack. My stomach churned, and I grabbed a barf-bag from the seat pocket in front of me just in case, but nothing came up. Maybe because I hadn't eaten since the night before. I looked over at Thamer, whose eyes were still closed, though his face no longer looked as tense as it had all day. No doubt he was more relieved than I to leave Iraq behind. I still hadn't had the heart, or the chance, to tell him that my country's leaders expected him to return to Baghdad when we were done with him. But I knew that moment was coming.

We landed safely in Kuwait, but we weren't out of the woods. The Kuwaitis welcomed us with all-but-open arms as we passed easily through every security apparatus between our arrival gate and the terminal, where we had to check in for our outgoing flight. But getting Thamer on a flight bound for DC still posed a challenge because although he had a reservation, he still lacked a visa. We moved as fast as we could, hoping the faster we moved, the less likely someone would figure out that we had just smuggled a bioweapons scientist out of Iraq.

We handed Thamer's passport to the United Airlines ticket agent. The agent checked it against the manifest in his computer, and his face grew puzzled as he continued to punch computer keys. He took the passport into a backroom and was gone a long time. Something was wrong. We all checked our phones for the time. Our flight would be boarding shortly.

The agent returned, shaking his head. "I'm sorry, gentlemen. He has no reservation."

I turned to Jim, who had been in charge of booking our flights. "Jim, what the hell is he talking about?"

"I made his reservation and doubled-checked it, Steve. This can't be right."

While Kevin, our master of charm, worked his way up the chain of command, begging United's Kuwaiti reps to keep checking their system, Jim and I tried to come up with a Plan B. The flight was full, so buying a new ticket wasn't an option. If only we could leave the airport, find a hotel for the night, and try again the next day. But that was out of the question because Thamer had no visa. If he left the secure area of the airport, they'd never let him back in.

"Listen, I'm telling you, we made the reservation!" Jim shouted.

"Again, if you had a confirmation number, or a copy of the reservation, I might be able to help you."

There was no point berating Jim about failing to bring those things. He felt bad enough, and it wouldn't change anything. The supervisor urged us to give up and let them help the passengers still waiting in line. We refused to budge.

Kevin shook his head. "You don't understand," he said to the airline rep. "If Jim says he made this reservation, he made this reservation. You have no idea what we've been through to make this flight happen, and we're not giving up. So please, you've gotta check one more time!"

This time two agents walked into the backroom together and were gone some twenty minutes. The flight was surely boarding by now.

One of them reappeared with a smile on his face. They had found the reservation. They finally realized they had an incorrect spelling of Thamer's name in their system. It's not uncommon for Arabic names to be misspelled. The intelligence-gathering world often receives reports on bad actors who have names much like those of other bad actors and much like those of innocent people. It's difficult to keep track of who's who.

One such incident had happened during my fight to get permission to bring Thamer to the United States. At one point, an intelligence scrub of Thamer's record had revealed he was supposedly involved in criminal financial activity because of his association with a Hawala, an underground banking network based on ancient methods of long-distance trade involving paperless financial transactions. Many Hawala transactions are legitimate, used by migrants to send money home to their families who live in countries where banking systems are unsophisticated and unreliable. But terrorists often use Hawalas to fund their illegal, violent activities without leaving a paper trail.

Thamer's involvement with an illegal Hawala system almost scrubbed the entire operation. Initially, I was angry at myself for missing this bit of intelligence. I later became convinced it was a mistake. As it turned out, another Iraqi with a name similar to Thamer's had been involved in illegal Hawala transactions, and during our background search, his name got mixed up with Thamer's. From that point on, our team used extreme care in identifying anyone.

To add to the problem, older Iraqis often have no complete date of birth. Many were born before their government created a database of birth records. Many were born at home. To allow for some sort of age identification, many births were associated with major events.

"How old is Ameer?" an Iraqi might ask.

"He was born in the year of the big snow."

"Ah yes, of course."

That might be fine for their purposes, but it's difficult to put that in a computer database.

At least on this flight we didn't have *that* particular problem. Once the United supervisor was satisfied that their Thamer *Imhran*, with an h, was our Thamer *Imran*, without an h, they gave us our tickets. We were all poised to make a run for the gate before they closed the door to our plane. Then the agent threw another obstacle at us.

It seemed the Federal Aviation Administration (FAA) had instituted a new policy in response to a major security issue involving luggage not being thoroughly screened. Before this new initiative, Gryphon Airlines had no program for screening bags before they left Iraq. Those unscreened bags would arrive in Kuwait or other way stations, then get transferred to US carriers without ever being examined. I guess Gryphon Airlines assumed no security checks were necessary for flights leaving Camp Victory because everyone had to pass through security checkpoints to enter that base in the first place. Meanwhile, the US carriers probably passed the bags on assuming they'd already been checked. I could only imagine what may have been smuggled out under that setup.

The FAA finally caught on, and it so happened the new rule change coincided with our arrival that night at Kuwait International Airport. I'm all for security checks, but this posed a problem for Thamer. If Thamer wanted to take his bag with him, it would have to be screened. That would require that he go outside the secure section of the airport and re-enter as a regular passenger. We pulled Thamer aside and explained the problem. He understood there was only one solution. He wasn't concerned about the clothes; we could always get him new things, but the personal things bothered him, the family photos, the mementos. But we had no choice. With that, the man without a country also became a man without luggage.

We left his carry-on suitcase behind with the airport officials. That left him with nothing but the clothes on his back and his wallet, albeit a wallet full of US cash. I mentally added a shopping trip to the agenda when we arrived in DC.

It would take me weeks of calls and threats to convince Kuwait International Airport's security to send us Thamer's luggage, but eventually we got it.

We arrived at Dulles International Airport after a long but blessedly uneventful flight. Thamer was now safe in the US and, at least for the time being, that meant one more asset for our side and one less asset for the insurgents and the terrorists.

Kevin had greased the wheels prior to landing at Dulles, so we were met by competent and efficient personnel from ICE and Customs and Border Protections, who led us to a private lounge for an easier entry process than I ever thought possible. I stood by the desk, barely listening to the multitude of questions CPB officials asked our guest—the who, what, where, how, and why type questions. They were mandatory and not really concerning to me, so I stood nearby, practically nodding off while standing up.

A new day was dawning, and I was thinking about all we had gone through to arrive at this sunrise—all the hurdles, setbacks, false starts, and frustrations. I thought about all the plan A's that turned into plan B's and then C's and then turned into "fuck it," we have no plan. Most of all, I marveled at Thamer, the man we had often referred to in covert conversations as "the package." What he had endured was astonishing, yet now he softly murmured answers to yet more questions with the calm demeanor of an ordinary tourist, not a man who had been interrogated under grim and terrifying duress.

While we waited, I asked Kevin to send an email to Dr. McCarthy, who was anxiously awaiting word of our safe return with "the package."

"Steve, look at this." Kevin handed me his phone to show me Dr. McCarthy' response.

It read, "You are great Americans."

Dr. McCarthy wasn't the type to offer such accolades, so it was very strange to read it. Great Americans, really? I appreciated her gratitude, and I knew she meant it, but even at that proud moment it just didn't sound right to me. Here we were bringing back a scared Iraqi that we ourselves had imprisoned and tortured. We invaded his country, killing thousands of people, as well as losing our own heroic American soldiers for a war that didn't need to happen. I hold the men and women that served in Iraq in high esteem. They served with honor. They did what they were ordered to do to protect America. They gave their hearts and souls and their lives. They are my heroes. As for the politicians that sent them there, well that's another story. I will gladly give my life for my country in return for all that it has given me but at that moment I didn't feel like a great anything.

For a moment though, I set aside thoughts of the terrible costs of war so I could let in this one shining ray of accomplishment. I smiled at Kevin. Despite the odds and all the forces against us, we had prevailed. We helped one decent man, and in so doing also served our country. After our long ordeal this was a crowning moment, but beyond that one smile, I was too tired to celebrate.

A lot more work still lay ahead.

Thamer passed the test of the border agents and rose to unsteady feet. His face had a bewildered look that told me he couldn't believe he had arrived in the place he had dreamed of for so long.

When we stepped out of customs, I smiled at him and asked, "What do you say now, my friend?"

"Thank you, my good friend. I am anxious to help and get to work."

It was May 30, 2008.

I bid farewell to the team as they prepared to take Thamer to yet another gate to await yet another flight, to our debriefing location. Meanwhile, I took a taxi home so I could say hello to my family, get a good night's sleep, and pack fresh clothes. All so I could turn around the next day and head back to Dulles.

I walked in to find a very happy wife. I hadn't contacted Carmela since I'd left home, and I knew she must have been worried. She never spoken aloud her fear that I might be hurt or maybe killed in the line of duty. It had always been a possibility of my work, and we would spend only minimal time talking about such things before we let it all fall into the background, just a fact of our lives. We spoke very little of the mission I'd just returned from, instead choosing to bask in the comfort of being home together, safe. That night, however, she did comment on my new beard. To my surprise, she liked it, so I decided not to shave.

The next day I boarded another flight, this time bound for Miami, Florida, where it was time to debrief Thamer and find out why he was so important.

Chapter 22

MIAMI, FLORIDA—JUNE 2008

I'D CHOSEN MIAMI FOR THAMER'S debriefing partly because it was far enough away from DC to avoid interference from bureaucrats. The same agency insiders who had initially refused to support our mission were already lined up to stick their noses into our interviews once we'd gotten Thamer to the US. Our team had shouldered the risks and hard work to get him here, and I wasn't about to let DC power-mongers screw it up by turning an opportunity to gather useful intelligence into a circus of competing political agendas. We had also chosen Miami, because it was host to plenty of international travelers and multiethnic residents, which would make it easier for Thamer to blend in.

A few weeks before we left to pick up Thamer in Iraq, I went to Miami to find a suitable location for the debrief. I initially worked out a deal with the folks from SOUTHCOM, the US military's Southern Command, to use their facilities. They had everything we would need: ease of access, space and privacy. It was a perfect location, a controlled and secure military installation. Unfortunately, their security personnel had reservations about allowing a foreign national into their facilities, especially one from a country where we were currently fighting a war. They rescinded their offer.

My liaison at SOUTHCOM tried to give me an "I'm sorry it didn't work out gift"; he got in touch with the FBI to ask for alternatives. They considered allowing us to use one of their safe houses, which sat in a peaceful suburban neighborhood. But when I explained that we'd need the residence for a month, they grew worried that we would burn it. That is to say, they were concerned that our constant use of the safehouse would draw suspicion from neighbors, rendering it an *un*safe house.

Then I found my own safe location in Miami Beach. I convinced our new FBI contacts to help us by conducting an electronic sweep of the location to ensure we weren't bugged. Then, shortly before our team was supposed to head to the site, I received a message from my FBI contact. He said, much to his embarrassment, FBI headquarters had advised him it was against bureau policy to conduct a sweep on a non-FBI case. Setbacks. All in a day's work.

The safe location was close enough to the beach to be inconspicuous among the crowds. In essence, we would be hiding in plain sight. I took care of the security sweep myself so everything would be ready when it came time to finally uncover the vital information Thamer possessed.

I arrived the next day and went straight to the location to meet with Thamer and my team. Then the scientific debriefing team whose members I cannot divulge started to trickle in for what we knew would likely be a month-long session. Our goal was to get every bit of information Thamer had about weapons of war, primarily biological weapons, focusing on forensics and low-level production techniques. Over the course of the next month about ten or so scientists would be coming and going, grilling Thamer almost non-stop.

Because we only had thirty days with Thamer, we wasted no time. I escorted him from his room to the separate suite we'd set up for the debrief. That first day there were at least a half-dozen bureaucrats and scientists gathered around Thamer with laptops, notebooks, and recorders. He looked from face to face as they introduced themselves, nodding and blinking, as if trying to memorize each name.

Dr. McCarthy secured an interpreter, Dr. Kay Mereish, PhD, an expert in medical sciences and reserve Colonel in the Army. She specialized in the field of "medical intelligence." Dr. Mereish was also the Chief Inspector for Biological Weapons for the United Nations Monitoring, Verification and Inspection Commission which looked for these weapons in 2002 - 2003 before the second Gulf War. She later stated publicly in her role as Chief Inspector that Iraq did not have weapons of mass destruction in the leadup to the war. Later, Dr. Kay Mereish would be awarded the Department of Homeland Security's Distinguished Service Medal for her years of service in helping to protect the Homeland. She is reputed to be one of the best at translating technical information. A transcriber was on hand to take electronic notes.

Thamer's initial tension gave way to earnestness as he unfolded the story of his work for the Iraqi government. It was as if he were finally unburdening himself to people who would understand, people like him—fellow scientists who weren't here to shake him down for evidence that didn't exist or to punish him for the crimes committed by his tyrannical former employers. They were here to learn.

A lot of the questions and answers were so full of scientific jargon that it all left me struggling to keep my eyes open, even though it was still early in the day, but I didn't dare leave the room, not even for a breath of fresh air that smelled like something other than fast food. I didn't want to miss anything.

I'm glad I hung in there despite not understanding much of the science. As I listened, the more I began to read between the lines of the technical talk, especially when one word came up over and over. It was the word that finally unlocked the mystery for me, the mystery of why we needed to find Thamer. Other government microbiologists had been cut loose on the dangerous streets of Baghdad, and I had long scratched my head over why this one man was more important than so many others. The reason was now revealed:

Anthrax.

Thamer was an expert on weaponizing anthrax. Someone in the United States had learned to weaponize anthrax with deadly consequences and they were still on the loose.

A week after the September 11 terror attacks, letters containing anthrax spores began arriving at several news media offices throughout the eastern US. On September 19, 2001, one of those letters was opened by Robert Stevens, a photojournalist for *the Sun*, a tabloid owned by American Media, Inc. based in Boca Raton, Florida. He had no way of knowing that the coarse brown, granular material inside was anthrax spores. Four days later, he entered a hospital with an undiagnosed illness that caused vomiting and shortness of breath. By October 5, he was dead.

The first post-9/11 anthrax letters had a Trenton, New Jersey postmark. Two more anthrax letters, bearing the same Trenton postmark, arrived three weeks after the first mailing. The letters were addressed to Senators Tom Daschle of South Dakota and Patrick Leahy of Vermont. At the time, Daschle was the Senate Majority leader and Leahy was head of the Senate Judiciary Committee. The Daschle letter was opened by an aide on October 15, triggering a shutdown of the US government mail service.

The unopened Leahy letter was discovered in an impounded mail bag on November 16; it had been misdirected to the State Department mail annex in Sterling, Virginia due to a misread zip code. A postal worker there, contracted inhalation anthrax and survived but never fully recovered from the lung damage. The anthrax toxin in the Senate letters was more virulent than in the first batch, this time a highly refined dry powder consisting of about one gram of nearly pure spores. Whoever was developing anthrax for terrorism was getting better at it.

In all, at least twenty-two people developed anthrax infections, from the letters, eleven of whom developed the more deadly inhalation variety. Five died of inhalation anthrax, and the nation panicked. It was the worst biological attack in US history. Someone, somewhere was using a bio agent to kill people and tried to kill two top US government officials. Was it related to the 9/11 attacks? Was it state sponsored or some rogue? What type of skills does it require to weaponize anthrax? What other bioagents could they unleash?

We had no answers, but what we did know was that we were not prepared for an act of biological terrorism. The subsequent investigation code named Amerithrax was one of the largest and most complex in the history of US law enforcement. The case involved interviews of more than 10,000 witnesses thousands of grand jury subpoenas, execution of eighty searches and recovery of over 6,000 potential items of evidence.

Simply put, biological terrorism is the use of naturally occurring viruses and bacterium to inflict sickness and death, and weaponizing them means to put them in a form that would make them easy to spread and difficult to detect. Someone weaponized anthrax by reducing the bacterium to tiny microspores almost undetectable that could be easily inhaled.

Anthrax is one of our top concerns because of its natural presence in soil making it easily accessible. It's a bacterium that lives in soil, and the disease outbreaks it causes typically affect only domestic livestock, including sheep and cattle. Humans only occasionally contracted the disease and only when someone came in direct or indirect contact with infected animals. That sort of contact can cause severe skin ulceration, malignant pustules, or a form of pneumonia called Woolsorters Disease. As horrific as all that can be, that type of infection isn't usually deadly and can be treated by antibiotics; however, if spores are inhaled they can migrate to lymph glands in the chest where they proliferate, spread, and produce toxins that often cause death. Weaponizing anthrax by turning the bacterium into easily transportable spores could be done in a lab by someone with the right skills. But maybe someone figured out a way to do it outside of a lab.

There's nothing new about the use of bioagents in warfare. The practice dates back to the 1300s when Tartar (Mongol) warriors besieged the Crimean city of Kaffa. During the siege, many Tartars died at the hands of the plague, and their lifeless bodies were hurled over the city walls. Some researchers believe that this tactic of exposing an enemy to disease-riddled bodies may have been responsible for the spread of the Black Plague throughout Europe. If so, 14th century biological warfare caused the eventual deaths of around twenty-five million Europeans.

The phrase *biological weapon* conjures images of spies smuggling secret vials of deadly viruses, bacteria, or toxins into a country and setting them loose to spread contagions. Because infectious diseases can be transmitted from person to person, the potential for large loss of life is high. There are many other bioagents such as smallpox, botulism, plaque, tularemia, and viral hemorrhagic fevers.

These germs if intentionally or accidentally released could kill thousands, if not millions. The mobility of our society with high speed air travel makes mass infections throughout the world very real. All of this was on our minds as we looked to bolster our defenses against further attacks. This kind of threat became such a worldwide concern that offensive biological weapons were outlawed by the Biological Weapons Convention (BWC) in 1972, and as of 2019, 183 countries had ratified or acceded to this treaty. The reasoning for such a treaty is simple: a biological attack could result in a catastrophic number of sick people and fatalities with long-term consequences to civilian populations and economies, and its ripple effects could affect the entire world in wildly unpredictable ways. The possibilities are terrifying. Many signatories to the BWC do pursue research into bioweapons defense or options to defend against biological attack, which is not prohibited by the BWC. The United States is one of them.

Relative to military strategy, a significant problem with a biological warfare attack is that it would take days to be effective and therefore might not immediately stop an opposing force. Some biological agents—especially smallpox, plague, and tularemia—can be transmitted in aerosol form, but an agent transmitted by this mechanism can also hit unintended populations, including friendly forces or civilians. Some have called bioweapons "the poor man's nuclear weapon," but that description isn't accurate because it suggests that all bioweapons are easy to weaponize. They're not. If they were, we'd all be in big trouble.

Our ability to defend against them would depend on our ability to develop medical countermeasures, which are expensive and difficult to manufacture quickly. What's more, we'd have to spend billions of dollars and conduct years of research to develop vaccines for every possible bioagent. That's not feasible.

But at that moment we were faced with anthrax, we needed to gather every possible bit of information about its production as a weapon, and Thamer was a source for that information. Someone in the US had already used anthrax to murder five people and attempted to murder two high-level government officials and poisoned dozens more. Was that just the beginning? The United States was completely unprepared for an anthrax invasion or any other biological invasion and if a murderer could use anthrax as a weapon, what other bioweapons could they create?

How many people were involved? How could terrorists living in the US "cook up" a bioagent and what would be the tell-tale signs and signatures? Where were they and when might they strike again? Our concerns were so great and our capabilities so limited that the United States created the National Biodefense Analysis and Countermeasures Center, a lab dedicated to fighting bioterrorism. Dr. McCarthy was a key player in helping to stand up that organization.

IN FEBRUARY OF 2003, SECRETARY of State Colin Powell went before the United Nations Security Council and presented evidence that, according to the US intelligence community, proved Iraq had misled inspectors and had hidden weapons of mass destruction.

"There can be no doubt," Powell warned, "that Saddam Hussein has biological weapons and the capability to rapidly produce more, many more." His testimony was made even more dramatic when he held up a vial that he said could contain anthrax. He was demonstrating that a vial as small as the one he was holding could kill hundreds, if not thousands of people. Six weeks after his testimony, we invaded Iraq. Although Secretary Powell was right to be concerned about the use of biological weapons, his testimony proved incorrect, thanks to faulty intelligence. No WMDs were ever found.

I would later learn that Secretary Powell, a man I deeply respected and admired, would come to regret his support of the war as would Great Britain's Prime Minister Tony Blair, who would later go on to say, "I express more sorrow, regret and apology than you can ever believe." General Powell was a good soldier who fell in line with his boss, President George W. Bush. Our justification to invade was based on bad intelligence, and that mistake cost the lives of thousands of our troops as well as thousands of innocent Iraqis and tore the lives apart of many like Thamer Imran. But at the moment we had a problem on our hands, and we needed to learn everything from the man I'd been trying to find for two years.

ON THAT FIRST DAY, WE LEARNED that at one point Thamer had led Iraq's biological weapons plant at Al-Hakam, which produced 500,000 liters of biological agents in 1989 and 1990. Between 1985 and April of 1991, Iraq developed anthrax, botulinum toxin, and aflatoxin for biological warfare, and two hundred bombs and twenty-five ballistic missiles laden with biological agents were deployed by Iraq by the time Operation Desert Storm began. Al-Hakam continued operating until 1996, when the facility was shut down and sealed by UN weapons inspectors, and the remaining biological stocks were destroyed. The facility was blown up by the US Army in the 2003 invasion. UN weapons inspectors were convinced that prior to the US invasion, Iraq possessed no WMDs. On January 12, 2005, White House spokesperson Scott McClellan told reporters that the physical search for WMDs was over—having found no weapons. Despite that revelation, the war continued on for another six years.

WHEN IT CAME TO THAMER'S INVOLVEMENT with anthrax, he understood the unwritten rule: do what Saddam wants you to do or die. Still, there were a few who defied him.

When Saddam became president of Iraq in July of 1979, Dr. Hussain Shahristani was his chief scientific adviser. Saddam wanted to redirect atomic energy research to military use, and Dr. Shahristani refused to do it, explaining to Saddam that it violated Iraq's participation in the Non-Proliferation Treaty. Later, Dr. Shahristani raised a human rights violation about people being imprisoned. Although he knew that in the secret-police state of Iraq his complaint would eventually get back to Saddam, he felt he needed to speak up about these abuses. He trusted that his importance to Iraq's atomic program would save him from being arrested or worse. He was a brave man, but he was wrong.

On December 4, 1979, plainclothes Iraqi security agents seized him in his office. He was taken to the basement of Baghdad security headquarters and tortured for twenty-two days. His hands were tied behind his back, he was hung up, and his torturers used a cattle prod to blast electricity into his genitals and other parts of his body. When he broke into a cold sweat—a sign that he was about to pass out—they took him down, revived him, and began again. This went on day and night. His tormentors hoped he would eventually return to the nuclear program and do Saddam's biddings, so they stopped short of inflicting permanent, debilitating injuries. But Dr. Shahristani didn't support Saddam's plan and was kept in prison. His refusal led to a death sentence that was later commuted to life in prison, and he was kept in solitary confinement for eight years in Iraq's notorious Abu Ghraib prison.

During the 1991 Gulf War, he managed to escape from Abu Ghraib and fled to Iran. He had been held captive for eleven years. While in Iran and later Great Britain, Dr. Shahristani told human rights activists that while being held by Saddam at Abu Ghraib, he saw other prisoners who'd been burned on their genitals and toes and branded with hot electric irons. Some had holes drilled into their bones or had other parts of their bodies dissolved in a tub of sulphuric acid. After the fall of Saddam, he returned to Iraq where he assumed several leadership positions in the new Iraqi government and later wrote *Escaping to Freedom*, a book about that extraordinary part of his life.

By 2008, the perpetrators of America's anthrax attacks, a.k.a. Amerithrax, were still at large, and the FBI and other law enforcement and security agencies were fervently working to find those responsible. We needed to figure out how terrorists could make anthrax without our intelligence community knowing about it, and Thamer was the perfect person to help us. When Thamer had dreamed of becoming a biologist, he never imagined he'd end up working with deadly bioagents cultivated to kill. But in Saddam's regime, he had no choice. Now he was making the choice to help us.

After the first couple days of Thamer's debrief, I suggested we protect him from exhaustion by keeping the crowds in the room small and rotating the scientists through in shifts. This meant the scientists had to meet regularly to debrief each other and review tapes, but that worked well too, because it allowed them to clarify what they needed to know and to amass a strong and cohesive collection of information. We brought in food to keep everyone going.

From time to time, I continued to stop in and listen to the debrief. Most of it continued to be highly technical information that went over my head. Still, it was important for me to stick around because I was the resident expert on Thamer.

As the weeks rolled on, Thamer seemed to relax into his role. He became animated as he was able to expand at length on his favorite subject, microbiology, this time knowing that his knowledge would be used for good. He talked with his hands when making an important point, he smiled often, and sometimes he even laughed. His laughter was infectious, so that even when the joke was about some little detail only the scientists would understand, I laughed along.

There were several elements included in our overall strategy to bolster our defenses against a bioagent attack, and intelligence was the key element. Another important factor in our strategy was to gather information that could help us come up with a robust plan to disrupt the activities we uncovered. And last but not least came the elements of resilience and recovery; in other words, what would we need to do to recover from an attack, and how could we improve that approach to be able to recover in the quickest possible time with the fewest possible casualties? All of this was on our minds as the scientists pressed on.

Thamer had answers to some of our questions, and when he didn't, he helped guide us to find the answers ourselves. He seemed nervous whenever he couldn't answer a question, and I knew he worried that he'd be sent back to Iraq should he fail to tell us everything we wanted to know. His value and the decision to keep him or send him back was not mine to make. I didn't know what the government would eventually do but my orders until rescinded were to bring him back to Iraq. We had thirty days and that was that.

Thamer was under no illusions and no guarantees were made. I didn't have the heart to tell him though I knew I had to that the government's plan was to return him to Iraq when this was over, regardless of the level of his cooperation and the value of his information. This was troubling for me. If I was up front with him, it might discourage his cooperation; on the other hand, holding back the truth didn't sit well with me. I hoped that fate would intervene before I became the bearer of the bad news that could cost him his life.

Chapter 23

MIAMI, BEACH, FLORIDA—JUNE 2008

AS THE DAYS PASSED, I BECAME Thamer's lifeline. My job was to keep him focused and engaged. More than that, I was the guy he turned to with his worries. After the long and laborious debriefing sessions, we would end the day walking around South Beach and talking for hours.

After the ravaged war zone of Baghdad, this sunny tourist destination swarming with overfed vacationers and bikini-clad women provided a welcome break, at least for me. Although Thamer enjoyed the weather and the beautiful beaches, the sight of nearly naked men and woman traipsing around was shocking to him. Of all the places to introduce Thamer to American culture I chose Miami Beach! Even for Americans Miami Beach is an eye opener, so for this proper family man from the Middle East, it caused a kind of cultural and sensory overload.

On occasion, we stopped at one of the many outside cafés. It felt surreal to finally be able to sit and just chat with the man I had tracked so long, no longer 6,000 miles away, but face-to-face. I wanted to learn as much from him as he did from me. The two of us enjoying lunch on a beautiful day with no barriers, bombs, or other elements of war between us was perfect. We never spoke business; we both needed a break from it all, and this was our chance.

I began to develop a sincere respect for Thamer. His laughter was contagious, and the inner peace he possessed puzzled me given all he'd been through. I admired that he never seemed down and genuinely seemed able to live in each moment as it came.

"Inshallah, Mr. Steve" (If God wills it) is a phrase he used often, and that I think gave him the strength to accept things as they came with no sorrow or regret. In some ways, I wished I were more like him. Thamer had the kind of engaging personality and a way of disarming people with his unaffected sincerity and gentle humor. Where he was gregarious, I was reserved. Where he expressed gratitude and took time to give thanks for life's gifts, my life was fast paced with a hundred balls in the air. I enjoyed my talks with Thamer because he made me slow down. He'd often tell me, "You need to relax, my good friend."

Often, I would see Thamer looking around and taking in the abundance of the United States, which I think it was a bit overwhelming. One day he told me about his father, Abdul Rahman.

"My father owned a small café where he sold tea and fruit. We didn't own a car or television set and had no phone, but we did have a small radio that we would gather around to listen to music and news. I think back now and it wonders me how my father was able to bring up a family of eleven from the small amount of money he earned. I used to watch him ride his bicycle to work. My mother and father could barely read and write, so they were strict on my schooling. All my family called me 'bookworm' because I loved to read!"

He told me his favorite books were detective stories by Maurice Leblanc, who wrote about a gentleman detective, thief, and master of disguise named Arsène Lupin. Lupin was the French counterpart to Sherlock Holmes, whose stories Thamer also loved when he could find them. He read for hours, often getting so lost in a story he imagined himself one of the characters.

The only thing he didn't love about school was math. His mother had to get after him to do the math homework he hated.

"It's boring!" he complained. "It has no story to it!"

I loved hearing about life in Iraq, and Thamer opened my eyes to a view of the world I had yet to consider. War had been cruel. It took the lives of relatives and friends and had caused him to endure humiliation, imprisonment, and torture. But instead of making him bitter, those experiences had given him even greater appreciation for the preciousness of all he had. I found that quality inspiring.

Only one thing tempered Thamer's natural good humor, and that was persistent worry about his family every day they were apart. He worried about his wife and children constantly, but also about his brothers, sister-in-law, father, cousins—all of them. The war was still raging and bombings were going on all around Baghdad even in the market areas. Whenever he spoke of family, it was as if he could see their faces before him, all counting on him.

The violence in Iraq was a topic I tried to keep out of our conversations, but he kept returning to it. Once, while we were on that topic, I asked Thamer if he'd been better off before the war or now. He told me he appreciated the sacrifice of our young Americans and our desire to bring them freedom, but then he admitted he'd been better off before the war. He said that although Saddam was a brutal dictator, most average Iraqis didn't experience his brutality or even hear about it. And those who did know about Saddam's atrocities were afraid to say anything bad against him. Thamer told me that satellite television dishes, which might have been able to carry news from outside of Iraq were reserved for the Iraqi elite, so average Iraqis saw what the government told them to watch and nothing more. If people had suspicions about the crimes and cruelty of Saddam Hussein, they were spoken of merely in whispers between people who shared an intimate trust. So though the outside world may have known about these crimes, many Iraqis did not and merely went about their lives.

Thamer's existence before the invasion had been quiet and peaceful. Back then, he'd had a home, a career, and a simple life. Now all of that was gone.

I did my best to answer the voluminous number of questions Thamer threw at me about American life, while tempering my own questions about his life because it clearly grieved him to talk about the things he loved about Baghdad that had vanished, and it worried him to talk about the dangerous new realities he had left his family to face without him.

He was a sponge: a man who wanted to learn all he could to help him fit into this new land. So many of America's sights and sounds called up the country of dreams he'd fallen in love with through movies and books. Yet, encountering real live Americans had left him mystified as he struggled to reconcile the hedonistic circus he witnessed in South Beach with the more traditional values of family and home that I told him about through my stories about the joys of growing up in a big family, talking with my wife over a home-cooked meal, and watching my boys grow into accomplished young men.

I had a sense that Thamer returned my respect for him, that he saw us both as men who prized knowledge, sought the truth, served our fellow humans, and loved our families. I knew he would make any sacrifice to protect his family and secure their future. I too would do everything I could to protect my family but I thanked God my belief had never been tested as Thamer's had already.

One balmy Friday when the sun was setting, Thamer and I strolled to an outdoor café on South Beach's popular Lincoln Road, a colorful pedestrian mall lined with palm trees, with outdoor restaurants and cafés, and people out for a stroll. It had been a long week and we both needed to unwind.

"Can I offer you a cigarette?" He held out a pack.

"No thanks," I said for the umpteenth time, and then, unable to refrain, I reminded him, also for the umpteenth time, "You know you could die from doing that."

He shrugged. "Inshallah, my good friend."

His head pivoted in every direction, unable to keep up with the sensory overload of Lincoln Road at sunset, with its blaring Latin music and model-perfect men and women parading past in Gucci, Prada, and Rolex. He smiled and shook his head as if to say it was all too much. After years hiding amid the ruins of Baghdad, the rampant wealth gliding past us must have seemed obscene, but I knew that wasn't why he shook his head. More than once, he'd revealed that the idea of his family thousands of miles away living in hell was always on his mind. The ostentatiousness and self-indulgence of our surroundings shot a glaring spotlight into those thoughts. I wondered if I'd made a bad choice bringing him to Miami.

We strolled down Ocean Avenue toward its many restaurants and clubs and picked yet another outdoor café. While we sat there, two half-naked ladies on rollerblades rolled toward us, and as they closed in, I saw they were topless. I had visited Miami before and such sights didn't much faze me anymore, but it dawned on me this sort of exhibitionism wasn't allowed in his country or under his religion. As the ample ladies coasted past us, I caught Thamer gaping. But he didn't look as displeased as I'd expected.

"Thamer, what are you looking at?" I teased.

He blushed crimson. "God put them there. What can I do? It is not my fault, Mr. Steve, you must believe me."

He studied my face as if trying to gauge my reaction. I was embarrassed too, for putting him in this situation, but decided to make the best of it.

"Well, I guess we'll just have to blame God for this." Then I broke out laughing. He sighed and smiled. I think he wasn't so much offended by the semi-nudity as he was concerned with my opinion of him for having looked. Occasionally when we took an outdoor break, I'd catch Thamer looking at the ladies.

Again, he would invoke God as the culprit, and again I'd say, "God is a pretty good guy, isn't he?" Then he'd give me a thumbs up! Thamer was being Americanized before my eyes. And nowhere did that seem more apparent than when we broached the subject of ice cream.

One day Thamer and I passed a Häagen-Dazs ice cream shop, and this sight excited him more than it ever had my boys, even when they were little. He insisted, "I must treat you. Wait here!" Before I could reply, he scurried inside. After a long absence, he reappeared with two cones piled so high with oversized scoops of ice cream they looked ready to topple.

Those cones must have cost him fifty dollars, but the look on his face told me they were worth every penny. I'll never forget him standing in the doorway, multiple shades of ice cream dripping down both hands, wearing the biggest smile I had seen on his face yet. He handed one of the cones to me, and I promised myself I would do everything I could so that sooner than later he could hand one to his wife.

The sun went down, which delivered welcome relief from the heat and turned down the volume on the American excess. Later, that evening, Thamer and I sat at a beachside restaurant, and our waiter came to light our table's candle. I felt glad of the change in atmosphere until I looked up and saw the alarm on Thamer's face. I couldn't imagine why the simple act of lighting a candle had jolted him.

"Does the power go out here, too?" he asked me. I wasn't sure if he was being sarcastic but that didn't appear to be his style.

Then it dawned on me. "Oh! No, it has nothing to do with electrical power. They light the candles to create a nice atmosphere."

I fell silent, pondering how I took for granted what was almost a luxury for him. Thamer had grown used to having electricity for only a few hours a day, and sometimes not at all. He had lived through sweltering hot summer days praying that the fuel for his foul-smelling generators wouldn't run out and cause his family's limited food supply to spoil.

Thamer fell silent as well, probably pondering the same thing. Then he said, "Seems like a waste of a good candle!"

I smiled at my good friend.

"STEVE, HE'S GONE! HE'S GONE!" The breathless guy yelling and running toward me in the hotel hallway was Scott, an assistant to Dr. McCarthy.

"What do you mean he's gone? Who's gone?"

"Thamer!"

"Whoa! What're you talking about?" I was sure this must be a mistake. Thamer had nothing to gain and everything to lose by running away, and he knew it.

"I just came from his room and it's completely empty. The maids are cleaning it, and everything's gone!"

That sounded bad, and I could think of no reasonable explanation. Sweat beaded my forehead, an ice pick of fear stabbed my gut, and a steamroller of panic knocked the wind out of me. My mind raced. I thought, I can't believe this is happening! Thamer was my responsibility, and if I lost him, we were all screwed. An Iraqi bioweapons scientist who we smuggled out of Iraq on the loose in the US? I could imagine nothing worse. Had escape been his plan all along?

"Let's go!" I said to Scott. "Show me."

With Scott in the lead, we ran to Thamer's room as countless terrible scenarios ran through my mind. We startled a maid as we charged through the open doorway. Sure enough, the room was vacant, all traces of occupancy gone except for the two maids still cleaning the room.

"I didn't see him this morning so I came to check on him, and I found it empty." Scott remained breathless with panic. I stood in the doorway in disbelief, trying to figure out what I needed to do next. This was entirely on me. Thamer was my responsibility. Great. An ex Secret Service agent loses his man! What else could go wrong?

I addressed the startled maids "Excuse me, the man in this room . . . did he check out or did he move to another room?"

"Yes, sir," one of them said. "He is gone."

"Do you know when he checked out?"

"A few hours ago, I think." Her voice shook.

As bad as I felt for scaring her, she couldn't be as scared as I was. I rubbed my forehead, which I always did when I was stressed. All I could think was, shit-shit-shit, this is bad. I took a shuddering breath. Okay, calm down, let's think this through. I walked over to the window and looked down at the street then berated myself—don't be stupid, he checked out hours ago, why would he be waiting on the street?

I continued to stare out the window, contemplating my call to DC to report Thamer's disappearance while the maids tiptoed around us to resume their duties. Then, in the fog of my thoughts, I noted something was off about the cars and pedestrians. I'd been in Thamer's room before, and had looked out this window, but I couldn't place what had changed. I stood there for a few minutes, puzzled, while Scott caught his breath.

Then it hit me, prompting a faint smile, which turned into an uncontrollable laugh, much to my colleague's chagrin.

"What's so goddam funny? He's gone!"

"Scott, yes, this is the last room on the left as you come out of the elevator, and yes, the occupant is gone, but you're missing one piece of the puzzle, my good friend," I said, adopting Thamer's term. "We're on the wrong fucking floor."

Scott stepped back and swung the room's main door to check the number on the other side. My esteemed colleague had decided to check on Thamer, gotten his floors mixed up, and gone to the wrong room. With Scott running ahead and me following, I hadn't bothered to check which floor we were on. I tried to stop laughing because Scott looked beyond embarrassed, but I couldn't.

We then ran to the right floor and banged most enthusiastically on Thamer's door.

He opened it. "Hello, my good friends! Is something wrong?"

We said nothing at first, just stood sweating and silent, a couple of idiots.

"No, nothing's wrong," I said. "We'll see you at the usual time?"

"Of course." Thamer looked at us as if he was concerned that we might be suffering from a mutual mental breakdown of some sort, which I suppose we just had.

"Is there anything else that you need?" he asked.

"Oh no, we're okay." Still, I didn't move.

"Okay then, my good friends, I will see you later." Thamer slowly closed the door, shaking his head as we both just stood there.

That little episode only lasted about twenty minutes, but it felt like it had taken about twenty years off my life.

THE QUESTIONS THAMER ANSWERED seemed endless, both in and out of the briefing room, and as hours grew to days and days grew to weeks, I realized that Thamer and I were not so different. We were both married former government workers with grown children. We had both served in the military, he in the Iraqi army and I in the US Navy, and we both had graduate degrees. We also both took a keen interest in world events. Between debriefing sessions, our private conversations grew to encompass international relations, war, politics, economics, and the role of science and technology in all of it. We marveled at the series of events that had landed both of us in the center of a maelstrom, set in motion by terrorists who had little to do with either of our two countries.

The more I got to know Thamer, the more convinced I became that, no matter where we come from, no matter which flag we hoist, people share a common humanity. We all dream of a good life for ourselves and our families. No ideology or dictator can ever change that. Whether getting rid of Saddam was worth the cost is debatable. All I know for certain is that a lot of innocent Iraqis were killed—men, women, young, old—people with no ill will toward the US. They were victims. In many ways, they were hostages, millions of them held captive by chains of fear, first at the hands of a vicious dictator and then at the hands of fanatical insurgents after our country took the dictator down. While I applaud our troops for their heroic work in keeping America safe, I question our leader's "nation-building strategy" that turned our troops into police signed on for years of commitment, sending many of them to their death for reasons that made no sense. Was there more to our invasion strategy than getting rid of a dictator—like Iraq's oil perhaps? Maybe, but nothing I could come up with that would be worth the cost paid.

In March of 2003, I had watched the statue of Saddam Hussein topple on TV and felt convinced that my country was rescuing Iraq's twenty-six million people from a tyrant that possessed weapons to kill millions. In 2007 and 2008, I slipped into the streets of Baghdad in hopes of saving a single man, and by then I had realized that our intervention and the chaos that followed as thousands of foreign fighters poured into Iraq, unintentionally made it an even more dangerous and corrupt country than it was before. There was no doubt that a portion of the vast amount of money being pumped into the country was being siphoned off by crooked politicians. Since 9/11, America's war on terror has killed more than half a million people in Iraq, Afghanistan, and Pakistan. Few families in the region have been left untouched.

Fifteen of the nineteen men who carried out the 9/11 Terror Attacks against the United States were Saudi Arabian, but we've never taken the war on terror to their country. We remain one of Saudi Arabia's staunchest allies.

Sometimes it felt easier to ask Thamer about the past than his opinions about the current war. One day, we got to talking about the Iran-Iraq War, which killed two of Thamer's brothers. I expressed sympathy for his loss. Then I said, "Do you mind if I ask you a question about that war, my good friend?"

He grinned at my use of his usual term for me. "No problem. I'll try to answer if I can."

"Do you believe Iraq's invasion of Iran was just?"

He paused before answering, "Mr. Steve, you must understand that in our country outside news was difficult to get. We only heard from our government."

I asked what he remembered hearing. He said the Iraqi government bombarded its people with propaganda to convince them Iran was stealing their land and planning an imminent invasion. He was much younger then, more inclined to believe what his government had to say, including that the only way to prevent an invasion of Iraq was to turn the tables and invade Iran instead. He believed his government again when its propaganda machine reported that Kuwait was stealing oil that belonged to the Iraqis, thus justifying Iraq's invasion of that country as well.

"Loyalty to my country, this is what I believed in," Thamer told me. "I did not understand. I was tricked by a dictator who sacrificed his own people to get more power."

I had interrogated hundreds of subjects over the previous three decades, I had a knack for ferreting out the truth, and I was never more certain about anything than this: Thamer spoke with the simple, direct, humility of an honest man.

I KNEW IT WAS DANGEROUS TO GET TOO friendly with the subject of a mission. I had learned that from my days as a detective: never trust an informant or get personally involved in a case. Many an investigator has been burned by violating this tenet. But my instincts told me I could trust Thamer. I called him "my good friend" not to echo him, and not to manipulate him, but because I felt genuine kinship with him. In fact, Thamer was one of the most important friends a man like me could ever have: a friend in need. My team and I had succeeded in bringing Thamer to the US to help our country, and I'd promised myself I would return the favor and help Thamer, but the Homeland Security Council had made it clear: we had thirty days to question him, and then we had to take him back.

DR. MCCARTHY FLEW DOWN TO CHECK our progress. I invited her to join me for a coffee break at a café around the corner and told her how I felt.

"It makes no sense to send him back," I said.

"I agree. He's still a risk to be captured and have his skills used against us," she replied.

"It defies comprehension if we give him nothing for his cooperation but maybe a death sentence. Because that's what happens if we take him back. Every time we go in and out of Iraq with him it increases the odds that his cooperation will be discovered."

"That's true," she said, "but some of the higher ups won't see it that way. As long as America isn't pulling the trigger, they won't care. I think we have to sell them on what's in it for them. I mean, what's in it for America if we keep him here."

I said, "We need to make clear that he's in danger of being captured, and his skills at biological warfare could still be used against the US. So why risk sending him back?"

She agreed. We just had to get other people higher up the chain of command to agree. We were committed to fight this with everything we had. Then she started making a lot of phone calls.

Chapter 24

ANNAPOLIS, MARYLAND JULY—2008

I STILL HAD TO PLAN FOR THAMER'S return to Iraq in case all our efforts and arguments failed, so I reluctantly started to work on logistics. My biggest concern was how to avoid making Thamer vulnerable to arrest upon reentering the country. We were now hearing reports about employees of the former regime being picked up by the new government only to disappear without a trace.

This was a difficult time for me. Thamer knew that cooperating with us guaranteed him nothing, that all possibilities had been expressed verbally but nothing had been promised, and there was nothing in writing. Yet I knew that in his heart, he had never given up hope that the United States would keep our promise to help him and his family. I believed that spending so much time with American scientists who seemed so eager to work with him gave him great hope. I also believed that spending so much time with me, an American who had developed a friendship with him, probably gave him even greater hope.

During our final week in Miami, I confessed to Thamer that, although I was doing everything I could think to help him stay, my superiors had agreed to no such thing, and I was by no means certain I would succeed. Ever the gentleman, he simply said, "I know you are doing your best, Mr. Steve."

I was sitting alone in my hotel room when my cell phone rang. It was Dr. McCarthy again. She had returned to Washington but checked in with me every day about Thamer's status. My initial hello must have sounded over-eager because she interjected before I could say more, "I'm sorry, Steve. No news today."

"Are you serious? Can't they see what's happening here?" With each word I got more wound up.

"I know," she said.

"I know you know. I'm sorry if I sound like I'm blaming you."

"I'll call you as soon as I hear anything."

I hung up the phone thinking maybe my wife's right, maybe I am too personally involved. We had two days left, and I paced the floor of my room, trying to figure out how on earth I'd break the news to my friend that we were sending him back to hell. Then my phone rang.

I grabbed it without looking at the number. "Yeah?"

"Steve, we got the okay from the top."

It was Dr. McCarthy. Lost in the fog of sleep deprivation, I didn't process what I'd just heard. I replied, "What?"

"We got the okay from the top."

I was stunned. I stared at my face in the mirror and listened to my thoughts process what she'd just told me. It was official: Thamer could stay.

I gasped, "Are you *serious*?!"

"I know."

I didn't know how Dr. McCarthy did it, but I knew she had worked nonstop to make this happen. "Thank you" didn't begin to cover how I felt, but it was all I could think to say.

The rest of the conversation was pure celebration. Not of any personal victory but of the realization that somewhere in the often-cynical bureaucratic machinery of Washington, justice and compassion had prevailed. We talked about what to do next but I was only half-listening, imagining Thamer's reaction when I told him. The moment I hung up, I ran to Thamer's room and banged on his door. He rushed to open it, a look of alarm on his face.

"I just got the good news. You're not going back to Iraq!"

He smiled. It was as broad a smile as when he held the two giant ice cream cones. This was the humble, grateful smile of a man who has just escaped death, a man who has laid everything on the line and won his life back. He accepted the news with his signature grace, humbleness, and thanks.

"Mr. Steve this is such good news for me, thank you, thank you, my good friend."

Thamer had his reprieve and was a happy man. I too was a happy man who just dodged a bullet of my own. But Thamer's good fortune was tempered.

"Has there been any talk about my family?"

"I'm sorry, but I don't have any information about that."

On occasion he would bring the topic of his family into our conversations. He wanted them to join him in America, but he never forced the issue. He knew that our interest was in him and not his family. He was the proliferation risk. It was his skills that could be a threat to us if he were captured. He felt that if he pushed too hard the whole thing could collapse.

"Let's get you settled first, and we can talk more later."

"Yes, of course."

I knew he was happy but at the same time crushed. The future of Thamer's family would have to wait. There was much to do. The sudden and unexpected decision to keep Thamer in the US created a new problem. I had been so busy planning for the worst, that I had no plan for the best. I had made no provisions for Thamer to settle in for a longer stay. The scientific debrief was over, and now I had an Iraqi refugee on my hands, a refugee who was now also my friend. With an uncertain path before us,

Thamer and I left Miami together and headed north to DC, and all I could think was, "What am I going to do with him?"

Jim had gone back to his previous assignment with the Marines, and Kevin to his with ICE, so I was solo on this one. I know that they would be happy to hear this news but notifying them would have to wait.

At the airport, I gave our taxi driver directions, then climbed in back with Thamer and asked, "Have you ever heard of Annapolis?"

"Anna-polis?" I smiled at his delightful Arabic pronunciation, which made it sound like two separate words: Anna and polis. "Yes, I think I have. Why do you ask?"

"Because, my good friend, that's where we're headed."

In the perpetual state of exhaustion I'd fallen into, I'd been able to think of only one place to take him: the cheap but comfortable hotel where Carmela and I had stayed when I transferred from the Boston Field Office to Washington. That was back in 1993. I could only hope it was still there, that it hadn't fallen into decay. Anyway, this was no time to be selective. These were only temporary quarters, as they'd been for Carmela and me back when we were waiting for our house to be built.

Thamer was starting a new life, and I knew he'd be grateful wherever I put him. That was his way. Although I wanted to invite Thamer to my home, I knew it wasn't the right thing to do because this was still an active case, and my assignment hadn't ended. Despite my deep connection with Thamer, I couldn't let my personal feelings cloud my judgment.

The hotel was still there, a little outdated, but still clean and decent. Most importantly, the location wasn't far from my own home, which would make it easier for me to keep an eye out for him and help him transition. I checked him in, barely able to keep my eyes open and stumbling through my conversation with the clerk. It had been a long day. Hell, it had been a long month.

"Okay, my friend, I'll be back at 8:30 tomorrow morning to

pick you up. We have a lot to do. Here are my numbers if you need me tonight. I asked the clerk at the front desk to help you if you need to get ahold of me."

"Thank you so much, my good friend," Thamer said.

For the first time, I left Thamer on his own. This whole thing was built on mutual trust now, me trusting him not to run off, him trusting me to come back.

I drove away thinking, "Okay, Steve, what do you do now?"

I got home, gave Carmela a warm but brief hug hello, and collapsed into bed, falling asleep around the time my head hit the pillow. Not the most affectionate homecoming after a month apart, but Carmela understood. She'd been married to me for more than two decades, and she knew to hold off on asking about my trip, not because I didn't want to talk about it, but because I had nothing left in the tank. But surely this assignment would come to a close soon.

Later, I told her about Thamer, and she was ecstatic.

"I would love to meet him," Carmela said.

"Maybe one day."

THE NEXT MORNING, AS I DROVE TO Thamer's hotel I saw him standing out front with a worried look on his face. I pulled under the awning and rolled down the passenger window.

"Good morning, my friend."

"Good morning to you," he replied.

"It's a beautiful day."

"Yes, it is. You did say 8:30, Mr. Steve, didn't you?"

"Ahhh, yes, I did." I looked at my watch, which had an 8:40 or so look to it.

Thamer's expression turned stern as he opened the door and climbed in. I got the message: he was a punctual person and expected me to be the same. Every time we met after that, I made it a point to be on time.

First things first—I got him a cell phone with a pay card so he could buy minutes as he went. I needed to be able to call him at a moment's notice, and I wanted him to be able to stay in touch with his family from time to time.

"How is your family," I asked as we drove. "Are they safe and well?"

"Oh yes, but they are missing me," he said with a laugh. "They are well, but they had many questions about my situation."

This was Thamer's way of asking me about the future of his family. Unfortunately, I had no idea what the government's long-term plan was for Thamer. I just had to make sure he was safe and still cooperating with us.

WHEN THAMER CALLED HIS FAMILY, I was never part of the conversations. This was his private time. If there were any problems with his loved ones in Iraq, Thamer kept them to himself. He always told me that everyone was fine, and he never complained.

One sunny day, I picked him up for lunch, and, wanting to take advantage of the beautiful weather, I took him to a restaurant overlooking Spa Creek in downtown Annapolis. This historic district along Chesapeake Bay had lured me to Annapolis when I first moved to the DC area. It seemed a fitting place for a foreign national to fall in love with our country, with its colonial architecture reminiscent of America's founding. The domes of the Maryland State House and the Naval Academy dominate the city, marked the oldest institutions of their kind in the country. Many of the red brick buildings lining the marinas have stood since the days of the Revolution, and the people who live there exude a strong sense of community, bonded to history.

I asked the hostess for the table with the best view of the creek, and it didn't disappoint. Sailboats floated by, a warm breeze catching their white sails. We sat by a small canal with docking areas where boaters would tie up their boats and stop in for lunch or dinner at the restaurants on the water. Annapolis is a beautiful city, and Thamer seemed to enjoy the stunning views that could make a guy forget that anything was wrong in the world.

We enjoyed a leisurely lunch and pleasant conversation, and then Thamer became very quiet. He gazed silently across the water, then turned to me and said, "Mr. Steve, you saved my life."

Now I was the silent one. No one had ever said anything like that to me before. I didn't know what to say in response, so I nodded and smiled, trying to absorb the enormity of his words, the significance of it all from his side of the situation. I felt humbled and maybe even a little embarrassed. As usual, Thamer had made a big statement with great subtlety. We sat there for a long time in silence, looking out across the bay.

WHEN I WASN'T WITH THAMER, I WAS in my office working with Dr. McCarthy to come up with a stable plan for Thamer's long-term stay in the US. First, I had to notify ICE and US Citizenship and Immigration Services (USCIS) that he wasn't going back to Iraq as planned. Then, I had to work out a better living arrangement, an interim one in the DC area that didn't involve hotels, and after that, a long-term home where he could hopefully settle with his family. Dr. McCarthy had a contact who would help us.

"Thamer," I said, "We found an apartment for you in Virginia."

"Virginia, what about staying here, Mr. Steve?"

"I'm sorry," I told him, "but Annapolis is a bit far from DC, and it would be hard for us to keep taking you back and forth."

As usual, Thamer took the news in stride. I didn't care to be that far from him, but the matter had been decided.

Dr. McCarthy's connections helped us find Thamer an apartment that would be flexible enough on lease agreements to allow for a quick move, given his fluid situation. The condo was comfortable and inviting, just what Thamer needed to give him a sense of home life and permanency after months of living out of hotels. Meanwhile, the government was paying Thamer as a consultant. It was a temporary arrangement until Dr. McCarthy and I put a plan together to allow Thamer to continue providing his assistance with forensic information in return for a modest salary to pay his bills. Yet, it was not Thamer's own comfort and security that worried him.

"Mr. Steve, what of my family? What will happen to them? They are still in danger, aren't they?"

"I understand. We'll do what we can."

It was an exchange we repeated often, and I was careful not to make promises. The truth was, it had taken a herculean effort to get Thamer to the US, and to now go back and fight for permission to get his family would be another enormous challenge. I had been told, "we're interested in him, not his family." I knew what that really meant. It was a lot of work to sponsor a family: visas, finding the money to fund them, language assistance, green cards, medical care, enrolling them in schools, and the list goes on. Nobody wanted to take that on.

It had been several months since Thamer had seen his family, and as each day came and went, I saw the flicker of doubt in his eyes, and heard the diminishing hope in his voice that he would see them anytime soon, but whatever I might keep from him, I couldn't prevent him from following the news reports coming out of Iraq. Each time I heard a report of a market being bombed, or Iraqi citizens being killed, I felt a chill. I prayed each time, please God, don't let it be anyone in Thamer's family. It felt terrible, praying for such things, knowing that if it wasn't his family it would be someone else's. The news was disheartening to me. I could only imagine what it did to Thamer.

He kept in contact with Eman, their children, and other relatives through letters and phone calls. He told me they promised him they wouldn't leave their homes unless it was necessary, and I let these reports reassure me. Thamer's time in prison had taught them all to keep a low profile. But such caution could protect them only so much. The insurgents had adopted a strategy of inserting themselves within the populace, which not only made it difficult for our troops to root them out but also turned a lot of innocent Iraqi civilians into potential collateral damage, putting them smack in the middle of the violence.

A comprehensive classified report was being drafted, containing the intelligence Thamer shared with us, so I needed his mind clear and sharp to concentrate on giving us any additional forensic information that he might have left out in Miami, but he was clearly preoccupied. He would invite me for tea, and we'd be talking about how his day went when he would stop midsentence, his mind thousands of miles away.

Although I hate cigarettes, I often sat outside with him when he smoked, to keep him company and maybe help him cope with the troubles that preoccupied him.

"Ah, Mr. Steve, please join me." He would say, and then offer me a cigarette. "Would you like one?"

"No, thank you."

He looked crestfallen every time I refused. I came to learn that in his culture, to refuse a friendly offer like this was like refusing friendship, an insult. He didn't understand that in my culture making such an offering to a man who doesn't want it is like saying, "What's a little cancer between friends?"

He looked so bereft; I didn't have the heart to explain. Instead, on occasion, I lit up and joined him. It seemed to comfort him to talk to me over a cigarette, bonding over this one activity that gave him some pleasure.

Whether we were at his house or out and about, he often picked up a newspaper or watched news broadcasts. I did my best to distract him from these things, to keep him from learning details of the latest bombings in Iraq. It was worrisome how many civilians were dying in public markets.

One day at his apartment he reached for a paper, and I said, "Come on, my good friend, let's get out of here today, and go see some sights."

"Of course, my good friend."

Thamer knew what I was up to, and he was all for it, always up for any excursions that might take his mind off his troubles. On one occasion we visited a science museum that held his interest for a couple of hours. Afterward, we did the one thing Thamer never tired of: we sat at an outdoor café and talked about American culture. He wanted to understand it all, so he could be a part of it.

One day while we were in a hotel restaurant, news flashed on a television about another bombing at a public market in Iraq. I don't remember the death toll. Neither of us spoke, but it was as if I felt both of our hearts seize in our chests as we wondered whether someone he knew had gone to the market that day. Although he didn't say so, I knew that at those moments Thamer wanted to return home to his family, but we both knew it would be a death sentence to send him back now.

In essence, cooperating with a foreign government without the approval of his country's government could be looked at as treason. It did not matter that our country and his country had both put him in an impossible position, leaving him with only two options: cooperate with the Americans, or perhaps die at the hands of the scientist killers. It did not matter that the US was helping rebuild Iraq, in effect helping his country run things. Iraq was a sovereign country, and its leaders, such as they were, expected their country's sovereignty to be respected. Thamer could never go back.

Thamer would build a life in the United States. But now, what about his family? There was no question they'd be in danger if word got out that he was helping us. The Iraqi government still had a warrant out for Thamer's arrest, and insurgents had proven they could exact revenge on almost anyone, anywhere, anytime. Any of these actors might kill Thamer's family as a warning to others not to aid our coalition forces. The threat was very real.

We were most concerned about his wife and sons. His daughter, Farah, was married with children of her own and not only was moving her whole family impractical, they were deeply attached to their Baghdad home. Because Farah's last name was different from her father's and because she was now part of another extended family, we believed she was relatively safe. But the wife and sons were still vulnerable, no question. We had to go back and get them out.

Chapter 25

BAGHDAD, IRAQ—OAKTON, VIRGINIA—AUGUST 2008

MONTHS HAD PASSED SINCE THAMER'S arrival in the US, and among countless other things on her plate, Dr. McCarthy now added the issue of what was to become of Thamer's family. Weeks of stonewalling and rejection to get permission for our team to go back for his family eventually forced her to take it to the top. She went again to the Secretary of Homeland Security, Michael Chertoff. She was smart and very persuasive, and fortunately for us, we had a secretary who was forward thinking and possessed a great measure of common sense, which was lacking in many of our political leaders.

I was sitting in my office one day when Dr. McCarthy walked in.

"We got the approval," she said with a grin.

"That's awesome!" I exploded, cutting her off as I reached for the phone to call Thamer with the news. I was so excited I misdialed the first time but then calmed down to get it right.

"Hello, my good friend."

"Ah, hello my good friend," I answered. "I have good news."

Thamer was silent. I knew he knew what that meant. He knew that we were trying hard to bring his family to the US and that finally I was calling with the good news he was hoping and praying for.

After several seconds, he spoke. "My family will be joining me?"

"Yes."

"Thank you, thank you, my good friend!" he said over and over. He was high as a kite. I wished I could have been there in person to celebrate the good news, but there was no time.

It had been an ordeal getting Thamer to the US, and the prospect of doing it all again for his family was daunting, but we had to go back. For a man like Thamer, life without his family would have felt pointless. I reached out to Jim and Kevin and asked for their help again. It was strange being a contractor asking the government guys for help; usually it's the other way around, but these guys had become trusted friends. Still, I wasn't sure how they'd react to my coming to them again, hat in hand, asking them to contribute more than duty required. I should have known they wouldn't disappoint me. They were eager to help me.

While we began planning to extract Thamer's family, other serious concerns confronted me at my job. Thamer was only one among many vulnerable scientists and technicians. Getting Thamer's family to the United States and getting them settled in their new lives remained my priority, but it was no longer the only project I was responsible for. My responsibilities had been expanding over the previous year or so, and my assignment now included researching whether some displaced scientists with less-than-honorable intentions might find their way to the United States.

I was assigned to the Intelligence and Analysis Directorate at DHS, and I helped them create and implement a rudimentary screening program so we could track the activities and where-abouts of all scientists visiting the US who had knowledge of or worked directly with WMDs.

I continued to juggle all that while working overtime to secure the approvals and prepare to launch the final phase of

Project Zebra. It was a lot, and I was about to jump back into the fire, so I decided it was time to sit down with my own family and tell them what was going on. I took Carmela, and our younger son, Jared, out to a restaurant not far from our home in Annapolis.

Carmela wanted to know, "What's the occasion?"

"I've been so busy with work lately we haven't had enough time together as a family."

That was true, but there was more to it than that. I hadn't yet told them I'd be returning to Iraq. I figured the news might go over better on a full stomach. I knew my wife wouldn't be happy. After I'd settled Thamer into his new town home, she'd told me more than once how relieved she was that I was through with all the nefarious stuff. At the restaurant there was a long wait for a table, and I knew Carmela and Jared could tell something was on my mind, so I decided to get the bad news out of the way while we waited for our table.

"So one reason I wanted to bring you both here is that I thought it was important to spend time together as a family before my next assignment. I have to go back to Iraq–just for a short time."

Carmela clenched her jaw but said nothing. I knew she wasn't angry with me, just worried. I didn't blame her. We watched the same news. Together, we turned to Jared, both of us concerned about his reaction.

He could tell we were waiting for him to say something. "Does this involve the same case you were working on last time you went?"

"Yes, it does." He didn't know the details of Project Zebra, but he had a general idea of what I was up to.

"Dad, you've been working this case for a long time, and you're going back to Iraq for a third time."

"Yes . . ." I wondered where this was going.

"And you're doing this all . . . for the sake of *one* man?"

I sat motionless. His words hung in the air. The question made sense, but I wanted to explain there was more to it than that, that we were at war with enemies who might as well be invisible because we couldn't see them coming, that we needed to do all we could do to protect ourselves against unpredictable threats we knew little about, that Thamer was part of that effort.

However, in the end, I gave him the only part of the answer I felt sure of, "Yeah you're right, Jared. I'm doing this all for the sake of *one* man."

My son's choice of words that night have stayed with me since. If we were doing this for one man, was it worth the effort? What is the worth of one man's life? One man's desire for freedom? One man's hope for his family? What price should a man be ready to pay to protect all he loves, family, country, honor?

This mission begged a lot of questions, and I didn't have a lot of answers.

FOR OUR THIRD FORAY INTO IRAQ, KEVIN, Jim, and I agreed we needed an interpreter fluent in Arabic to join the team. Not just someone we could grab on the fly once we arrived. We had learned from the previous two trips that the simplest miscommunication could have dangerous consequences. And this time the need for language help was even more critical. While Thamer spoke passable English, his family was a different story. Thamer's wife and younger son spoke no English. His older son knew some English but not enough to give us confidence he'd be able to follow our instructions, much less relay them to his family. By luck and timing, we were able to get Dr. Mereish to help us once again. Kay was fluent in Arabic, and she agreed to meet us in Egypt. With that, we had our team.

Jim, Kevin, and I flew out of Dulles as usual, but this time we passed through Frankfurt and landed in Cairo. Kay had landed shortly before us and was waiting to greet us when we stepped off the plane. We had a couple of nights layover before our final hop into Baghdad, as those flights only ran on certain days at certain times. So the four of us left the airport and headed into the city.

Jim, a good logistics man who seemed to know people every-where, had arranged for two friends to meet our team at the Cairo airport. We carried our luggage outside the secure area into an impenetrable mass of people waiting to greet arrivals, and as much faith as I had in Jim, I had my doubts we'd ever find his contacts in this sea of people. But Jim is tall and eagle eyed. He spotted our greeting party right away and waved. I shook my head and laughed when I spotted his two friends enthusiastically waving back; they were two good-looking young women.

"No wonder you wanted to handle logistics, Jim," I shouted to compete with the noise of the crowd. "You guys never give it a break."

"What can I tell you, man?" Jim grinned.

"Where did you meet these girls?"

"On the Internet."

"What? Are you crazy? They could be anybody."

"It's okay. I know them. They're sisters."

"Tell me you're kidding."

"Don't worry. They're only going to escort us around Cairo."

I came to find out the two sisters were Iraqis who had fled their country and were trying, like thousands of other Iraqi ref-ugees, to get to the US. They'd been living in Cairo for several months and knew the city, and they became valuable in helping us get around. Jim told me they knew nothing of the reason we were there, and they never asked. Whatever their stories, the two women greeted us warmly, then led us through a madhouse of young Egyptian men all competing for the chance to give us a ride. It was a herculean effort to get past this horde. The young women were fluent in Arabic of course, which came in handy as they directed us to an area where the supposed legitimate taxis were located.

They walked down the line of cars and negotiated with two drivers to transport the six of us, plus luggage. It took plenty of shouting before they settled on a price they assured us was fair.

The three guys would go in one taxi with the luggage, the three gals in the other.

Kevin took one look at our taxi and wanted nothing to do with it. "I'm not getting in there! It's a piece of shit. Look at that thing."

"Come on, man, let's just get to the hotel," I said.

I laughed hysterically at the sight of Kevin reluctantly collapsing his six-foot-three-inch frame to fit into the back of that tiny hunk of junk. For a moment, I doubted that Jim and I would be able to squeeze in with him, much less fit our luggage. But we made it. As the shortest, I squeezed in front with my knees against the dash.

Our driver tore away from the curb, the taxi with the three women hot on our tail, and already I wondered if Kevin was right and we shouldn't have gotten into this deathtrap. It was a third-world James Bondo special: no air conditioning, lamb's wool seat covers, a collection of bobble-head dolls across the front dash, broken mirrors, operated by a small chain-smoking Egyptian driver named Ishaq. I was still searching for my non-existent seatbelt when we shot into the crowded, breakneck traffic of Cairo.

With less than inches to spare on both sides, Ishaq forced his way between the other cars at homicidal speeds. There were no lanes, no speed limits, no apparent rules. Honking cars zigzagged in every direction without regard for pedestrians. Ishaq's head swiveled in every direction except toward the road ahead as he spewed a litany of what must be Arabic profanity, given the choice physical gestures that went with it. I was amazed he was able to drive without looking forward. I clutched the edges of the seat and didn't know whether to laugh or scream. That ride rivaled the wooden roller coaster in Revere Beach that used to scare the crap out of me as a kid.

The taxi squealed to a stop that threatened to send me through the windshield, and the driver announced the name of our hotel. Kevin, Jim and I looked at each other and let out a deep breath. The girls arrived moments later and tumbled out, chattering cheerfully, as if this sort of thrill ride was routine in Cairo.

Kevin, on the other hand, roared as he unfolded from the car, "That was un-fucking-believable!"

"Do you believe that shit?" Jim agreed.

"That guy's an asshole!" Kevin shouted, well in earshot of our crazy driver.

"You know he speaks English," Jim said.

"I don't give a shit," Kevin said. "Fuck him!"

I put an arm around Kevin's shoulder. "You should apply to the State Department diplomatic corps. With your communication skills, you'd be a shoo-in."

We all agreed on one thing, it was a toss-up whether the dangers of Iraq could be any scarier than that taxi ride.

As usual, we had no choice but to run much of this operation by the seat of our pants because there were so many variables that couldn't be planned in advance. For one, we still had to figure out our best strategy for getting into Iraq without attracting attention. Meanwhile, over the next couple of days, we made contact with Thamer's family in Baghdad to tell them for the first time that we were on our way to get them out. We hadn't been able to risk telling them until this last moment, lest things fall through or they let a whisper fall into the wrong ears. We also contacted the DHS attaché in Baghdad to work out what the rest of our instructions would be.

We tried to get as much as possible lined up while still in Cairo because once we got to Iraq, we'd have to hit the ground running, and though we had to make a slew of calls, we still ended up with a day of downtime. We decided to head out to see as much of Cairo as our limited time allowed, especially the sight I had always dreamed of: the pyramids of Giza.

Thanks to books and movies, the pyramids had become the stuff of legend for me, and I was thrilled to be able to see them for real. We stood in a hot, dusty, crowded line to get our tickets, and it was worth it. One step through the entry gate, and I was astounded. Considering when they'd been built, the enormity of the pyramids and the Great Sphinx defied logic. It was a bucket list moment for me that I will never forget. But despite my awe at the pyramids, my mind quickly shifted to what lay ahead. We left the splendor and craziness of the Nile River, the pyramids, and the Giza City markets behind and made our way back to Cairo.

The next day we were off to Baghdad, and I spent the two-hour flight trying to convince myself that a woman and her two teenage sons would be no more difficult to smuggle out of Iraq than one wanted middle-aged man. Deep down, I knew this extraction was likely to be harder than it had been with Thamer. More people meant more problems.

As on our previous trip, we arranged as safe a meeting location as we could find. We needed a place where Eman and the two boys would feel safe. A place where it was normal for them to be at that time of day. As soon as we connected, they would become our responsibility and keeping them safe was all we could think about. We picked an area off an exit on Route Irish past the Winged Man statue. Once again we would have to deal with those pesky car bombers that hung around the on and off ramps. However, the situation on Route Irish had gotten much better.

With the help of Kay, we gave Eman detailed instructions including the exact date and time we would meet them, the location, the vehicles we would be driving, what to bring, and what not to bring. We emphasized the importance of having their phones charged and turned on so we could maintain constant contact in case we had to call the meeting off at the last minute or change plans on the fly. I asked Kay to confirm with Eman more than once the make, model, and color of the car they would meet us in.

On our end, Kevin, Jim, and I again got help from a contingent of two federal agents to provide ground support. I could tell by the looks on the team's faces as I gave them instructions that I was over-explaining, repeating myself, and ramping up the intensity in general. I couldn't help it. I was more nervous about this trip than the last. I believe Thamer could have forgiven me if something had happened to him the last go-around, but if something were to happen to his wife or sons, who knows? If something bad happened to Thamer's family that would be a tough one for me to swallow.

Once again, we'd be traveling with passengers who had no visas, so we'd have to rely on the SPBP option to get them through security. And once again, there was a chance that might not work. The idea of SPBP was that the person in question had some benefit to offer the people of the United States, and Eman and her sons offered nothing our government needed, except to the extent that we could argue they were essential to the well-being of our asset, Thamer Imran.

On the day of the pickup, we reconnoitered at Camp Liberty, assembled our tiny convoy of two armored SUVs, and gathered our equipment and protective armor. I triple-checked the vehicles and weapons, and for the umpteenth time went over who was assigned to each vehicle, where Eman and her two sons would sit, and who would provide cover while we grabbed the family and their belongings and hustle back to the base. Every team member responded to my instructions with a firm nod and terse confirmation: "Yes, sir . . . You've got it, Steve . . . Yup, Yup, Affirmative"—until I turned to Kay.

"Kay, you'll be riding in my vehicle in the back."

"Okay," she said. "No problem, Steve."

"We have an M-4 for you. Do you want it?"

"Is it loaded?"

"Well, it isn't right now, but you'll need to carry a loaded weapon or it won't do you much good." The uncertain look on her face gave me pause. "You do know how to use it?"

Kay didn't answer, which made me nervous, but she was an army reserve colonel, surely she'd fired a weapon before? I pulled her aside, and a brief discussion revealed she had very little weapon experience. She was a PhD scientist, and a direct commission type of officer; in essence, a brain with a uniform. She assured me she'd received some training, but when I handed her the M-4, the shakiness with which she handled it gave me little confidence.

I took a deep breath to keep from losing my cool. "Kay, you're going to ride in my vehicle, so why don't I just keep your weapon up front with me. If something happens just follow my lead. We're not going to do anything foolish. We'll just drive on through any trouble." I hoped that was true.

She looked relieved. "That would be fine."

"Okay then." I was relieved too. The last thing I needed was one of my own team members blowing my head off from the rear seat.

What I really needed was all the help and protection I could get, not more people to worry about. But we needed Kay to translate and her presence would indeed be welcomed by Eman and her boys. So that was that. I reminded myself that her translation skills had already proved valuable, and I might find her a lifesaver before the day was out. I had come to like Kay from our time in Miami, and I respected the work she'd done with the UN Weapons Inspection Teams. I just wanted all of us to be safe, so, the weapon stayed with me.

I addressed the whole group again. "Remember, everyone, move in fast, make the switch, and get out fast."

With that, we all took our positions in the two vehicles, with me in the front passenger seat of armored SUV Number Two. Then we hit the gas, and we were off.

It took about half an hour to get off base, make our crawl through some shabby streets, and reach our destination. Our timing was perfect as we arrived at the same time as the transport car Eman had described. Jim provided cover, while Kevin and I jumped out, ready to grab the family and their baggage.

Everything looked okay so far, but then that's usually the case until something unexpected happens.

Eman and her sons stepped out of their car, and we went into motion to load them into the SUVs. We rushed Eman into SUV number one. Then, Thamer's oldest son opened their trunk and pointed at the sight that almost made me lose it. I couldn't believe the trunk was crammed full of bags, and I mean crammed! Eman had been told repeatedly to make sure she brought only what they absolutely needed. So, she brought their entire house. There was no room for all this in the SUVs, and even if there were, there was no time to load it all. The longer we spent loading, the greater the risk we would be spotted and targeted.

"Are they shitting me?" Kevin said. "Look at these bags! Their whole house is here!"

"Look, Kevin, we don't have time to scream at them. Let's just grab these, stuff as many as we can, and go."

I tried to lift the first suitcase, and it was so heavy, I could barely move it. To make matters worse, the youngest son, just stood there staring at us. He was wearing earbuds and holding his cell phone, bouncing to music as if he didn't have a care in the world, not lifting a finger to help us. Here we were in a war zone, trying to keep him from getting killed, and he was acting like an American teen on a boring family road-trip.

"Hey you, yalla, yalla," I screamed in my limited Arabic to be heard over whatever he was listening to. "Take those damn earphones out and grab a bag!"

He spoke no English, and "yalla, yalla," meaning "come on" was all I could manage. But from my pointing and yelling, I could see he knew exactly what I was talking about. Still, he hesitated, looking from me to the bags.

"Let's move!" Teenagers, I thought, doesn't matter what country they're from, they're all clueless.

Jim wasn't loading any bags because his job was to provide security by keeping his weapon ready to fire at a moment's notice.

He grew twitchy, angry eyes darting from us loading the SUVs to the locals gawking at us. There were always Iraqis watching. Anyone could see that Jim didn't like how long this was taking.

"Steve, we got to get outta here, fast!" he yelled.

With SUV's stuffed to the limit, we somehow managed to load every last bag and still have room for the teenagers. We got out of there without incident—except that my back was killing me for the next couple of days.

We wouldn't return to Cairo but would fly to Kuwait City as we had done with Thamer. We got the entire family's SPBP paperwork approved, but there was still a chance their lack of visas would hang us up on our way out of Iraq if Gryphon Airline's security decided to go by-the-book. Despite that possibility, we had decided to use Gryphon Air again because of our success with them the last go-around. And this time, we had something in our favor: these Iraqis weren't wanted. Once again, through a little bit of BS, and a whole lot of bravado, we got them onto the plane.

We'd been careful to explain the protocols for air travel to Eman and the boys before we picked them up in Baghdad, especially what passengers can and cannot take on a plane. Given the amount of baggage, I asked Kay to explain the rules to them again, in detail. For extra measure, I had her double check what they were carrying on their persons to make certain they were clean. It seemed to work. We boarded the flight without incident. The short flight was also uneventful.

Then we arrived at Kuwait International Airport, and again ran into their wall of ever-present complications with flight reservations. We'd survived so many mishaps by this point in Project Zebra that I found myself waiting for inevitable disaster. Again, United had no record of Eman or her sons on the flight manifest, and this time the ticket agents were immune to more than an hour of arguments.

We had no choice but to repurchase all three of the Thamer family's tickets. Kevin put them on his personal credit card. I held my breath while the agent ran Kevin's card.

The agent said, "Okay, your payment was accepted."

I collapsed against the ticket counter as I said to Kevin and Jim, "Christ, will anything go right?"

They leaned against the counter with me, and our eyes said what we dared not speak aloud: it's been an honor working with you gentlemen, but let's never do this again.

I led the way through the throngs of people waiting to get through security. I motioned to the security officers that the group behind me was with me. Eman was directly behind me. I went through the metal detector with no problem. So did Eman. Her bags did not. Officers pulled her aside to further check her bag. I've never seen anyone so terrified. Her eyes seemed to take up her whole face.

I assured her this was a random check, happens all the time in the US, no problem. I wouldn't have been all that surprised if the Kuwaiti security agent had been rude to her. She was an Iraqi, and her country had invaded and decimated Kuwait in the first Gulf War. But the agent was efficient and polite. I remained patient as he felt through her bag. This went on for a couple of minutes until I noticed his facial expression change from poise and calm to a scowl of suspicion. Something was definitely wrong.

His hand came out of her bag holding one of the largest knives I had ever seen. It looked more like a sword. Everyone around us froze, including the other waiting passengers. Then all hell broke loose, security agents shouting in Arabic, Eman chattering away in a high-pitched voice, passengers visibly upset and backing away. I stood there in disbelief, sure we were all going to wind up in Kuwaiti prison cells, charged with terrorism, or at the very least, that Eman and her boys would be deported back to Iraq. This sort of stuff in the US leads to automatic arrest, game over.

The security forces pulled us aside. Then they pushed us in front of them, first one way then another. Here! No over here! I had no idea what anybody was saying, but there seemed to be confusion over what to do with us and where to take us. Other people who had been standing behind us were diverted to other lines. It was a mess.

I stared at Eman in disbelief as she seemed to plead with the men. What was she saying? "Geez, I didn't realize I couldn't bring a four-foot sword in my bag"? I wished she would shut up. I felt sure she was only making matters worse. In that part of the world, always on alert for terrorist activity, security guards don't tend to listen to excuses from people who bring weapons aboard planes.

I said, "I told you to bring only what you needed, and you need this?" Then I gave up and called out, "Where's my interpreter, where the hell is Kay? Kay!"

Kay appeared from the crowd and hurried to my side.

I hissed, "This is your responsibility! Deal with it!"

She sprang into action. I stood dumbfounded amid a cacophony of shouts, threats, and exhausting explanations I couldn't understand. After half an hour of this, expressions softened, voices quieted, and then, music to my ears, someone chuckled. We were allowed to pass through, minus every traveling Iraqi mother's weapon of choice, which as Kay learned was a kitchen knife—one that apparently meant a lot to Eman, though I never knew why.

"Kay, what the hell did you tell them to get us out of this?"

"I explained that Eman has never flown before"—which was true— "and didn't have the sophistication to understand the prohibitions on bringing items like the knife on the plane."

"And they bought that?"

Kay cocked an eyebrow at me. "They're allowing us to pass aren't they?"

I promised myself, next time, Steve, look through the bag yourself. Then I promised myself, better yet, don't let there be a next time.

We all boarded the plane, and I collapsed into my seat with the realization that I'd made it out of war-torn Iraq, only to narrowly escape being thrown in a Kuwaiti jail because Eman wanted to bring along the sword of Ali Baba.

THE FLIGHT TO AMERICA WAS LONG AND a bit bumpy, but Eman and the boys handled it well for first-time fliers. We arrived at Dulles, where ICE agents escorted us all to a room to wait for Eman and her sons to undergo their lengthy entrance interview. I watched the three of them waiting to be processed, faces unreadable, manners polite but reserved. Eman broke the silence only once, to tell me, via Kay, how grateful she was for our efforts to help her family.

After that, she and her sons stared into space, apprehension and hope warring on their faces, refugees overwhelmed by a new reality. They hoped to soon be reunited with Thamer, but they knew that would happen only if they passed this final test. And they probably realized that if they were accepted into America, they might never again see the only home they'd ever known.

They passed the test, and we walked out of the airport into warm summer afternoon.

Kevin and Jim had said at the start that they wanted to be there for the family's reunion. But now that it came down to it, they looked like the walking dead. Knowing they needed a break, I said, "Guys, I can finish this last leg without you. You've done all that I've asked and more, and I can't thank you enough. Go get some sleep."

I thanked Kay, too. She had been a huge help. Without her intervention at Kuwait International, Eman and the boys might well have been shipped back to Iraq.

We all shook hands and hugged, slapped shoulders and backs. My chest swelled with the realization we three had just gone through the kind of experience most people couldn't even conceive of, that our mission had built among us the kind of comradeship that comes once in a lifetime. And then they were gone.

I had started this mission without a team, and it seemed fitting to finish that way.

A young ICE agent helped Eman and the boys into a large van for the trip from Dulles to their new home. I sat up front with the agent, who would double as our driver. I called Thamer on the cell phone I had bought for him when he first arrived and told him we were on our way. His voice shook with joy.

On the drive, I occasionally looked back at Thamer's wife and sons as they took in the sights around the Washington DC area. I could only imagine what was going through their minds. Without Kay to translate we uttered few words. The ICE agent handled the heavy traffic with relative ease and got us to the Virginia townhome unscathed.

We pulled into the parking lot, and Thamer was waiting as I had known he would be, outside and on time. I tried to imagine how Eman saw him. She probably noticed he had gained a few pounds, Americanized already.

Thamer had admitted to me his frequent doubts this day would ever come. I never blamed him for that. I'd had my doubts too. I stepped out of the passenger side and opened the sliding door. Then one by one, they stepped out, Eman, Mustafa, Usama. Thamer moved toward them in a gesture that had become familiar to me: arms outstretched, head tipped to one side, wearing that smile I now knew so well. As he drew closer, I saw his eyes welling up. Then he did something completely surprising: he veered past his family to wrap his arms around me.

"You did it, my good friend!" His voice was exuberant. "You did it. You kept your word. Thank you."

"You're welcome," I replied.

It was an emotional moment for both of us. Without losing another second, he greeted his family with hugs, pausing to give thanks to Allah for their safe travel. It was quite a sight to see. If Thamer's smile had gotten any bigger, I think his head would have exploded. His journey had been a long, hard one, his experiences harsh and brutal, but now his belief in "Inshallah" had been validated. What he thought might never happen just happened. He looked every bit like a man who became whole again.

"Welcome to our new home," he said to Eman and the boys. Then he invited the ICE agent and me inside for something to eat. Unfortunately, I couldn't accept his hospitality because the ICE agent was my ride, and he had to leave.

"Then, my good friend, I would like a picture with you and all of my family."

"Of course, my good friend. I'd like that very much."

We handed Thamer's cell phone to the ICE agent, and the Imran family and I posed in front of their new home in America. When I see him in that photo now, I think, that's a man who looks complete. The people in the picture chronicled almost five years of terror, turmoil, sorrow, separation, fear, and despair, all to reach this moment. That Thamer wanted to include me in the photo of the moment he and his family were reunited, safe and poised to begin a new life—is one of the proudest moments I've ever experienced.

They were tired and needed to rest, so I bid them farewell. The ICE agent offered to drive me home, but it was out of his way, and anyway, I wanted a moment alone before reuniting with my own family. I asked him to drop me off at the nearest Metro station.

I sat on the Metro train bound for Annapolis, looking out the window as it crossed the Potomac and reflected on how much the previous two and a half years had changed me. I had been consumed by Thamer's plight, and now it was over. I had been so angry in 2001, standing atop Ground Zero, mourning the dead and vowing vengeance against men I'd never met.

Now I am grateful that instead I ended up rescuing a man I'd never met, and in so doing, found the most unexpected friendship of my life. I felt sad it had all come to an end, but reminded myself that in Thamer's world there will always be time for a friend.

AFTERWORD

FOR ME, THE END OF PROJECT ZEBRA marked the start of a lonely time. The band had broken up, and we'd never get back together again. Jim was sent to Afghanistan to continue the war on terrorism, and Kevin was transferred to the Arizona and Mexico border to fight the drug and human traffickers that prey upon all of us.

I would think of them often and hoped that they were safe. As for me, I went back to my cubicle taking on other projects. Each day rolled into the next with endless tasks that gave me no satisfaction. Despite being busy, I no longer had the sense of purpose that Project Zebra brought me. I missed my friends and the camaraderie we shared. I missed the funny moments, the adrenaline filled ones, the scary ones, even the embarrassing ones, and the crazy ups and downs of a crazy case that consumed two and half years of my life. Though now I had more time to spend with my family, which was something I cherished, I realized that even the love of family can't fill every void.

I came to realize that my life had been one of belonging to something that was important, at least to me. My time in the military, as a police officer, as a Secret Service agent and working with my guys on Project Zebra meant that I was part of group, part of a team with a mission and a purpose. Now all that was gone. How do you replace thirty years of belonging to something bigger than yourself? I didn't have a clue. I felt empty.

I stayed in touch with Jim and Kevin now and then, mostly via email, but as time passed, we got in touch less and less. Then one day, I got a message from Jim. He was on leave and asked me to meet him at a coffee shop near Chinatown. It was great to see him again, mismatched clothes and all.

He was carrying a package wrapped in brown paper, and after some small talk he handed it to me.

"This is from Kevin and me."

I opened the package to reveal a framed picture of the three of us in a marketplace in Cairo. The photo also had a cutout that contained a coin commemorating Project Zebra. I felt the rush of brotherhood that comes from trial by fire. Jim said he'd had one made for each of the three of us, and that Kevin kept his on the wall in his office in Arizona. He said, "When people walk in and ask him what it's about, Kevin tells them, 'That's a picture of my friends and of the best case I ever worked on.'"

Months after Project Zebra ended, The Department of Homeland Security held their annual awards ceremony at their headquarters in Washington, DC. Kevin and Jim were selected as honorees. I felt proud to sit in the audience along with their families and friends as framed medals were presented to each of them and their citations were read aloud commending their work on Project Zebra. The pride on the faces of Jim's parents who lost their son Robert in the attack on the Pentagon years earlier brought tears to my eyes.

Thamer and I called each other often. We would talk about his family and my family, his work and my work, funny anecdotes and serious worries. We would talk about everything except politics. For the longest time, we never mentioned the war that had brought us together. Then one day I blurted, "Do you think the Americans did the right thing, invading Iraq?"

Thamer paused, and then he spoke slowly and deliberately. "Well, the purpose was to remove the dictator and to build democracy. They removed the dictator, although Hussein certainly was not the only dictator in the region, but they failed to achieve the second goal, to build democracy. Not only that, they gave Iran the chance to interfere in Iraqi internal affairs. There were so many mistakes made during the war, which allowed terrorists to cross the borders." He sighed. "Mr. Steve, I know of no one in Iraq who is better off, or even as well off, as before the war."

"How do you feel about Americans after all you've been through?" I was a little nervous to ask that one, but I had long wondered about it, and I figured it was time to hear what my friend thought, for better or worse. I knew I could count on Thamer to tell me the truth.

"Oh, now, American society like other societies has the good people and the bad people," he said. "Since I came to the United States, I've been treated in a good manner wherever I go. I've found that people here sympathize with me and my family due to what happened to my country."

"What's your biggest regret?"

He laughed. "My biggest regret is getting into the field of biological weaponry! That's what got me into this mess in the first place." His voice sobered. "But I thought I was serving my country and making it stronger among the other countries. And to be fair, it has given me a knowledge I can use here now."

"Why did you choose to work with anthrax?"

"Oh, I didn't choose," he said. "I was forced to work in this field. If I refused, I might have been terminated from employment or imprisoned."

"Did Iraq plan to use anthrax against Iran?"

"That I don't know. We were just told the work was to get our country stronger for defensive purposes, just in case another country attacked us with such a weapon."

"What's your biggest worry now?" I asked.

"I worry that something will happen to someone I love. The biggest worries, they are always personal."

In March of 2011, my phone rang and I recognized Thamer's number.

"Hello, my good friend!" he shouted the moment I picked up, breathless with excitement. I hoped this meant he had good news.

"Hello to you," I said, "You sound happy."

"We got them, Mr. Steve! We got them!"

"Got what?"

"Our green cards! They came in the mail today, and I wanted to tell you right away!"

I was so ecstatic for my friend that I almost dropped my phone. And he had more good news. He was hired by a contracting firm in the southwestern US, where he continued to use his skills to help our government.

The official War in Iraq is over from our perspective, but it continues for those who remain there. In the end, did the United States do anything right by the Iraqi people? Generals don't win wars, privates win wars, or so says the time-tested truism. Iraq is the latest, perhaps most challenging, example of that belief. The victories in Iraq are often hidden from view by a hostile press, bureaucratic paperwork, or secrecy and locked doors. Yet they are there, small untold stories of men like Thamer. Their stories underscore the importance of helping our friends, keeping our promises, and honoring the humanity we all share.

I learned a lot from my time searching for Thamer. I learned about true commitment and friendship and the importance of perseverance. I came to understand at a greater depth, the inner workings of government bureaucracy, and sadly that sometimes the greater good takes a back seat to the personal needs and reputations of those in charge. I now realize with more clarity how vital it is for all of us who serve America's government to let go of turf wars in favor of working together, to fight our real enemies and not each other. My eyes were opened wide to the hidden evils of war not seen on the front pages and how the innocent suffer. But above all, I learned in a most profound way, how wrong my hatred was of a country and its people and of a man I didn't even know.

Although the final tally of the Iraq War is debated, according to a study by researchers from the University of Washington, Johns Hopkins University, Simon Fraser University, and Mustansiriya University that covers the period of March 2003 until June 2011, more than 460,000 Iraqis are estimated to have died from direct and indirect actions attributed to the war. In addition, 4,809 coalition troops were killed, 4,491 of whom were Americans. Tens of thousands were wounded and displaced. Entire families were wiped out. Many Iraqis disappeared never to be found. The estimated cost of the war: two trillion dollars.

On December 30, 2006, Saddam Hussein uttered his last words "Allah Akbar" (God is Great) before he was dropped from the gallows. The brutal dictator had his day of reckoning, but in the end, we must ask ourselves was the price paid in the suffering of hundreds of thousands worth a noose around one man's neck? I suppose the Iraqi people will make that determination.

For many Iraqis, the pain of the war will never go away, and they'll live forever with the nightmares as will our heroic American soldiers who did their duty and gave their all.

The battle continues for my good friend, Thamer, and his family. He is a man in the middle, caught between two countries, overtaken by historical events not of his making. He's a special friend, and I cherish that. But I hope he becomes more than that for those who read this story, I hope he serves as a symbol of the hundreds of thousands of people we don't take into consideration when we go to war, the innocent victims who always bear the cost, sometimes in blood, of one government's fight against another.

Thamer and Eman now live in an undisclosed location in the United States. He continues to help the US and is deeply grateful to have been offered his new life. Thamer remains a dear friend, today and forever. I retired at the end of 2018, and

I live in Maryland with Carmela. Our boys are out in the world and thriving.

One day in the spring of 2019, I picked up the phone to catch up with Thamer and got the greatest of news. On September 24, 2018, Thamer and Eman raised their right hands and became US citizens. Thamer and I shouted at each other like two little kids. That this very good man who had endured isolation, imprisonment, and even torture had now made his way to becoming a full-fledged American citizen—well, I thought I just might explode with happiness for both of them.

After we calmed down, Thamer asked me to hold on because he had a surprise for me. There was a moment of silence, then a woman's voice said, "Hello, Mr. Steve, this is Eman." They were her first words to me that didn't involve an interpreter. Eman was speaking English! I complimented her on her language proficiency, and she proudly went on to tell me how she was getting along and how well Usama and Mustafa were doing.

At the end of the call Eman said, "Mr. Steve, thank you for all you did to give us a new life." I was humbled by her words and reminded myself of the immense satisfaction that comes from believing that your work has some purpose, that you contributed to something bigger than yourself, and in some way made life better for someone else. Every single day, people like Kevin, Jim, Maureen McCarthy and countless others put forth their best efforts and sometimes risk it all to keep our country safe. They have my undying gratitude. In this case, the work was important to my country, to national security, and to the well-being of countless people around the world who might unknowingly be spared tragedy because of the intelligence and work that Thamer and people like him continue to provide.

I hung up the phone and smiled—for myself, for Thamer, and for his family. And I smiled for my team. We'd kept our promise. If only for the sake of one man.

Fires broke out frequently as we hoped against hope that someone would still be alive under all of this. After a while, I prayed that they all died quickly. I knew we couldn't get to them in time and the thought that they would continue to suffer was unbearable. This image is courtesy of Nancy Olds USSS/FSD.

My team at Ground Zero. They gave everything they had. Despite being on one knee, America rose up and came together on 9/11, and in the days and weeks that followed. We refused to stay down. This image is courtesy of Stephen Phillip Monteiro.

Ground Zero. Getting ready to hit the "pile." I'm on the left with my team. It was impossible to work with the masks on for very long, so we took them off and, despite the poison air, kept going. It was later estimated that the air contained over 2,500 contaminants. Many got sick and more died in the aftermath than during the initial attack. This image is courtesy of Stephen Phillip Monteiro.

I stopped to witness our flag, torn and tattered but still flying. It's a sight I will never forget. It gave us the inspiration to keep going. This image is courtesy of Stephen Phillip Monteiro.

Tight quarters on a C130 with US Army troops heading to Baghdad. I was proud of our men and women in uniform. The soldier to my left thanked me for being in Iraq doing whatever I was doing . . . at my age! This image is courtesy of James Elseth.

Jim, Kevin, and me "kitting up," ready to hit the ground in Iraq. We hoped we could get to Thamer in time and that he would want to meet with us. So much was unknown. This image is courtesy of James Elseth.

"Finding Thamer." My team getting ready to rendezvous with the Gray Bird of Baghdad. We were finally going to meet the man I thought was a ghost. This image is courtesy of Kevin Kelly.

Getting ready to "exfiltrate" Thamer out of Iraq. We hoped we had wallpapered him with enough documentation to get him through. If we failed it was game over. It was a smuggling job extraordinaire. This image is courtesy of Stephen Phillip Monteiro.

Before heading south to debrief Thamer, Jim and Kevin made a stop at a place Thamer always wanted to visit. This image is courtesy of Kevin Kelly.

Thamer; his wife, Eman; his sons, Usama and Mustafa; and me. The Imran family chronicled almost five years of terror, turmoil, sorrow, separation, fear, and despair, all to reach this moment. That Thamer wanted to include me in the photo of the moment he and his family were reunited, safe and poised to begin a new life, is one of the proudest moments I've ever experienced. This image is courtesy of Stephen Phillip Monteiro.

My Team: From left to right, Lt. Colonel Jim Elseth, USMC, HSI Special Agent Kevin Kelly, and me in Cairo. The end of Project Zebra broke up the band. Jim was sent to Afghanistan to fight terrorists and Kevin to the border of Arizona and Mexico to fight drug and human traffickers. I could not have accomplished what I did without them. They represent the best of America. This image is courtesy of Stephen Phillip Monteiro.

ACKNOWLEDGMENTS

I WROTE THIS BOOK NOT FOR MYSELF but for the thousands who died and suffered in the Iraq war. I wrote this book not to pass judgment but to enlighten and add to the discourse on the evils of war and the sorrow that comes from everything it touches. I wrote this book to ask questions and create dialogue and debate on how we can go forward and learn to resolve our differences without the need for death and destruction. Whether I succeeded at all is up to the reader.

There are so many to thank that helped me write this book. First and foremost, I'm eternally grateful to my good friend Thamer, who sat with me for hours recounting details and patiently answering my never-ending questions. He never wavered and stuck with me to the end. His friendship and support is something I will always cherish.

I would especially like to thank Dr. Maureen McCarthy for the faith she had in me and for her courage to face down great odds at a personal cost to protect her country. She is a fighter and an inspiration.

A special thanks goes out to my teammates Kevin Kelly and Jim Elseth, who refreshed my memory and inspired me to go for it. I also want to thank my sons, Ryan and Jared, who gave me some great ideas and cheered me on.

Writing a book is harder than I thought and more gratifying than I could have ever imagined. None of this would have been possible without the support, direction, and guidance of Cara Lopez Lee and Jodi Fodor. Their dedication to this project, along with their outstanding editing skills, made it all possible. I learned so much from both of them, for which I am truly grateful. I would also like to thank my agent, Andy Ross, who pointed me in the right direction and showed me the correct way to write a book proposal, and the staff at SparkPress for their diligent work in helping to bring this story to light. To friends, family, and colleagues that I may have left out—thank you. Your support means everything to me.

And to our first responders and those wearing the uniform of our country who put it all on the line every day to keep us safe: you have my undying gratitude.

Last but not least, I want to thank my wife for her encouragement and support. Whenever I started to fall, Carmela, you were always there to pick me up and put me back on course. You never failed me.

In Remembrance

For those that died on 9/11
and since, and for the men and women who wore
the uniform of our country and gave their lives in the
Global War on Terrorism: may they never be forgotten.

And for all the innocent Iraqis that perished:
may their deaths not be in vain.

———————————————

"Blessed are the peacemakers,
for they shall be called sons of God."
—Matthew 5:9

ABOUT THE AUTHOR

STEPHEN PHILLIP MONTEIRO IS AN EXPERT IN security, forensics, intelligence, and bioterrorism. He spent more than twenty years as a Special Agent with the US Secret Service and served in the US Navy, where he was trained in cryptology. He was a member of the elite Presential Protective Division at the White House and served as the Special Agent in Charge and director of the Forensic Crime Laboratory. Later, he became a Senior Advisor to the Director of Weapons of Mass Destruction Intelligence for the DHS focusing on bioterrorism and received the Director of National Intelligence Meritorious Unit Citation for his work on Iraqi scientists. His expertise has led to appearances on episodes of *The Forensic Files*, the National Geographic Channel, and the History's Channel's *America's Book of Secrets*, as well as local newscasts. He currently resides in Annapolis, MD.

Author photo © The Annapolis Photographer

SELECTED TITLES FROM SPARKPRESS

SparkPress is an independent boutique publisher delivering high-quality, entertaining, and engaging content that enhances readers' lives, with a special focus on female-driven work. www.gosparkpress.com

Mission Afghanistan: An Army Doctor's Memoir, Elie Cohen, translation by Jessica Levine. $16.95, 978-1-943006-65-6. Decades after evading conscription as a young man, Franco-British doctor Elie Paul Cohen is offered a deal by the French Army: he can settle his accounts by becoming a military doctor and serving at Camp Bastion in Afghanistan.

The Journalist: Life and Loss in America's Secret War, Jerry A. Rose and Lucy Rose Fischer, $16.95, 978-1-68463-065-3. A collaboration between Lucy Rose Fischer and her late brother, The Journalist tells the story of Jerry Rose, a young journalist and photographer who exposed the secret beginnings of America's Vietnam War in the early 1960s. He interviewed Vietnamese villagers, embedded himself with soldiers, and wrote the first major article about American troops fighting in Vietnam.

Behind the Red Veil: An American Inside Gorbachev's Russia, Frank Thoms, $16.95, 978-1-68463-055-4. Frank Thoms went to Russia seeking to understand himself—and to empathize with Russians living in a deteriorating Communist society. In Behind the Red Veil, he takes readers inside the culture of "the enemy," inviting them to discover both Russia and its people for themselves.

The Restless Hungarian: Modernism, Madness, and The American Dream, Tom Weidlinger. $16.95, 978-1-943006-96-0. A revolutionary, a genius, and a haunted man . . . The story of the architect-engineer Paul Weidlinger, whose colleagues called him "The Wizard," spans the rise of modern architecture, the Holocaust, and the Cold War. The revelation of hidden Jewish identity propels the author to trace his father's life and adventures across three continents.